Contents

List of tables and boxes

Tables

Boxes

INTERNATIONAL APPROACHES TO PROSTITUTION

Law and policy in Europe and Asia

Edited by Geetanjali Gangoli and Nicole Westmarland

Published in Great Britain in May 2006 by

The Policy Press
University of Bristol
Fourth Floor
Beacon House
Queen's Road
Bristol BS8 1QU
UK

Tel +44 (0)117 331 4054
Fax +44 (0)117 331 4093
e-mail tpp-info@bristol.ac.uk
www.policypress.org.uk

British Library Cataloguing in Publication Data
A catalogue record for this book is available from the British Library.

Library of Congress Cataloging-in-Publication Data
A catalog record for this book has been requested.

ISBN-10 1 86134 672 7 paperback
ISBN-13 978 1 86134 672 8
ISBN-10 1 86134 673 5 hardcover
ISBN-13 978 1 86134 673 5

Cover design by Qube Design Associates, Bristol.
Printed and bound in Great Britain by Hobbs the Printers, Southampton

Notes on contributors

Kristina Abiala is Senior Lecturer and Researcher in the Department of Gender Studies, History, Comparative Literature and the Study of Religions at Södertörn University College in Stockholm, Sweden. In 2000 she defended her thesis in sociology focusing on emotional labour in private service work. From commoditisation of sociality, she then researched irregular female migration and sexual trafficking in and from Eastern Europe. She is part of a network of researchers and journalists in Western Russia and Sweden working to establish stable information exchange and to improve the situation of women. She is also part of a research group planning to study Swedish policy on gender equality, where she analyses gendered sexual politics.

Gill Allwood is Reader in Gender Politics at Nottingham Trent University, UK, and author of *French feminisms: Gender and power in contemporary theory* (London: UCL, 1998) and *Women and politics in France 1958-2000* (London: Routledge, 2000, with Khursheed Wadia). She has published a number of journal articles on feminist movements and theories, women's representation and prostitution. She is a member of the editorial boards of the *Journal of Contemporary European Studies* and *Modern and Contemporary France.* She is currently working on books on refugee women in Britain and France, and gender and public policy in France.

Alyson Brody completed her doctorate at the School of Oriental and African Studies, London, focusing on women and rural–urban migration in Thailand. Prior to this, she worked in Thailand on women's and children's rights issues. She is currently at the Institute of Development Studies in Sussex, UK.

Mei-Hua Chen gained her doctorate in Women's Studies at the University of York, UK. Her dissertation looks at the ways in which Taiwanese sex workers make sense of their daily lives. She currently teaches at the Graduate Institute of Gender Studies, Kaohsiung Medical University, Taiwan. She has published articles on issues such as abortion, surrogate motherhood and women and employment in Taiwan. Recently her research has concentrated on the inter-relation between sex work and the gendered labour market, and on the Chinese migrant sex workers in Taiwan.

Geetanjali Gangoli is a research fellow and Coordinating Officer for the Violence Against Women Research Group at the School for Policy Studies, University of Bristol, UK. She has worked and published on law and feminism in India, issues of livelihood, poverty and the sex trade in India, comparative studies on domestic violence in China and the UK, and domestic violence and forced marriages in immigrant South Asian communities in the UK. She has also volunteered in feminist organisations, including Saheli and Forum Against Oppression of Women, in India, and the Truth About Rape campaign and Women in Black, in the UK.

Fouzia Saeed, a social scientist with a PhD from the University of Minnesota, is the author of *Taboo!: The hidden culture of a red light area* (Karachi: Oxford University Press, 2001), based on eight years of field research among prostitutes in Pakistan. Dr Saeed is well known in the activist circles of Pakistan's social movement, having worked for decades on women's issues especially those linked to violence against women, prostitution, women in the entertainment business, women's mobility and sexual harassment. Her work on violence against women spans more than 20 years and includes founding the first women's crisis centre in Pakistan in 1991. Her earlier work with the Pakistani Culture Institute led to the book *Women in folk theatre* (Islamabad: Lok Virsa, 1989). During her career she has headed the UN Gender Programme in Pakistan, served as Pakistan country director for Action Aid and currently is an international consultant in the field of gender and development. She maintains an associate status with Mehergarh, a non-profit research and leadership institute in Pakistan.

Yvonne Svanström is a researcher in the Department of Economic History at Stockholm University. She wrote her doctoral thesis on the 19th-century system of regulation of prostitution in Stockholm: 'Policing public women: the regulation of prostitution in Stockholm 1812-1880'. Her current research is focused on a comparative study of Sweden and the Netherlands and their policies on prostitution during the welfare state period. Among her recent publications are 'Criminalising the john: a Swedish gender model?', in Joyce Outshoorn (ed), *The politics of prostitution: Women's movements, democratic states, and the globalisation of sex commerce* (Cambridge:

Cambridge University Press, 2004) and 'Through the prism of prostitution: attitudes to women and sexuality in Sweden at two fins-de-siècle', *NORA – Nordic Journal of Women's Studies*, no 1, 2005.

Nicole Westmarland is a research fellow in the area of gender, violence and abuse at the University of Bristol, UK. She has a PhD from the University of York, UK, on Rape and Human Rights. She is the author (with Marianne Hester) of *Tackling street prostitution: An holistic approach* (London: Home Office, 2004) and has published a number of journal articles and reports on violences against women. She is also known for her feminist activism in groups such as the national Rape Crisis (England and Wales) group and the Truth About Rape campaign. Current work includes research on the perpetrators of domestic violence.

ONE

Introduction: approaches to prostitution

Nicole Westmarland and Geetanjali Gangoli

Prostitutes. Whores. Prostituted women. Toms. Sex workers. Entertainers. Hookers. Natashas. Working girls. Prossies. Market women. Women abused through prostitution. Sauna staff. Common prostitutes. Tarts. Ladies of the night. Madams. Self-employed workers. Trafficked women. Comfort women. Women involved in prostitution. Street walkers. Brothel workers. Victims of commercial sexual exploitation.

In no particular order, these are some of the many terms used to describe women involved in prostitution. What is immediately evident is how many different terms there are; there are far more words to describe women who sell sex than there are for men who purchase it. But there is another purpose for starting the book with this list of terms – to demonstrate how the words that are used to talk about prostitution reflect different approaches to prostitution.

Pick up a book or article about prostitution and the general approach to prostitution that the author is taking soon becomes clear. The language used to describe women involved in prostitution can sometimes give more information about the author than does the title of the book or article. The term 'sex worker' and any words relating to 'trade' or 'work' imply a different approach to prostitution from the terms 'women abused through prostitution', 'prostituted women' and 'commercial sexual exploitation'. In reading these terms, certain value judgements are made about an author and their approach to prostitution. In some cases only those books with 'appropriate language' (where what is deemed 'appropriate' varies from reader to reader) will be read and cited.

In this book all the authors (including ourselves) have used the terminology of their choosing, for example 'sex workers', 'prostitutes' or 'women involved in prostitution'. This did not happen by accident; we did not begin editing the chapters and then start debating which terms we should use. When we started the book we already knew that we as editors did not use the same words when talking about prostitution. To dictate to the authors the language they should use to talk about prostitution would, in our view, be taking editorial power more than one step too far.

Situated knowledges – our approaches to prostitution

The issue of prostitution brings to the fore many of the contradictions in feminist politics, and the ambivalence in dealing with issues of sexuality reflected both in Asian (Gangoli, 1998) and Western feminist politics (McElroy, 1991). There are many theoretical positions on prostitution, which tend to pivot on a dividing line between those who view prostitution as work and argue that sex workers should be given the same rights as others in the labour market (eg International Committee for Prostitutes' Rights, 1988; Bell, 1994; Durbar Mahila Samanwaya Committee, 1997) and those who view prostitution as a form of abuse serving to continue the oppression of women (eg Dworkin, 1981; MacKinnon, 1993; Jeffreys, 1997).

Rightly or wrongly, consciously or unconsciously, we have both been characterised (partly by ourselves but mainly by others) as taking different positions in the prostitution as sex work/prostitution as abuse debate. Nicole Westmarland is seen more as belonging to the 'prostitution as abuse' school (that prostitution is abusive to women and should be classed as a form of violence against women), and Geetanjali Gangoli to the 'prostitution as work' school (that women in the sex trade are engaging in legitimate work). Indeed, some people expressed concern about our working together on this book. It was suggested that our views on prostitution were so diverse that our differences would be insurmountable, rendering the project unworkable. We, however, believed that this was the very reason why the book was needed and why we should work together rather than apart.[1]

We have both interviewed women and children involved in prostitution, Geetanjali in India and Nicole in England. Despite taking different approaches to prostitution, the reason we believed that we could work together on this book was because we share a common worldview. We are both fighting for a world that is based on an equitable world order and have previously worked together on domestic violence research (Donovan et al, 2005; Gangoli et al, 2005) and in the activist arena (in the Truth About Rape campaign and Bristol Women in Black). In this book we do not advocate a particular way forward or promote a specific approach. We try to avoid morally dictating which approaches are universally 'right' or 'wrong', and focus instead upon how it is understood in different places in different times under different circumstances. In doing so, we hope to begin the development of a more nuanced approach to understanding prostitution in the international arena and to contribute to the emerging literature that seeks to explain prostitution as a complex phenomenon where gender, economics, power, class, age and 'choice' intersect (O'Connell Davidson, 1999).

First, however, we offer a brief insight into how our own personal views on prostitution have developed in order to 'situate' or 'locate' our knowledges (Haraway, 1991). These are shown in the two boxes that follow and are based on a 'stream of consciousness' exercise that we did together specifically for this book.

Box 1.1: Personal reflection – Geetanjali Gangoli

I have grown up in India, and been part of the Indian feminist movement, which has always taken up issues of poverty, class and caste, along with violence against women. I know that women and men in India and in the rest of the world aren't equal by a long shot, but also know that all men aren't equal either. Men get hurt because of poverty, class, caste and race. So poor men, black men in white societies, Dalit men in caste-ridden India also suffer discrimination and violence. But these factors – poverty, class, caste and race – all affect women too, and in ways that are sometimes similar to and sometimes different from the way they affect men. For instance, caste oppression and poverty may push some women into the sex trade, but may also push men into bonded labour or some other location that hurts and harms them. But maybe the sex trade is the area that is most gendered. For instance, men in the sex trade are often the most vulnerable men, they are the ones that are least integrated into patriarchy, like gay men who are different from the norm and young poor socially excluded boys. So I believe in a sense that prostitution is the most extreme form of the reality we are living in – where commoditisation and sexualisation of women is acceptable, but men who don't conform to the ideal norms are also commodified and sexualised, just as the women are.

Interviewing women in the sex trade in India, I found that the women I interviewed came from different backgrounds, ages, regions and castes. Some of them had been sold into prostitution by their parents, others by their husbands, some entered the trade because their mothers were in the trade and they couldn't get any other jobs or find any other livelihood. Some came from families that were so poor that their wages as prostitutes were the only thing that kept their families alive. Some were thrown out of their marital homes after being widowed or divorced, and not accepted by their natal homes and so ended up in sex work. So the problem isn't always only within prostitution, it's out there in the real world. I remember speaking to an activist in Nepal who works with women repatriated from India after raids in brothels in Mumbai or Kolkata, who said that she was really frustrated by the governments of India and Nepal. Both the governments wanted better border controls, but she feels that the only way to end trafficking into prostitution was to end global poverty, inequality and structural and family violence against women. But the structural issues are so big that they can almost seem insurmountable in the short term. And that's the reason that I think that prostitution should be treated as work; it's partly pragmatic. Prostitutes are there, and they will starve if they are not in sex work, so I will support all efforts that give them rights while they are there. In the same way, I support struggles opposing violence against women in marriage. Those women are in the situation and exiting isn't always possible because of structural reasons, so I believe they should be supported whether they stay in the marriage or leave.

Box 1.2: Personal reflection – Nicole Westmarland

I grew up in the North-East of England and my involvement in the women's movement has centred on violence against women. When I began researching prostitution I was convinced from the start that the two approaches (prostitution as work/prostitution as abuse) would not be as distinctive as they are sometimes made out to be, and that a lot could be gained by people from different approaches coming together and finding a way forward for women in prostitution. As a young woman, early in my academic career, I sometimes used to feel intimidated when faced with women from the 'prostitution as work' position; I started becoming more defensive instead of listening and trying to engage with what they were saying, which only resulted in both 'sides' pushing away from each other even further. The more defensive you get the more difficult it becomes to listen properly to other arguments.

One case in particular set me thinking. A woman had left street prostitution, had moved away from the area with a man who used to be her client and was engaged to be married to him. When do we cross the line between prostitution and a sexual relationship? She is living with him, and he is financially supporting her. How different is this from someone living with or married to a man upon whom they are completely financially dependent? There are no binary opposites, but rather a very large grey area that probably contains more questions than answers.

I strongly believe that the women involved in prostitution whom I have met in England are being hurt by prostitution and drugs. In most cases it was men who were the source of this harm. This is probably because I have seen a distinct group of women, mostly controlled by drug use and with very distressing life experiences in the past. They may sometimes believe that they have chosen prostitution because of the networks they have and the limited options open to them, but I cannot see how they have had any real choices. I have met a small number of women in other countries that I don't feel the same about, who are drug free and have stable lives, and I accept that to some extent they are choosing. So I end up in part back to Geetanjali's position that some prostitutes may be choosing to work in prostitution in a world where sexuality is commodified. There are lots of things we don't choose freely. This is not to say that I think all prostitution should be treated as work, but to recognise that my approach is not necessarily in conflict with Geetanjali's – it is just that we have researched prostitution in completely different contexts. In England and Wales I have met a woman who has had sexual intercourse for a pack of cigarettes; another for a can of cola; another for a takeaway meal. Many for drugs. What would happen if they didn't gain these objects? Would they starve? Unlikely. Are their wages from prostitution keeping their families alive as in Geetanjali's research? Probably not. Are they really choosing whether to have sexual intercourse for these objects? No. And this is why I think that prostitution in this context should be treated as abuse, not work.

The structure of this book

For the rest of this book we try to move away from our individual perspectives on prostitution. Is it violence against women? Is it work? Is it both? Is it pleasure? Is it choice? While all these debates are important and valid in themselves, this book is about contextualising approaches to prostitution: to discover how prostitution is understood in different places, in different times, by different people, in order to understand the context in which specific policies and legislation are situated.

This book is divided into two parts. The first (Chapters Two to Five) looks at prostitution in Europe, and the second (Chapters Six to Nine) in Asia. The rest of this introductory chapter picks up on some of the themes that the authors of the different chapters were asked to address. Most of the book is about street prostitution and the main focus is on adults.

Part One, on prostitution laws and policies in Europe, opens with a chapter on England and Wales, by Nicole Westmarland, focusing on the changing perspectives to prostitution over time – and the background to the government's 2006 Coordinated Prostitution Strategy. Chapter Three, on France, by Gill Allwood, looks at the way in which French law has recreated prostitution as a security issue. The following contribution on Sweden by Yvonne Svanström explains the move in 1999 to a new policy that criminalises only the clients of prostitutes, and Chapter Five, by Kristina Abiala on the Republic of Moldova focuses on the state's concern to tackle trafficking, leaving debates about prostitution largely silenced.

Part Two, on Asia, has chapters on prostitution in India by Geetanjali Gangoli, looking at the shift in parts of the country from toleration to legalisation in response to a perceived AIDS pandemic (Chapter Six); and on prostitution in Pakistan by Fouzia Saaed, addressing the impact that rising religious fundamentalism has had on prostitutes' lives and laws (Chapter Seven). Chapter Eight, by Mei-Hua Chen, looks at Taiwan, where licensing of some forms of prostitution has been replaced in the 1990s by increased criminalisation of some activities associated with prostitution. The final chapter, by Alyson Brody, focuses on Thailand, explaining the forms of legalisation that Thailand has chosen to tackle the issue of prostitution there.

Why these countries?

The countries were chosen as good examples of contrasting policy perspectives, with different historical and political trajectories regarding prostitution across Europe and Asia. In Europe, France has recently taken a stricter perspective to women involved in prostitution, but only punishes some men as buyers, while England and Wales are moving towards a more lenient welfare-based approach to women involved in street prostitution, while taking a more punitive stance towards the buyers. Sweden and Moldova take opposite perspectives to one another, with Sweden criminalising only the buyer and Moldova criminalising only the women involved in prostitution. In Asia, India has a toleration system with regard to prostitution, but concerns about the spread of the HIV virus are pushing policy makers to recommend moves towards the prostitution-as-work position, but a deep-seated morality makes the operation complicated. Pakistan has experienced 'Islamisation' with profound impacts on women in prostitution, who are subjected to moral policing. In Taiwan, there is simultaneously tolerance and criminalisation of prostitution, with partial legalisation of the trade, while Thai prostitution has been characterised as catering to the pressure of international tourism, and solutions in the form of legalisation have been the response.

The impact of political structures

Politically, the countries are quite different from one another. In Europe, Moldova stands out as being particularly different from the others in this book. Between 1940 and 1991, Moldova was governed from Moscow under communist rule (as the Moldovan Soviet Socialist Republic). Now independent for over a decade, it still has many problems, for example the judiciary and government function poorly, and there is some evidence of corruption and links between government officials and organised crime. Moldova has the smallest population (around 4.3 million) out of the European countries analysed here (at around 61.2 million, France has the highest). As the only Eastern European country, Moldova also stands out from the rest in economic terms; it is the only European country out of those chosen for this book that is not a member of the European Union. Trafficking out of the country has been the main policy concern in Moldova, leaving prostitution rarely discussed by the government.

In contrast, prostitution has been on the political agenda in Sweden, France, and England and Wales at various points over the last decade. Influenced by a high proportion of female policy makers and the state's gender equality discourse, in Sweden prostitution began to be conceived in policy terms as a form of violence against women in the late 1990s. Around this time, prostitution entered the public agenda in France, and the right-wing government elected in 2002 pushed policy making even further down the security and law and order path. From the 1950s until recently, there had been no serious consideration of prostitution legislation in England and Wales. When New Labour gained power in 1997 it embarked on a large range of constitutional and legislative reforms. After lengthy consultations and legislative reviews of sexual offences (which included some but not all prostitution laws) and domestic violence, a review of policies relating to prostitution was announced by the Home Office in 2004, and a new Coordinated Prostitution Strategy was published in January 2006.

The four Asian countries that we have chosen – Pakistan, India, Thailand and Taiwan – are diverse in some aspects of their political and social structures. Politically all four countries have different systems of governance. Although India and Pakistan share a past and a geographical boundary, following independence from colonial rule they took on distinct and separate identities. Pakistan has emerged as an Islamic state, while India is notionally a secular country, and prides itself on its democratic structure. Taiwan has also experienced colonialism from the Japanese. Thailand, as all the Asian countries discussed, has been a predominantly rural economy but has – like India and Pakistan – experienced the economic and social consequences of globalisation and structural adjustment.

Prior to 1947, India and Pakistan had a common geographical boundary, hence the legal colonial controls over prostitution in the form of the Contagious Diseases Acts – a form of licensing the trade – were the same. In both India and Pakistan, the precolonial forms of the sex trade – the devadasi (religious prostitution) and tawaif (courtesan) systems – continued under colonialism, and continue in some form to date, although they are often difficult to distinguish from the brothel system. Historically both these systems are associated with music and dance. The British army in India and Pakistan had a policy of supporting the creation of such regulated zones around cantonments, railway stations and working-class areas in urban centres where young single men lived, and these have survived in urban centres of India (Mumbai, Kolkata and New Delhi) and Pakistan (Lahore and Multan).

The system of prostitution in colonial Taiwan was based on racial differentiation and, as in India and Pakistan, there was some effort by colonialism to control sexually transmitted diseases (STDs) through licensing prostitution. After the Second World War, policing prostitution was regarded as an issue for the Chinese nationalist ideology and efforts were made to correct the 'improper social atmosphere' that had been brought about by Japanese colonists. However, there were some efforts through a form of licensing to satisfy the perceived sexual urges of single young soldiers, from mainland China.

Thai prostitution has a different historical trajectory, and has been attributed to patriarchal values inherent in Buddhism, the collapse of slavery in the early 20th century and local cultural values that elide extra-marital sex with financial exchange. In Thailand, the sex trade has only developed into a full-scale industry in the past few decades, as an effect of two separate, but interconnected events – the Vietnam War and the explosion of tourism.

The status of women

Across Europe and Asia, women bear the brunt of poverty, in that they are more likely to live in poverty than men in the same country. In Europe, women from England and Wales, France and Sweden, however, are financially well off compared to women in Moldova. Moldova is the poorest country in Europe, in contrast to the others, which are among the richest.

Women in the European countries have a number of rights guaranteed under the European Convention on Human Rights; however, in practice women may find it difficult to take action if their rights are violated. Women from the International Committee for Prostitutes' Rights and those attending the World Whores' Congress have argued that the human rights of sex workers guaranteed under the European Convention on Human Rights are being breached under a number of Articles, including: Article 2 (Right to life), arguing murderers of prostitutes are rarely prosecuted; and Article 8 (Respect for private and family life), arguing that anti-pimping laws put their whole families at risk of arrest (International Committee for Prostitutes' Rights, 1988). Arguments could also be made that prostitution breaches women's right to be free from torture, inhuman and degrading treatment (Article 3) and the prohibition of slavery and forced labour (Article 4), particularly for trafficked women. All four countries are also all signatories to the 1979 Convention on the Elimination of All Forms of Discrimination against Women. Violence against women and other forms of gendered inequality are raised as issues in all of the chapters. Both Kristina Abiala and Yvonne Svanström show that widely held views about women need to be questioned, in particular the mythology of the 'strong Moldovan women' and the 'gender equal' image of Sweden.

There are some similarities to women's status in all the Asian countries that we are looking at. In all the countries we are examining, women have a number of constitutional legal rights. In India these include right to equality and equal protection under the law, right to equal pay and legal protection from sexual assault and domestic violence. In Pakistan, women have full rights of equal citizenship within the constitution of Pakistan, while in Taiwan, women theoretically enjoy equal rights to obtain child custody and rights to property. In reality, however, women in all the countries experience a range of economic and social hardships, including domestic violence, limited access to the public sphere, low literacy rates, high death rates during child birth, restricted access to opportunities, including education and employment, and a generally inferior status in society.

Women in India and Pakistan suffer the ill effects of dowry demands that reflect their low status in society, while in Taiwan and Thailand, young single women experience a sense of obligation towards their parents. Both these factors have implications for entering the sex trade. Dowry is often cited as a reason for entering the sex trade as there is often pressure on young women to 'earn' dowry for themselves or other female members of their families, while a sense of filial obligation can also be a cited reason for entering the sex trade, as young women consider it their responsibility to look after their parents or other members of their family. What is interesting to note here is that while the logics behind dowry and filial obligation seem to be different – dowry is a sense of women being seen as economic burdens on their parents, of which filial obligation is the reverse – they both lead to increased pressures and oppressive practices on women, including violence against women.

Thai women experience the effect of global tourism, which is perhaps less obvious in the other areas that we are looking at. However, all the societies we are looking at experience the social and economic consequences of globalisation, including increased impoverishment, which have specific gendered consequences. These include women being subjected to increased and changed forms of violence both within the home and within the market. Globalisation in India has meant that agricultural waged labourers (predominantly women) have had to experience the shift from a barter system (which allowed them to feed their families and not experience the vagaries of inflation) to a cash economy and pressure from the market. This has led to decline in food consumption, with a consequent increase in interpersonal violence against women in the home (Krishnaraj, 1999).

The Asian countries have very strong women's movements that have responded to specific challenges faced in their countries. For instance, the contemporary Indian women's movements have responded to issues of poverty, dowry-related violence and globalisation, while in Pakistan, women's organisations have struggled against an increasing Islamisation of the society, which has attempted to control women and women's sexuality in different ways. In Taiwan, as in India and Pakistan, women's organisations have existed since the 1920s but feminist organisations devoted to radical social changes only emerged in the 1980s. Across the four countries, the issues of prostitution and women in prostitution are only recently becoming issues of debate within feminist movements as feminist issues.

Legal structures in relation to prostitution

Law and policy relating to prostitution across the countries are heavily influenced by different approaches to prostitution. Globally, nearly all states have a policy on prostitution of some kind, even if it is not actively enforced (Outshoorn, 2004). Until recently, in England and Wales, the predominant perspective has been one of reducing public nuisance, and laws have criminalised not the selling of sex, but rather the activities that surround it (loitering, kerb crawling, etc). However, the 2006 Coordinated Prostitution Strategy aims to achieve a reduction in street prostitution, not only for reasons of public nuisance and the safety and quality of life of residents living in communities affected by prostitution, but also to reduce the incidence and prevalence of commercial sexual exploitation. In France, legislation comes from a security perspective, underlined by a right-wing law-and-order government and strict immigration policies. From this perspective, women face increasingly high penalties, including imprisonment and deportation, if convicted of soliciting or even 'passive soliciting'. Buying sex from a woman involved in prostitution is only a criminal offence if the woman is classed as being 'particularly vulnerable'. Policy makers in both France and England and Wales have watched the implementation and impact of Sweden's new legislation with great interest.

In Sweden, a new law was introduced in 1999 that criminalised only the buyer, and not the seller, of sex. This was a radical move and is based on the perspective of violence as abuse. The maximum penalty is imprisonment; however, as Yvonne Svanström highlights in Chapter Four, no man has yet been sent to prison for this offence. In contrast, in Moldova the act of selling sex is a criminal offence, but the buying of sex is legal. In Chapter Five, Kristina Abiala describes how the idea of criminalising the buyer is viewed as an amusing one by male officials in Moldova.

Although the four Asian countries have different legal systems, what they share is the desire to control sex work. As we have seen, the Contagious Diseases Acts were in operation in colonial India and Pakistan, intended to keep women in prostitution clean from STDs. However, the post-colonial legal structures in both these countries are dissimilar. After independence, India adopted the 'toleration system' under the 1956 Suppression of Immoral Traffic Act (henceforth SITA), later amended to the 1986 Immoral Traffic in Women and Girls (Prevention) Act (henceforth PITA). Under these Acts, prostitution was tolerated, but there were strong efforts by the state to control it by creating penal provisions for soliciting, seducing, activity in the vicinity of public places, procuring, detaining, brothel keeping, abetment to brothel keeping, renting premises for the purposes of prostitution and living off the earnings of a prostitute. PITA recognises male prostitution by including male prostitutes in the category of soliciting or seduction for prostitution. In addition to these provisions, women in prostitution are subjected to provisions in the Police Acts in different states of India that aim to control 'indecent behaviour' and 'public nuisance'. There have been recent attempts to legalise sex work in parts of India, in an effort to counter the perceived threat of AIDS and STDs, because women in the sex trade are seen as vectors of these diseases. The proposed laws are not meant to protect them but to look after the interests of clients.

In Pakistan, however, there were efforts to dismantle the red-light areas in the 1950s and 1960s. Unlike India, toleration was not an option. However, with the breakdown of red-light areas, sex workers moved to residential areas, creating a backlash from residents of these areas and so the red-light areas were reopened. In the time of Zulfiqar Ali Bhutto, in the early 1970s, the communities from the red-light areas enjoyed a respite, with some degree of police protection. However, during Zia-ul-Haq's time (1977-88), there was an effort to Islamise the country and prostitution was seen as an evil practice; the government's approach was to eradicate it by harassing sex workers and clients. In addition, the Hadood Ordinances (ostensibly a tool to check adultery) were used against sex workers as a tool for extortion. This, however, meant that sex work spread outside the red-light area to where police presence was not so visible. Thus, not only did the government's approach not eradicate prostitution, but it also helped to spread it to areas outside the more visible red-light areas. Zia's policies continue to plague women in sex work in Pakistan, partly because feminists have not focused on the rights of sex workers, even though the ill effects of the Hadood Ordinances were felt equally by sex workers and women outside the sex trade.

In Taiwan, from the late 1950s to 1997, some forms of prostitution were legalised, and during this period there were 'special businesses' constituting the two major sex sectors of modern Taiwanese sex industry since. These included 'body-selling' and 'pleasure-selling'. Commercial sex in 'body-selling' sector involves providing explicit sex to clients, and relations between clients and workers are more commercialised; while 'pleasure-selling' involves a whole range of different services and the relations are more personalised to cater to clients' diverse demands. Women in the 'body-selling' sector usually suffer more from police harassment, while the 'pleasure-selling' sector is much more tolerated. Existing Taiwanese regulations regarding prostitution include criminal law, the Social Order Maintenance Act (SOM), and the Act for Prevention of Child and Juvenile Involvement in Commercial Sex. As in India, the criminal law does not criminalise prostitutes, but makes pimping, trafficking of women and children, and running and managing brothels felonies. However, the SOM criminalises prostitutes and people who solicit for prostitution. As in India, the law tolerates clients and penalises women in the sex trade, while in Pakistan, both prostitutes and clients are penalised in a moralistic legal system.

In Thailand, the 1966 Service Establishments Act effectively legitimised places where sex work could be conducted, following a brief period that made it illegal in 1960. Till then, as in India and Pakistan, prostitution had been legalised, and regulated by the 1909 Control and Prevention of Venereal Disease Act, which introduced licensing for brothels and required brothel owners to ensure that women in the trade were free of STDs. The Entertainments Act is ostensibly designed to control sex work but, in reality, provides loopholes for owners of bars and brothels but no protection for sex workers. Legalisation provides no benefits or protection to sex workers but to pimps and clients.

Debates around decriminalisation and legalisation

Another reason to work on this joint project was to understand the different systems of laws relating to prostitution that exist through the world. The main forms are: prohibition or abolition, toleration, legalisation and decriminalisation. *Prohibition* or *abolition* criminalises all aspects of prostitution, that is, the sale of women's sexual services for commercial purposes. Prostitution is therefore illegal. *Toleration* does not abolish prostitution per se. The basis of the toleration prism is that prostitution is a 'necessary evil' that must be controlled so that public decency and order are not affected. *Legalisation* permits prostitution, but under the aegis of the state. Under this system, women involved in prostitution are allowed to practise prostitution if they obtain a licence from the state. The licence is given if the women fulfil certain conditions: these could include a minimum age and health standard. Legalisation equates prostitution with work, but effective protection under law is not always given. Here, too, the underlying assumption is that prostitution is necessary for the effective running of a stable social order and that prostitutes should be subjected to controls lest they adversely affect public order and health. *Decriminalisation* involves removing provisions that criminalise aspects of prostitution, such as soliciting, brothel keeping and living off the earnings of prostitution. A distinction is made between voluntary prostitution and prostitution involving force and coercion. Decriminalisation allows scope for criminalising non-voluntary prostitution and child prostitution.

Although an issue of little debate in Moldova, Kristina Abiala describes how there is general agreement between government and non-governmental organisations that prostitution should not be legalised: a position that is supported by the international community. A minority view does exist for legalisation, but this is more related to the tax revenue it would create than to the right of women to sell sex.

In the other European countries – England and Wales, France and Sweden – there has been more debate. In Sweden and France debate in the late 1990s and early 2000s was extensive, with new policies developing from this debate. Yvonne Svanström explains that in Sweden debate now centres on the pros and cons of the new legislation rather than on whether prostitution is a phenomenon wanted in modern society. As the implementation of the 2006 Coordinated Prostitution Strategy gets under way in England and Wales, it is likely that the same thing will happen, and the strategy rather than prostitution will become the issue under discussion.

There are very active debates on decriminalisation and legalisation within feminist organisations in India, Taiwan and Thailand, but very little on the issue in Pakistan. In Pakistan, there have been some debates around health issues relating to women in prostitution but not on decriminalisation and legalisation. This is possibly because, while Pakistan has a vibrant women's movement, it has been confronted by other political debates, including basic human rights of women under an increasingly Islamised society.

In India, while NGOs and women's organisations have views about the merits of one type of legal system over another, there is a general consensus that existing laws are not effective. Some sex workers' organisations believe that some women enter sex work voluntarily. In all cases, legalisation can help to improve their lives and will prevent excesses by the police. Proposals include repealing all laws that victimise women in prostitution, recognition of voluntary prostitution, a legal recognition of the families of prostitutes as a legitimate unit and effective criminal law intervention in the case of rape, sexual abuse and coercion. Other organisations argue that prostitution is not work, but a form of oppression and should not be legalised. They look at prostitution as resulting from trafficking and force and argue that no woman would choose to enter prostitution voluntarily. Therefore, women and children in the trade should be protected and offered safe ways to exit the profession. Debates in Taiwan are similarly divided into two camps – abolition and decriminalisation. The abolition camp also stresses links between trafficking and commercial sex; while the decriminalisation camp looks at prostitution as a way of promoting sexual liberation. Therefore women in the sex trade should be treated the same as women in any other form of labour.

In Thailand, as in India, existing laws have been attacked as insufficient. While one camp, including Coalition Against Trafficking in Women (CATW), argues that existing laws offer no protection to victims of forced prostitution, others, including Global Alliance Against Traffic in Women (GAATW), argue that the law does not recognise the complexities involved within trafficking situations, including recognising trafficking to sites other than prostitution or voluntary entry into the trade. CATW views consent as a kind of false consciousness, while GAATW feels that some women do enter the trade voluntarily. Both CATW and GAATW have been influential in other parts of the world, including India and Taiwan, where the arguments have been adopted (and adapted) in local situations.

The chapters that follow

In this introduction we have explained how and why this book came about and why we chose the countries described in the chapters that follow. While emphasising context, we have attempted in this chapter to show how prostitution laws and policies operate across Europe and Asia. We have focused on areas where comparisons can be made. However, the individual chapters show that there are other key issues faced in relation to prostitution that vary according to time and place. Drugs, poverty, male violence, migration, trafficking, social stigma and discrimination in relation to sexual health are factors emphasised to varying degrees in the rest of the book. Although organised into two parts by continent, the chapters are not sequential and can be read in any order.

Note

[1] Previously, arguments have broken out between authors who state they have been misinterpreted and unfairly criticised by others. See the journal *Violence Against Women*; here Raphael and Shapiro (2004) and Farley (2004) were criticised by Weitzer (2005a) and subsequently had replies to Weitzer published (Farley, 2005 and Raphael and Shapiro, 2005), who himself had a reply published in response to their replies (Weitzer, 2005b)!

References

Bell, S.R. (1994) *Reading, writing and rewriting the prostitute body*, Bloomington and Indianapolis: Indiana University Press.

Donovan, C., Gangoli, G., Hester, M. and Westmarland, N. (2005) *Service provision and needs: Children living with domestic violence in South Tyneside*, Bristol: University of Bristol.

Durbar Mahila Samanwaya Committee (1997) *Sex-workers' manifesto. Theme paper of the first national conference of sex-workers*, Calcutta: Durbar Mahila Samanwaya Committee.

Dworkin, A. (1981) *Pornography: Men possessing women*, London, Women's Press.

Farley, M. (2004) 'Bad for the body, bad for the heart: prostitution harms women even if legalised or decriminalised', *Violence Against Women*, vol 10, no 10, pp 1087-125.

Farley, M. (2005) 'Prostitution harms women even if indoors; reply to Weitzer', *Violence Against Women*, vol 11, no 7, pp 950-64.

Gangoli, G. (1998) 'Prostitution, legalisation and decriminalisation – recent debates', *Economic and Political Weekly*, 7 March 1998, pp 504-5.

Gangoli, G., Donovan, C., Hester, M. and Westmarland, N. (2005) *Service provision and needs: Black and minority ethnic women living with domestic violence in South Tyneside*, Bristol: University of Bristol.

Haraway, D.S. (1991) *Simians, cyborgs and women: The reinvention of nature*, London: Free Association Books.

International Committee for Prostitutes' Rights (1988) 'International Committee for Prostitutes' Rights world charter and world whores' congress statements', in F. Delacoste and P. Alexander (eds), *Sex work: Writings by women in the sex industry*, London: Virago, pp 305-21.

Jeffreys, S. (1997) *The idea of prostitution*, Victoria, Australia: Spinifex.

Krishnaraj, M. (1999) 'Globalisation and women in India', *Development in practice*, vol 9, no 5, pp 587-92.

McElroy, W. (1991) *Freedom, feminism and the state: An overview of individualist feminism*, California: Holmes and Meier Publishers.

Mackinnon, C. (1993) *Only words*, Harvard, MA: Harvard University Press.

O'Connell Davidson, J. (1999) *Prostitution, power and freedom*, Cambridge: Polity Press.

Outshoorn, J. (2004) Introduction: prostitution, women's movements and democratic politics', in J. Outshoorn (ed) *The politics of prostitution – Women's movements, democratic states and the globalisation of sex commerce*, Cambridge: Cambridge University Press, pp 1 20.

Raphael, J. and Shapiro, D. (2004) 'Violence in indoor and outdoor prostitution venues', *Violence Against Women*, vol 10, no 2, pp 126-39.

Raphael, J. and Shapiro, D. (2005) 'Reply to Weitzer', *Violence Against Women,* vol 11, no 7, pp 965-70.

Weitzer, R. (2005a) 'Flawed theory and method in studies of prostitution', *Violence Against Women*, vol 11, no 7, pp 934-49.

Weitzer, R. (2005b) 'Rehashing tired claims about prostitution, a response to Farley and Raphael and Shapiro', *Violence Against Women*, vol 11, no 7, pp 971-7.

Part One
Europe

TWO

From the personal to the political: shifting perspectives on street prostitution in England and Wales

Nicole Westmarland

Introduction

In July 2004, the Home Office announced the largest review of prostitution law and policy since the 1950s. The aim of the review was to provide a basis on which a realistic and coherent strategy to prostitution could be developed. Similar consultations and reforms had just been completed in relation to other forms of violence against women, including domestic violence, rape and other sexual offences. Based on findings from Home Office evaluations (Hester and Westmarland, 2004) a consultation paper called *Paying the price* was published (Home Office, 2004). In his foreword to the consultation David Blunkett (Home Secretary at the time) acknowledged that many of the laws relating to prostitution were '... outdated, confusing and ineffective' (Home Office, 2004, p 5). Almost 6,000 paper copies of the consultation were distributed (in addition to the online copy) and the review team received 861 responses by the closing date in November 2004. In January 2006 the government published its new Coordinated Prostitution Strategy (Home Office, 2006).

Before the publication of the Coordinated Prostitution Strategy there was a lack of clear policy in relation to prostitution in England and Wales. Legislation was situated within a public nuisance framework where prostitution itself was not illegal but the activities associated with it were (for example soliciting, kerb crawling, procuring and brothel keeping). This framework emerged from the 1957 *Report of the Committee on Homosexual Offences and Prostitution*, widely known as the Wolfenden Report after its chairman, Lord John Wolfenden. It is perhaps more infamous for its recommendation that some homosexual acts be decriminalised; the committee applied the same logic to both prostitution and homosexuality: that certain acts, however immoral, should be an issue of private not public control.

> Certain forms of sexual behaviour are regarded by many as sinful, morally wrong, or objectionable for reasons of conscience, or of religious or cultural tradition; and such actions may be reprobated on these grounds. But the criminal law does not cover all such actions at the present time; for instance, adultery and fornication are not offences for which a person can be punished by the criminal law. Nor indeed is prostitution as such. (Committee on Homosexual Offences and Prostitution, 1957, p 10)

Of course, public opinions have shifted hugely since the 1950s, and it is not surprising that we should see a shift in how prostitution is understood and how it is described in government policy documents. Fast forward nearly 50 years, and we see a far different approach being taken:

> Prostitution can have devastating consequences for the individuals involved and for the wider community. It involves the abuse of children and the serious exploitation of adults.... We need to ensure we have in place a coherent legal framework and effective tools to tackle abusers and exploiters.... We want this paper to inform the development of a clear view of the brutal realities of prostitution ... (Home Office, 2004, pp 5-6)
>
> It is crucial that we move away from a general perception that prostitution is the 'oldest profession' and has to be accepted. Street prostitution is not an activity that we can tolerate in our towns and cities. Nor can we tolerate any form of commercial sexual exploitation, whether it takes place on the street, behind the doors of a massage parlour or in a private residence. (Home Office, 2006, p 1)

The 2006 Coordinated Prostitution Strategy keeps the reducing public nuisance vision in sight, but puts in place a more holistic approach towards achieving this vision through: prevention, tackling demand, developing routes out, ensuring justice and tackling off-street prostitution. No longer is a reduction in prostitution seen as needed purely to reduce public nuisance and prevent community complaints to the police. This chapter describes the background to the Strategy and some of the tensions that exist between different approaches to prostitution. The focus of the chapter is on street prostitution.

The national context

Women in England and Wales are well off financially when compared to women in the rest of the world, with the UK ranked 12th in the Human Development Index (United Nations Development Programme, 2004). However, it is still estimated that 25% of women live in poverty (Bradshaw et al, 2003). There is a large gender gap between the earnings of women and men, and the UK is ranked only 50th in the world in terms of the ratio of female-to-male earned income (United Nations Development Programme, 2004). On average, women's hourly earnings are around 80% of men's (Office for National Statistics, 2004): around 40% of women, compared with less than 20% of men, have a weekly income of less than £100 (Women and Equality Unit, 2003), and nine out of ten single parent families are headed by a woman (Office for National Statistics, 2004).

In 1997, the Labour Party was elected, ending 18 consecutive years of the Conservative Party being in power (1979-97). Hailing itself as 'New' Labour, the party set about modernising the government, which included attempts to increase the number of women members of parliament, and the introduction of a new cabinet position of 'Minister of Women' and a Women's Unit.

Before the 1997 general election, just 9% of MPs were women (Women and Equality Unit, 2005). This rose to just over 18% in the 1997 election, dropping slightly in the 2001 election to just over 17% before rising again in 2005 to nearly 20% (Women and Equality Unit, 2005). All-women shortlists are thought to be responsible for this pattern: the Labour Party introduced all-women shortlists between 1993 and 1996 (responsible for the rise in 1997); in 1996 it was found that such shortlists were unlawful under the 1975 Sex Discrimination Act (responsible for the fall in 2001); then the 2002 Sex Discrimination (Election Candidates) Act legalised the shortlists again (responsible for the rise in 2005) (Women and Equality Unit,

2005). Within the House of Lords, the proportion of women is slightly lower than in the House of Commons (with the House of Lords made up of 17.7% women), but women occasionally fare slightly better within the cabinet, representing 26.1% following the May 2005 reshuffle (Women and Equality Unit, 2005).

Despite the increase in the proportion of women MPs – now more than double the pre-1997 number in the Conservative government – the UK is still far from reaching proportional representation in terms of gender. Comparatively, the UK fares poorly. It is ranked 13th in the EU and 41st by the Inter-Parliamentary Union (which lists 184 countries). Before the 2005 election the Inter-Parliamentary Union ranking was 57th (Inter-Parliamentary Union, 2005).

The current Labour government has probably taken so-called 'women's issues', particularly violence against women, more seriously than has any UK government before it. In its first two terms it reviewed and updated rape and sexual offences legislation (resulting in the 2003 Sexual Offences Act) and domestic violence legislation (resulting in the 2004 Domestic Violence, Crime and Victims Act). However, there is no integrated approach to tackling violence against women, and no national violence against women strategy (Kelly and Lovett, 2005).

Many forms of violence against women are criminal offences, particularly physical and sexual violence. This includes rape within marriage, although this has only been a criminal offence since 1991. However, successful prosecutions (defined here as resulting in a conviction) are rare for all forms of violence against women. Home Office data shows that only 5.6% of rapes reported to the police result in a conviction for rape (Kelly et al, 2005). Research on domestic violence shows that this low conviction rate is not peculiar to rape, but rather a feature in the prosecution of male violence against women in general (Phillips and Brown, 1998; Hester et al, 2003; HMIC and HMCPSI, 2004; Hester and Westmarland, 2005).

In 1999, the Home Office launched its £250m Crime Reduction Programme (later increased to £400m when £150m was added for the expansion of CCTV). This was a huge programme of funded pilot projects and independent evaluations in an attempt to discover 'what works' to reduce crime and disorder, with the longer-term aim of implementing an integrated approach to reducing crime and increasing community safety. The Crime Reduction Programme was divided into 20 sub-programmes, or 'streams', and funding allocated accordingly. Included in these streams were the £6.3m

Violence against Women initiative, which funded and evalu projects on domestic violence, rape and sexual assault, as more general streams such as the £30m targeted-policing in

The £850,000 'Reducing Crime and Disorder Associated Prostitution' stream funded 11 projects and evaluations. O one hand, this represented a very small proportion of the Crime Reduction Programme's original £250m funding (0.34% – less than half of one per cent). On the other hand, however, the funding of prostitution projects from central government money was historically a new phenomenon (Sagar, 2001).

Different perspectives on prostitution within England and Wales

There are three dominant perspectives on prostitution within England and Wales: the 'prostitution as nuisance', 'prostitution as work' and 'prostitution as abuse' perspectives. However, it must be remembered that these are not mutually exclusive groups and there are some overlaps between the approaches. As already mentioned, the current legislative framework follows the 'prostitution as nuisance' perspective. The Crime Reduction Programme's 'Reducing Crime and Disorder Associated with Prostitution' stream has some aspects of each of the perspectives, particularly the 'prostitution as nuisance' and 'prostitution as abuse' perspectives. The prostitution stream started and finished at around the same time as the Violence against Women Initiative reported its findings to the same Home Office team, and had the same authors responsible for the published overview of findings (Hester and Westmarland, 2004 and 2005). Yet, in labelling it as its own stream outside the Violence Against Women Initiative, the Home Office was able to sidestep the issue of whether it was viewing prostitution as a form of abuse (Skinner et al, 2005). The title of the stream meant that it remained firmly within the boundaries of the 'prostitution as nuisance' perspective, suggesting it was aiming not to reduce prostitution per se, only the crime and disorder associated with it.

Outside government, all three perspectives can be found. Examples of the 'prostitution as nuisance' perspective can be found particularly within local community residents' groups, who complain about the impact that prostitution has on the lives of those living within their community. Prostitution can have a huge impact on communities, including: an increased fear of crime inside and outside of the home; a reduction in property prices; concerns for children playing in the area; and a decreased quality of life (Hester and Westmarland, 2004). Very established 'red-light' districts, or 'beats', can become 'tourist attractions', with men travelling from long distances to visit the district (Hubbard and Sanders, 2003).

Some communities have attempted to take the problem into their own hands and engage in vigilante behaviour to move prostitution away from their area (Hubbard, 1997 and 1998). This is sometimes fuelled by local media, describing women involved in prostitution using offensive terms such as 'the human scavengers polluting our streets' and 'street scum' (*Birmingham Evening Mail*, 27 July 1995, cited in Hubbard and Sanders, 2003).

From the 'prostitution as work' perspective, prostitution is a form of labour and should be treated as such. The English Collective of Prostitutes is part of the International Prostitutes Collective, and argues that the way forward is decriminalisation – the abolition of all offences that criminalise women involved in prostitution and kerb crawlers. They argue that the police and the courts should shift their priority from prosecution to protection and that benefits and the minimum wage should be increased so that women are able to leave prostitution if they want to. From this perspective, a huge step forward was made in 2003 when one of Britain's largest trade unions, the GMB, voted to allow women involved in prostitution to join.

There is no one group that campaigns against the policies advocated by the English Collective of Prostitutes. Its main opponents can probably be best characterised as the feminist movement to end violence against women. This may sound strange, given that ending violence against women is one, if not the primary, aim of the English Collective of Prostitutes. The feminist movement to end violence against women and the English Collective of Prostitutes both, therefore, aim to end violence against women. However, for many involved in the violence against women movement, prostitution is in itself a form of violence against women. From this perspective, it is argued that women involved in prostitution need human rights, not workers' rights (Bindel, 2003), and prostitution equates to the 'oldest oppression' rather than the 'oldest profession' (Bindel, 2006).

Laws and policies

Existing laws and policies on prostitution

There is a widespread belief in England and Wales that prostitution is illegal. In fact, the selling of sex for money or other benefits is not illegal, but some of the activities associated with it are. There are currently over 25 criminal offences on the statute books that relate to prostitution, although some of these will be reformed during the implementation of the 2006 Coordinated Prostitution Strategy. Prostitution itself is not defined in statute, but is generally understood to be the exchange of sexual acts for money or drugs. The common-law definition dates back to the case of *de Munck* in 1918, as 'a woman who offers her body commonly for lewdness for payment in return' (cited in O'Neil, 1999, p 181).

The current legal framework, as mentioned earlier, is largely based on recommendations from the 1957 Wolfenden Report (Committee on Homosexual Offences and Prostitution, 1957) and also the work of the committee that preceded it – the 1927 Street Offences Committee led by Lord Macmillan. Under section 1 of the 1959 Street Offences Act, loitering or soliciting for the purposes of prostitution is a criminal activity, punishable by a fine of up to £500 for the first offence and £1,000 for subsequent offences. Under the Coordinated Prostitution Strategy loitering and soliciting will be reformed and a more rehabilitative 'staged' approach introduced. More than two cautions for soliciting currently renders the label 'common prostitute' in the eyes of the law; a term that has long been thought to be an inappropriate one[1]. The Coordinated Prostitution Strategy promises to remove the term, which the Home Office has now accepted is a stigmatising one. Under the 2003 Criminal Justice Act, community sentences can be given to people with three or more prostitution convictions, and the 2003 Sexual Offences Act made the offence gender neutral. Although the 2003 Sexual Offences Act did not contain the same overhaul of prostitution laws as it did for other sexual offences, it did create the first set of offences related to the protection of children under the age of 18. These new offences include: paying for the sexual services of a child; causing or inciting child prostitution; and controlling a child prostitute.

Men who visit women involved in prostitution are known as 'punters', 'clients' or, most often, 'kerb crawlers'. Kerb crawling – the persistent soliciting of a woman for the purposes of prostitution either on foot or from or near a motor vehicle – became a criminal offence under the 1985 Sexual Offences Act. The two relevant offences are:

> Kerb crawl with persistence from a motor vehicle or in a manner likely to cause annoyance to the woman or nuisance to other people in the neighbourhood. (section 1)
>
> Persistently solicit in a street or public place. (section 2)

The maximum sentence if convicted for kerb crawling or persistent soliciting is a £1,000 fine. In 2002 kerb crawling was made an arrestable offence under the 2001 Criminal Justice and Police Act (meaning kerb crawlers could be taken into custody and questioned immediately instead of being summonsed to appear in court), and in 2004 it became possible to use disqualification from driving as an increased penalty. The Coordinated Prostitution Strategy clearly states that the focus of enforcement in the future will be on kerb crawlers rather than women involved in prostitution. The Strategy talks of 'disrupting the market', for which it sees tackling 'demand' to deter punters as key.

The introduction of Anti-Social Behaviour Orders, commonly known as 'ASBOs', added to the 'prostitution as a public nuisance' discourse. ASBOs were introduced under the 1998 Crime and Disorder Act and were first granted in 1999. They are civil orders (although have a maximum criminal penalty of imprisonment if breached) that grant local authorities additional powers to deal with behaviour deemed anti-social, broadly defined as '... behaviour which causes or is likely to cause harassment, alarm or distress to one or more people who are not in the same household as the perpetrator' (Home Office, 2003a, p 5). Examples of such behaviour in the guidance are: graffiti, abusive and intimidating language, excessive noise, fouling the street with litter, drunken behaviour in the streets, and dealing drugs (Home Office, 2003a). However, ASBOs soon began to be used on women involved in prostitution, with an analysis of cases showing that in 5% of cases the anti-social behaviour in question was prostitution (Campbell, 2002). Following early concerns that ASBOs were being used in a discriminatory manner because of a focus on women involved in prostitution (Jones and Sagar, 2001), some orders have now been made against men who kerb crawl (Matthews, 2005). The Coordinated Prostitution Strategy acknowledges that many of those who responded to the consultation document were concerned about the use of ASBOs for women involved in prostitution, concerned that they may exclude women from the geographical areas where service providers (for example, support/exiting projects, drug projects) are based. However, the Strategy states that ASBOs and ABCs (Acceptable Behaviour Contracts) are appropriate for use with women involved in prostitution as long as they are used as part of a wider strategy of support, possibly including the new 'Intervention Orders', which are designed to assist with drug-related anti-social behaviour. The Strategy also confirms that ASBOs and ABCs can be used in relation to kerb crawlers and pimps.

Although this chapter is predominantly about street prostitution, it is important to mention briefly the view the Strategy takes with regard to off-street prostitution. A 'brothel' is defined in case-law as premises from which more than one person is involved in prostitution. The Strategy proposes that an amendment should be made to the definition of a brothel, and that the new definition should allow two or three people to be involved in prostitution from the same premises in the interests of safety. The Strategy also promises that a UK action plan on trafficking will be developed.

Operation of laws and policies

Although many of the activities associated with prostitution are illegal, as described above, in practice many of these laws are not actively enforced. The policing of prostitution tends to be reactionary, led by community complaints and varying over time and place. When complaints in an area reach a high level the police sometimes launch zero-tolerance style 'crackdowns' on prostitution where a higher than usual police presence is put in place, often for a pre-defined period. The new Strategy suggests that such 'crackdowns' will focus predominantly on men as 'buyers' in the future, and those involved in prostitution will be signposted towards services that might help them leave prostitution. Some vice units allow 'unofficial' tolerance zones to operate, where women are urged to work in some areas rather than in others; however, in practice this has often led to confusion. Because it is unofficial, it is difficult to communicate to the women and other police officers where the specified areas are, particularly if this changes. Changes in senior police staff and/or complaints from residents have sometimes led to the specified area changing location with little or no notice.

Convictions and cautions for soliciting offences are far more frequent than they are for kerb crawling. In 2002, 4,102 cautions and convictions were recorded for soliciting offences compared with just 1,354 for kerb crawling. This suggests that the criminal justice system is either disproportionately targeting women over men as offenders or that it is easier to prove that soliciting has taken place than it is kerb crawling. Presuming the 'tackling demand' and 'ensuring justice' elements of the Coordinated Prostitution Strategy are well implemented, this pattern should begin to reverse over the coming years.

The number of cautions and convictions given for soliciting offences is already on a downward slope. There were 14,824 cautions and convictions given in 1990 compared with 4,102 in 2002. This represents a huge 72% decrease over time. This decrease has not been replicated in the number of cautions and convictions for kerb crawling, with the number reducing only slightly and without the constant decrease over time. In 1990 there were 1,650 cautions and convictions for kerb crawling compared with 1,354 in 2002. This represents an 18% decrease. These statistics are most likely to be indicative of law enforcement practices rather than any true reduction in the extent of prostitution (O'Neil, 1999). To some extent, they might also reflect a reorganisation of prostitution, with fewer women involved in 'street' prostitution and more in 'off-street' locations (O'Neil, 1999).

Convictions for living off the earnings of prostitution are rare, and cases are notoriously difficult to prosecute. Women involved in prostitution may be reluctant to give evidence against those who 'pimp' them, because of a lack of confidence in the police, fear of the pimp and/or because they are in or have been in a relationship with the pimp. Convictions and cautions for procuring offences and for brothel-keeping offences have both been falling over time since 1990. In 2002 there were just 41 cautions and convictions for procuring offences (compared with 444 in 1990) and just 12 cautions and convictions for brothel-keeping offences (compared with 150 in 1990).

Analysis of policies and interventions

It was clear that the legislative framework on prostitution was not working long before the announcement of the review. It had not worked in relation to the prevention of public nuisance. Police 'crackdowns' have generally led to 'functional displacement', where women commit other offences such as handbag thefts, shoplifting and cheque fraud, and then return to prostitution when the crackdown has ended (Hester and Westmarland, 2004). Local communities have not been protected from prostitution-related disorder. On 10 September 2003, a one-day count of anti-social behaviour took place (Home Office, 2003b). This count found that 1,011 complaints were made regarding prostitution, kerb crawling or sexual acts. They estimated that organisations' time spent dealing with these complaints added up to £167,000 per day, totalling £42m per year in England and Wales (Home Office, 2003b).

However, the current legislation hass not worked for women involved in prostitution either. The English Collective of Prostitutes argues that the government's policies have made women involved in prostitution even more vulnerable to violence and exploitation. In particular, they criticise: the use of ASBOs for increasing the number of women being sent to prison, thereby destroying families and putting more children into local authority care; the introduction of anti-trafficking legislation that they claim is primarily used to deport women with no evidence of force or coercion needed to prove the offence; and the targeting of kerb crawlers for arrest and possible disqualification of driving if convicted. They claim that these factors result in increasing violence and make women more vulnerable to pimps and others.

The current legislation does not seem to have worked in relation to kerb crawlers either. Men who kerb crawl have rarely been stopped by the police and even if they were, did not always face prosecution. It is difficult to evidence 'persistence', and men use a range of 'reasons' as to why they were in the area and talking to the women legitimately. Brooks-Gordon and Gelsthorpe (2003) found that denial (for example, claiming they were asking for directions) was the most frequent response given by men stopped for kerb crawling. Many then went on to 'plead' with the officers, particularly the male officers, for example: 'please officer, you'll ruin my life', 'you will break up my marriage' or 'I will lose my job' (kerb crawlers cited in Brooks-Gordon and Gelsthorpe, 2003, p 162).

The current prostitution legislation has also sent out confusing and mixed state messages, particularly in relation to children and young people. In 2000, new policy guidance was issued jointly by the Department of Health, the Home Office, the Department for Education and Employment and the National Assembly for Wales entitled *Safeguarding children involved in prostitution*. Here, they stated that 'children involved in prostitution should be treated primarily as the victims of abuse …' (DH, HO, DfEE and NAW, 2000, p 3). They explained:

> It is a tragedy for any child to become involved in prostitution. It exposes them to abuse and assault, and may threaten their lives. It deprives them of their childhood, self-esteem and opportunities for good health, education and training. It results in their social exclusion. (p 3)

This guidance therefore created a paradigm shift from a 'punishment' to a 'welfare' model (Ayre and Barrett, 2000).

It is still, however, possible for children involved in prostitution to be prosecuted if they are said to be 'persistently and voluntarily' returning to prostitution. The fact that children and young people can still be labelled as 'common prostitutes' under the law sits extremely uneasily with other government policies, and the abolition of the term within the Coordinated Prostitution Strategy is welcomed but also well overdue. In *Paying the price*, for example, the government seemed to accept unequivocally that children are abused through prostitution. For example, they asked for responses to the question 'How do we ensure that it is clearly understood that those using young people under 18 for sex are guilty of child abuse?' The answer to this must presumably start with preventing the labelling of abused children as 'common prostitutes' and removing the possibility of their arrest, prosecution and conviction. Between 1989 and 1999, there were 3,312 cautions issued and 2,327 convictions of children and young people aged under 18 (Home Office figures, cited in Hunter and May, 2004), although this number has thankfully fallen dramatically. The Coordinated Prostitution Strategy states as one of its objectives '… we must leave no one in any doubt that involving young people in prostitution is child abuse' (Home Office, 2006, p 1). The Strategy assures the reader that there were only three convictions of people under 18 in England and Wales in 2004. However, the number of arrests and prosecutions is likely to be higher (that is, a 100% conviction rate is unlikely), and the question of why even three young people who are experiencing child abuse should be convicted remains unanswered. The use of the criminal law for victims of child abuse is unacceptable and it is outrageous that the Coordinated Prostitution Strategy states that in exceptional circumstances children can still be prosecuted in this way: 'Guidance will remain firmly against the use of the criminal law in respect of children involved in prostitution save in the most exceptional circumstances – as a "last resort" where services fail to engage with young people and they return repeatedly to the streets' (Home Office, 2006, p 9).

If the 'last resort' should be used 'where services fail', perhaps it is the service providers and/or those who fail to provide adequate funding for services themselves who should be prosecuted. Is it really the child's or young person's fault that the services failed to engage?

Debates on legalisation and decriminalisation

From the public nuisance perspective, official tolerance zones or managed zones can be an attractive proposition, and there are often high levels of community support for such zones. Moving red-light districts away from residential to more industrial areas means a reduction in nuisance caused to neighbourhoods. In Liverpool, 83% of residents voted in favour of a managed zone, as did most women involved in prostitution (96%), with the latter naming added safety and no risk of arrest as the main incentives (Clark et al, 2004). However, local authorities do not have the power to create managed zones, with a need for primary legislation to be changed before Liverpool or any other city could go ahead with their creation. To the disappointment of residents affected by prostitution in Liverpool and some other areas, the Coordinated Prostitution Strategy firmly rules this out of the question.

The English Collective of Prostitutes is quoted as opposing such zones, with a spokesperson describing them as '... nothing more than an excuse to tolerate rape and other violence against prostitute women' (Carter, 2004). As mentioned earlier, the 'prostitution as work' perspective campaigns for the abolition of all soliciting and kerb crawling offences, claiming that prostitution should be treated as a job like any other and that government policies dramatically increase the amount of violence and abuse faced by women involved in prostitution.

Criticisms are also made of the wider women's movement as well as government policies. In 2003, the International Collective of Prostitutes released 'An open letter to the women's movement from the global women's strike'. In this letter, they described the picketing of a lap-dancing club in London by a number of well-known feminist organisations to end violence against women on International Women's Day as 'obscene'. They argued that these groups should have been campaigning against the Iraq war rather than against a lap-dancing club, accused them of being sexist and arrogant for thinking they know what is best for women who work in such clubs and for putting women at a greater risk of violence if such clubs are raided or closed down. In 2004, they made similar criticisms of a Reclaim the Night march held on International Violence against Women Day through Soho – an area of London with high levels of lap-dancing clubs and prostitution. Other groups have also been critical of the movement to end violence against women's approach to prostitution, for example a group called Cause for Concern was set up specifically to challenge and share their concerns about a kerb crawler re-education programme set up by a group of violence against women researchers (this is discussed later; for an overview of the arguments made by Cause for Concern, see Campbell and Storr, 2001).

In contrast to the 'prostitution as nuisance' and 'prostitution as work' perspectives, the movement to end violence against women has not needed to mount sustained lobbying campaigns. Although most would rather women were not criminalised and a welfare and empowerment approach was taken, the introduction of the power of arrest for kerb crawlers and the increased penalty of removal of driving licences have been welcomed with little lobbying needed. It is now the case, as others have noted, that England and Wales are moving further away from the 'prostitution as work' perspective towards the 'prostitution as abuse' perspective: 'Issues of abuse and coercion are beginning to dominate UK debate, both in the media and at official levels, encouraged by a Labour government with a programme of moral renewal' (West, 2000, p 110). This means that the movement to end violence against women has been in a relatively powerful position as regards the shaping of government policy in relation to prostitution. This is aided by the historically unique position that the movement to end violence against women currently has in England and Wales, with strong non-governmental organisations alongside a government seriously willing to address some of the issues it has raised (Kelly and Lovett, 2005). Looking at the position the movement is in now, it is sometimes hard to remember that little over a decade ago it was legal for a man to rape his wife in England and Wales.

From the 'prostitution as abuse' perspective, tackling prostitution means supporting women to leave while penalising the men who abuse them (from this perspective meaning all kerb crawlers and pimps). This does not necessarily equate to criminal penalties;

England and Wales' first kerb crawler re-education programme was developed and run by a group of violence against women researchers. Based on the North American 'john school' model, the first kerb crawler re-education programme was set up in West Yorkshire in 1998. The one-day programme aimed to shift the emphasis from the woman involved in prostitution and onto the kerb crawler, and by attending the programme the kerb crawlers were able to avoid prosecution (Research Centre on Violence Abuse and Gender Relations, 2000). Although this and other evaluations have found few or no men are stopped again for kerb crawling after completing such a programme (see also Hester and Westmarland, 2004), the length and geographical coverage of these evaluations mean it is not possible to be confident about the impact of these programmes. Comments from men following programme attendance, however, are promising:

> '... it opened my eyes to what was really going on and the women who are prostitutes are real people, not just objects to be used.' (Kerb crawler, quoted in Research Centre on Violence, Abuse and Gender Relations, 2000, p 17)

> 'Basically it was quite disturbing to be presented with the full implications of one's behaviour.' (Kerb crawler, quoted in Research Centre on Violence, Abuse and Gender Relations, 2000, p 17)

> 'It was a stupid mistake – after listening to the speakers I would like to give something back to the community.' (Kerb crawler, quoted in Hester and Westmarland, 2004, p 45)

The Coordinated Prostitution Strategy states that kerb crawler re-education programmes (funded by the offenders and offered as a form of court diversion) can be useful in reducing re-offending for men who have no previous convictions for kerb crawling or other sexual offences.

Key issues faced

Drug use

In England and Wales, drug addiction is central to street prostitution, leading to the argument that drugs are in fact replacing pimps (Miller, 1995; Melrose et al, 1999). Research shows that nearly all women (more than nine in ten) involved in street prostitution are using drugs (Barnard and Hart, 2000; Hester and Westmarland, 2004). Hester and Westmarland (2004) report that heroin is the drug most commonly used (in 88% of cases where drug use was disclosed), although there are an increasing number of women using crack cocaine (in 68% of cases where drug use was disclosed). Over half (58%) of the women who disclosed drug use were dual addicted, using both heroin and crack cocaine. These figures are far higher than have been found among women in the general population. British Crime Survey findings show that in general, women are less likely to use Class A drugs than men, that less than 0.5 per cent of women aged between 16 and 29 had used heroin within the last month, and the same figure had taken crack cocaine (Ramsey et al, 2001).

Drug use varies between those involved in street prostitution compared with those involved in off-street prostitution. Church et al (2001) found that nearly two-thirds (63%) of women involved in street prostitution reported that the main reason they were involved in prostitution was to buy drugs, compared with just 1% of women involved in off-street prostitution. The type of drugs used varies as well, with women involved in street prostitution more likely to use heroin and crack cocaine than women involved in off-street prostitution, and women involved in off-street prostitution more likely to use tranquillisers and amphetamines (Church et al, 2001).

There is no simple answer to the question of what comes first – the drug use or the prostitution. May et al (1999) found that 46 out of 67 women involved in prostitution (69%) had started using drugs before they became involved in prostitution; however, 18 (27%) had become involved before they started using drugs. A few (4%) said that their drug use had started at the same time that they had become involved in prostitution.

Once involved in prostitution, drug addiction can act as a factor to keep women involved. Research by May et al (1999) found that women involved in prostitution were spending between 75% and 100% of their money on drugs. Again, there was a difference depending on the location of the prostitution, with women involved in street prostitution spending an average of £525 per week on drugs, compared with an average of £270 per week for those involved in off-street prostitution.

Reasons for entry into prostitution

The 1957 Wolfenden Report suggested 'a bad upbringing', 'seduction at an early age', 'a broken marriage' or 'some additional psychological element in the personality of the individual woman who becomes a prostitute' as reasons why women may become involved in prostitution (Committee on Homosexual Offences and Prostitution, 1957, p 79). Since then, and particularly over the last decade, there have been a number of research studies that have found that there are a number of social factors that work in various ways to make involvement in prostitution plausible (Phoenix, 2001). These vary depending on age and personal circumstances. Pearce (2003) interviewed 55 young women and found that sexualised risk taking (eg getting into cars with strangers) and 'swapping' sexual acts for some form of gain (eg a roof for the night, a meal) were both associated with the risk of becoming sexually exploited through prostitution. It is also thought that the number may be increasing, as mobile phones and internet chat rooms are increasingly being used as grooming tools (Barnardos, 2004).

Typically, women are young when they first become involved in prostitution. Around half are aged 18 or under (May et al, 1999; Hester and Westmarland, 2004), meaning that at least their early experiences were ones of sexual exploitation. In a survey of Area Child Protection Committees across England, Swann and Balding (2001) found that three-quarters said that they knew of children being sexually exploited through prostitution in their area. Most of these children have a history of running away from home or care (Melrose et al, 1999; Pearce, 2003), many have lived in local authority care (Pearce, 2003; Hester and Westmarland, 2004) and have obtained few if any educational qualifications (Pitts, 1997; Hester and Westmarland, 2004). Experiences of abuse as children are also common (Hester and Westmarland, 2004).

As well as drugs, already discussed earlier, women give a variety of reasons as to why they first became involved in prostitution. While an abusive male acting as a 'pimp' is sometimes the main reason for becoming involved, it is more likely to be a female friend who first introduces them to prostitution (Hester and Westmarland, 2004).

Wanting money for 'nice things', to fit in with a peer group, a low level of self-esteem and to pay outstanding debts have all been associated with becoming involved in prostitution (Hester and Westmarland, 2004). Needing money for household expenses and/or to support their children is far more regularly cited as a reason for being involved in prostitution by women involved in off-street prostitution than those involved in street prostitution (Church et al, 2001).

Conclusions

This chapter has described the current legislative framework and different perspectives on prostitution in England and Wales. It has shown how policy and legislation have traditionally centred on the 'prostitution as nuisance' perspective; however, the 'prostitution as abuse' perspective has received more attention from policy makers in recent years and it is this approach that forms the basis of the 2006 Coordinated Prostitution Strategy.

Talking about academics at London Metropolitan University's Child and Woman Abuse Studies Unit (CWASU), Kantola and Squires (2004) highlight the influence they have had on shaping policy around the trafficking of women and children for sexual purposes: 'They have been able to gender the debate because their sexual domination frame is in sufficient ideological alignment with the moral order frame of the government' (p 78).

It is probably no accident either that Marianne Hester and I, at the time the Director and Coordinator of the International Centre for the Study of Violence and Abuse, were commissioned to write the overview report of the findings from the evaluation of the Home Office's Reducing Crime and Disorder Associated with Prostitution (Hester and Westmarland, 2004).

So did this mean that the findings of the review were a foregone conclusion? Was it inevitable that the new Strategy would follow the 'prostitution as abuse' perspective? An adaptation of the Swedish model where only the male is criminalised was certainly on the agenda but so were other possibilities, for example the review asked very detailed questions about tolerance zones. The differences between prostitution in England and Wales and prostitution in Sweden were an issue that the Home Office was very aware of; in particular, that Class A drug abuse is not as widespread in Sweden as it is in England and Wales and that Sweden has never had the same extent of prostitution as England and Wales has (Home Office,

2004; 2006). It was also unclear what impact, if any, the change of Home Secretary in 2003 would have. The only thing that was certain was that the existing legislation was not appropriate, had long been in need of review, and if it is to be another half-century before it is reviewed again, it is important that it is right this time for everyone involved.

Whether it is right this time for everyone involved will depend to a great extent who you ask. Some groups will be relatively pleased with the content of the Strategy and hope that implementation is fast and successful. Others will be angry, upset and disappointed by the Strategy. As time goes on it is hoped that the Strategy can act as an impetus for different groups to work together more closely to achieve what is best for women involved in different forms of prostitution, and that ideological positions do not get in the way of ensuring women's safety and well-being.

Note

[1] Between 1967 and 1981 five Private Member's Bills were introduced in the House of Lords to abolish the term, but none received a second reading (Kantola and Squires, 2004).

Recommended further reading

Hester, M. and Westmarland, N. (2004) *Tackling street prostitution: Towards an holistic approach*, Home Office Research Study 279, London: Home Office.

Home Office (2006) *A Coordinated Prostitution Strategy and a summary of responses to Paying the Price*, London: Home Office.

Kantola, J. and Squires, J. (2004) 'Prostitution policies in Britain, 1982-2002', in J. Outshoorn (ed) *The politics of prostitution Women's movements, democratic states and the globalisation of sex commerce*, Cambridge: Cambridge University Press, pp 62–82.

References

Ayre, P. and Barrett, D. (2000) 'Young people and prostitution: an end to the beginning?', *Children and Society*, vol 14, no 1, pp 48-59.

Barnard, M. and Hart, G. (2000) *Client violence against prostitute women working from street and off-street locations: A three-city comparison*, Swindon: Economic and Social Research Council.

Barnardos (2004) *Just one click: Sexual abuse of children and young people through the internet and mobile phone technology*, Ilford: Barnardos.

Bindel, J. (2003) 'Sex workers are different', *Guardian*, 7 July.

Bindel, J. (2006) 'Eradicate the oppression', *Guardian*, 18 January.

Bradshaw, J., Finch, N., Kemp, P.A., Mayhew, E. and Williams, J. (2003) *Gender and poverty in Britain*, Working Paper Series, no 6, London: Equal Opportunities Commission.

Brooks-Gordon, B. and Gelsthorpe, L. (2003) 'What men say when apprehended for kerb crawling: a model of prostitutes clients' talk', *Psychology, Crime and Law*, vol 9, no 2, pp 145-71.

Campbell, R. and Storr, M. (2001) 'Challenging the kerb crawler rehabilitation programme', *Feminist Review*, vol 67, no 1, pp 94-108.

Campbell, S. (2002) *A review of anti-social behaviour orders*, Home Office Research Series 236, London: Home Office.

Carter, H. (2004) 'Liverpool seeks first legal red light zone', *Guardian*, 5 March.

Church, S., Henderson, M., Barnard, M. and Hart, G. (2001) 'Violence by clients towards female prostitutes in different work settings: questionnaire survey', *British Medical Journal*, vol 332, no 7285, pp 524-5.

Clark, P., Bellis, M.A., Cook, P.A. and Tocque, K. (2004) *Consultation on a managed zone for sex trade workers in Liverpool: Views from residents, businesses and sex trade workers in the city of Liverpool*, Liverpool: Liverpool John Moores University.

Committee on Homosexual Offences and Prostitution (1957) *Report of the Committee on Homosexual Offences and Prostitution* (the Wolfenden Report), London: HMSO.

Department of Health (DH), Home Office (HO), Department for Education and Employment (DfEE) and National Assembly for Wales (NAW) (2000) *Safeguarding children involved in prostitution*, London: DH.

Hester, M., Hanmer, J., Coulson, S., Morahan, M. and Razak, A. (2003) *Domestic violence: Making it through the criminal justice system*, Sunderland: University of Sunderland.

Hester, M. and Westmarland, N. (2004) *Tackling street prostitution: Towards an holistic approach*, Home Office Research Study 279, London: Home Office.

Hester, M. and Westmarland, N. (2005) *Tackling domestic violence: Effective interventions and approaches*, Home Office Research Study 290, London: Home Office.

HMIC (Her Majesty's Inspectorate of Constabulary) and HMCPSI (Her Majesty's Crown Prosecution Inspectorate) (2004) *Violence at home: A joint inspection of the investigation and prosecution of cases involving domestic violence*, London: HMIC.

Home Office (2003a) *A guide to anti-social behaviour orders and acceptable behaviour contracts*, London: Home Office.

Home Office (2003b) *The one day count of anti-social behaviour*, London: Home Office.

Home Office (2004) *Paying the price:A consultation paper on prostitution*, London: Home Office.

Home Office (2006) *A Coordinated Prostitution Strategy and a summary of responses to Paying the Price*, London: Home Office.

Hubbard, P. (1997) 'Red-light districts and toleration zones: geographies of female street prostitution in England and Wales', *Area*, vol 29, no 2, pp 129-40.

Hubbard, P. (1998) 'Community action and the displacement of street prostitution: evidence from British cities', *Geoforum*, vol 29, no 3, pp 269-86.

Hubbard, P. and Sanders, T. (2003) 'Making space for sex work: Female street prostitution and the production of urban space', *International Journal of Urban and Regional Research*, vol 27, no 1, pp 75-89.

Hunter. G. and May, T. (2004) *Solutions and strategies: Drug problems and street sex markets*, London: Home Office.

Inter-Parliamentary Union (2005) *Women in national parliaments* (available at www.ipu.org).

Jones, H. and Sagar, T. (2001) 'Crime and Disorder Act 1998: prostitution and the Anti-Social Behaviour Order, *Criminal Law Review*, November, pp 873-85.

Kantola, J. and Squires, J. (2004) 'Prostitution policies in Britain, 1982-2002', in J. Outshoorn (ed) *The politics of prostitution: Women's movements, democratic states and the globalisation of sex commerce*, Cambridge: Cambridge University Press, pp 62-82.

Kelly, L. and Lovett, J. (2005) *What a waste – The case for an integrated violence against women strategy*, London: DTI.

Kelly, L., Lovett, J. and Regan, L. (2005) *A gap or a chasm? Attrition in reported rape cases*, Home Office Research Study 293, London: Home Office.

Matthews, R. (2005) 'Policing prostitution: ten years on', *British Journal of Criminology*, vol 45, pp 877-95.

May, T., Edmunds, M. and Hough, M. (1999) *Street business: The links between sex and drug markets*, Police Research Series Paper 118, London: Home Office.

Melrose, M., Barrett, D. and Brodie, I. (1999) *One way street? Retrospectives on childhood prostitution*, London: Children's Society.

Miller, J. (1995) 'Gender and power on the streets: street prostitution in the era of crack cocaine', *Journal of Contemporary Ethnography*, vol 23, no 4, pp 427-52.

O'Neil, M. (1999) 'Literature review of research on offences of sexual exploitation, Appendix D3', in Home Office *Setting the Boundaries*, London: HMSO, pp 177-94.

ONS (Office for National Statistics) (2004) *Focus on gender*, London: ONS.

Pearce, J. (2003) *It's someone taking a part of you: A study of young women and sexual exploitation*, London: National Children's Bureau in association with the Joseph Rowntree Foundation.

Phillips, C. and Brown, D. (1998) *Entry into the criminal justice system: A survey of police arrests and their outcomes,* Home Office Research Study 185, London: Home Office.

Phoenix, J. (2001) *Making sense of prostitution*, London: Palgrave.

Pitts, J. (1997) 'Causes of youth prostitution: new forms of practice and political responses', in D. Barrett (ed) *Child prostitution in Britain: Dilemmas and practical responses*, London, The Children's Society, pp 139-58.

Ramsey, H., Baker, P., Goulden, C., Sharpe, C. and Sondhi, A. (2001) *Drug misuse declared in 2000: Results from the British Crime Survey*, London: Home Office.

Research Centre on Violence Abuse and Gender Relations (2000) *Kerb crawler re-education programme report*, Leeds: Leeds Metropolitan University.

Sagar, T. (2001) 'Street prostitution: what works?', *New Law Journal*, vol 151, no 7000, p 1374.

Skinner, T., Hester, M. and Malos, E. (2005) 'Methodology, feminism and gender violence', in T. Skinner, M. Hester and E. Malos (eds) *Researching gender violence – Feminist methodology in action*, Cullompton, Willan, pp 1-22.

Swann, S. and Balding, V. (2001) *Safeguarding children involved in prostitution: Guidance review*, London: DH.

United Nations Development Programme (2004) *Human development report* (available at www.undp.org/).

West, J. (2000) 'Prostitution: collectives and the politics of regulation', *Gender, Work and Organisation,* vol 7, no 2, pp 106-18.

Women and Equality Unit (2003) *Individual incomes of men and women 1996/97-2000/01*, London: DTI.

Women and Equality Unit (2005) *Women's representation in politics*, (available at www.womenandequalityunit.gov.uk).

THREE

Prostitution in France

Gill Allwood

Introduction

Prostitution has been high on the public and political agenda in France since the late 1990s. This is due to a number of factors, including: the impact of UN debates and initiatives on related issues, especially child prostitution and pornography, and trafficking in human beings; the growing acceptance in international fora of a distinction between 'free' and 'forced' prostitution, which the dominant abolitionist position in France rejects; and changing patterns of migration, which have led to an increase in the number of migrant women and girls on the streets of French cities. Internally, there has been a rise in security discourse, which has changed the framework in which prostitution debates are situated. The plural left coalition government under the premiership of Lionel Jospin (1997-2002) was succeeded in 2002 by Jean-Pierre Raffarin's right-wing government, brought to power amidst widespread public concern with 'security'[1]. This has affected policy debates around prostitution and public perceptions of the issues that surround it.

The national context

France is an advanced industrialised country, ranked 22nd in the world in terms of GDP (World Bank, 2004), 16th in the UNDP's 2004 Human Development Index and 15th in the Gender-Related Development Index (UNDP, 2004). The principle of equality between men and women was stated in the preamble to the Constitution of 1946 and again in the current Constitution of 1958. French women gained the right to vote and to stand for election in 1944, and saw the recognition of a series of civil rights throughout the 1960s and 1970s[2]. They won the right to contraception in 1967 and to abortion in 1974. Rape was defined in criminal law in 1980, marital rape in 1990 and sexual harassment in 1992. The principle of equal pay for equal work was recognised in 1972, equality at work laws were passed in 1983 and 2001, and a high-profile campaign for equal political representation resulted in the parity laws of 1999 and 2000.

France has a well-established system of women's policy agencies dating from 1974 and attracted widespread interest in 1981, when it established a full Ministry for Women's Rights. Equality legislation is in place, ranging from equality at work (1983 and 2001) to parity in politics (1999 and 2000). However, in many respects, there is a clear gap between rhetoric and reality. The gender pay gap, the segregation of the labour market and the continued under-representation of women in areas of political and economic decision-making persist. Job insecurity, the concentration of women in part-time, low-paid work, and the feminisation of poverty are among the problems women face in the labour market.

French women have high levels of participation in the labour market[3]. In 2003, 81% of women between the ages of 25 and 49 were in work (Zappi, 2004b). However, in the ratio between men's and women's earnings France is ranked only 58th in the world (UNDP, 2004). The gender wage gap of 20% has not changed in 20 years (*Le Monde*, 8 March 2004). This is largely attributable to the (growing) gendered segregation of the labour market: 61% of working women are employed in just six (out of 31) employment categories, an increase from 53% 20 years ago (Ferrand, 2004). Within these categories, 66% of management jobs are occupied by men, and 34% by women (Zappi, 2004b), demonstrating that the segregation is both horizontal and vertical.

Since the late 1980s, job insecurity has increased, especially for women. Not only are women's unemployment levels two points higher than men's, but one in three women are in part-time work (compared with one in 20 men). In the majority of cases this is not through choice, and 80% of those who earn less than the minimum wage are women (*Le Monde*, 8 March 2004). Since 2002, there has been a further rise in economic insecurity (*Le Monde*, 8 October 2004). The number of people receiving the minimum state benefit has never been higher, and is increasing rapidly. It rose by 10.5% between June 2002 and June 2004. The number of people evicted from rented accommodation doubled between 1999 and 2004, rising by 29% between 2002 and 2003 (Bissuel and Guélaud, 2004). The number of people with serious debt problems increased by 22% in the same period. This primarily affects women living alone or with one or more children, unemployed young people with no qualifications, foreigners with no immigration rights and asylum seekers (Bissuel and Guélaud, 2004).

Officially, France has been following a policy of zero economic immigration since 1974. Visitors' permits are available for foreigners who meet certain criteria: for example, those who enter under family reunification procedures; those who are married to, and still live with, a French national; and those who can prove they have lived in France for at least ten years. These permits, which are marked 'private and family life', give the holder the right to work. Those who are found guilty of soliciting (whether actively or passively) have their permits removed. Asylum seekers are not automatically entitled to work, but may be given permission to do so, as long as there is not high unemployment in the sector in which they wish to work. Legitimate entry into the country has become more difficult, fuelling a trade in people smuggling. Changes in global migration patterns, the collapse of the Soviet bloc, and the perception that French laws are lenient have all contributed to the rise in the trafficking of women into France.

Different perspectives on prostitution within France

French prostitution debates are highly polarised, made up of those who see it as an inherent act of violence towards women, an attack on their human dignity and right to bodily integrity, and those who argue that what is wrong with prostitution is the stigma attached to it and the poor living and working conditions that women in prostitution endure. The former fight for the eradication of prostitution, while the latter tend to be involved in projects providing short-term solutions to immediate social and healthcare problems.

Abolitionists dominate the debate, forming a powerful and heterogeneous coalition of Catholics, advocates of traditional family structures, many feminists and large sections of the left. Support for abolitionism is further broadened by the ambiguity of the term. Originally referring to the abolition of the regulation of prostitution, of laws and policing practices that target and control prostitutes, it later came to mean the abolition of prostitution itself. Many participants in the debate manipulate this ambiguity to support a range of arguments. Until the Jospin government of 1997-2002, there was a broad abolitionist consensus from the 1960s, with sporadic moments of activism and debate, stimulated by police attempts to clamp down on prostitution, by suggestions by individual politicians that brothels be reopened, and by concerns about the spread of HIV/AIDS. Around the turn of the century a number of factors coincided, together raising the profile of prostitution as a public and political issue. External factors, including international debates, changes in policy in the Netherlands and Sweden, and the involvement of activists in transnational networks played an important role.

State feminists, influenced by feminist activists involved in the struggle against male violence towards women, entered the debate and began to seek policy solutions to particular constructions of the 'problem'. They played an important role in stimulating, structuring and publicising debate on prostitution policy. In 1999, the newly created Delegation for Women's Rights in the Senate chose prostitution as its first subject of enquiry. It produced a detailed and critical report, arguing that France's official policy of abolitionism was inadequately implemented (Derycke, 2001). Activist groups, such as the Bus des femmes, tried to impose their own definitions of the issue, and demanded action from local politicians, the police and the National Assembly in response to the appearance of women and girls trafficked from Eastern Europe by mafia networks and apparently working in conditions of slavery (Boucher, 2002b). The debate galvanised civil society organisations that had been working on the ground, providing social and health services to prostitutes in the hope of 'saving' them, as well as those who had been providing services in a context of AIDS prevention.

On 18 May 2000, the centre-left news weekly, *Le Nouvel Observateur*, published a declaration entitled 'The body is not a commodity', signed by 35 prominent figures from politics, the arts, academia and the medical and legal professions. Among its demands were that France and Europe officially confirm their commitment to the fight against all forms of prostitution; that they fight against pimping; and that they implement a coherent policy of prevention and rehabilitation, as well as assisting victims of trafficking. It prompted a first round of debate among intellectuals and activists in the media, addressing questions such as whether prostitution is a job like any other, a necessary evil, a useful service or a form of slavery. At the centre of much of the debate were the concepts of choice, autonomy and voice or agency (for example, Bruckner et al, 2000).

The framing of all prostitution as an inherent act of violence and violation of human rights has a tendency to construct prostitutes as victims who need to be saved and reintegrated into society. This can deny them recognition as subjects and agents. At a high-profile conference at UNESCO in Paris in 2000, organised by the abolitionist NGO, la Fondation Scelles, Phillippe Scelles, for example, declared, 'Prostitution is not an expression of women's freedom, but of their profound misery, the tragedy of destiny, a descent into hell' (UNESCO, 2000, pp 5-6). In a book published by the same organisation, *Le Livre noir* (Coquart and Huet, 2000, p 9), prostitution is portrayed as '… the alienation and destruction of women, men and children reduced to the state of sexual objects, of commodities in a global market, an attack on the integrity and the dignity of the human being, a negation and violation of human rights, neither "inevitable" nor a "necessary evil"'. In this view, the victims of prostitution are usually unaware of their own oppression and alienation. Senator Dinah Derycke (2001, p 26), who authored the report on prostitution and public policy for the Delegation for Women's Rights, states, 'One day or another, all prostitutes aspire to a life away from prostitution, *whatever they may say*' (my emphasis).

AIDS prevention and community health groups are deeply critical of what they perceive as a moralistic and paternalistic attitude towards prostitutes, to whom all voice and agency is denied until they see the light and agree to be 'reintegrated' (see Mathieu, 2001, p 24). These groups claim to give voice to prostitutes and to work in partnership with them to meet their needs. One group, Cabiria takes this further, presenting prostitutes not only as agents, but as rational decision-makers. The group's annual report (Cabiria, 2000) emphasises the agency of prostitutes, including migrants who choose to come and work in France:

> If the fact of prostituting may at first sight seem a submission to the system, from the perspective of the strategies of agents, one could consider that through prostitution these women make men pay directly and explicitly for what other women give freely or [charge for] indirectly in this same system of domination, thus gaining autonomy.

In direct opposition to the dominant state-sanctioned abolitionism, prostitutes' rights advocates, community health associations and some feminists called for the removal of the stigma attached to prostitution and for the recognition of the rights of sex workers. They argued that the state's blinkered commitment to abolitionism ignored difficulties, dangers and the denial of rights faced by prostitutes in their daily lives and that their existence and needs must be recognised, that they should be seen as subjects and agents, not victims. The associations Act Up-Paris, PASTT, Cabiria and AIDES Paris-Ile-de-France condemned the UNESCO conference, which, they argued, further stigmatised sex workers and denied them the right to use their own bodies. They argued that the sale of sexual services should not be confused with slavery and trafficking, and demanded that the government concentrate on improving the working conditions of sex workers and their access to health and social services.

Despite the irreconcilable dichotomies around which the debate was organised at this time, the central concern was what was best for prostitutes themselves. This is illustrated by the claims made by all parties that they spoke on behalf of/in the interests of/with prostitutes themselves, and that their opponents refused to give prostitutes voice and agency (Cabiria, 2000; Coquart and Huet, 2000; UNESCO, 2000; Louis, 2001; Mathieu, 2001). Whether the ideal outcome was seen as their escape from prostitution or improved living and working conditions with access to full citizenship rights as prostitutes, this was the heart of the issue. There was never any question of penalising prostitutes, who were positioned either as victims or as workers. By 2002, this was about to change.

Local residents' concerns about law and order, and the prominence on the right and the left of discourse focused on security in the 2002 election campaigns, led to the adoption of restrictive by-laws and to a heated debate between prominent intellectuals conducted in the national media in the summer of 2002[4]. This was fuelled by the suggestion by UMP deputy Françoise de Panafieu, that the brothels be reopened (*Le Figaro*, 1 July 2002). In the autumn, the new minister for the interior, Nicolas Sarkozy, tabled a Domestic Security Bill, and public debate focused on his proposals.

Laws and policies

Existing laws and policies on prostitution

France has been officially abolitionist since 1960, when it ratified the 1949 UN Convention on the suppression of trafficking and the exploitation of prostitution. Until 1946, when it closed its state-controlled brothels (*maisons closes*), France had been regulationist, and between 1946 and 1960, it maintained police files on prostitutes.

The foundations of state abolitionism were laid in a series of policy measures in the early 1960s, but for most of the following 30 years implementation varied locally, and prostitution rarely appeared on the political agenda. The exceptions were a brief mobilisation of prostitutes' rights groups against police harassment in 1975 and debates surrounding a suggestion in 1990 by the former minister for health (1986-88), Michèle Barzach (RPR), that state brothels be reopened in order to reduce the risks to public health associated with unregulated prostitution[5].

State policy on prostitution has been two-pillared. The first criminalises the exploitation of prostitution, bans brothels and makes soliciting an offence. The second is intended to support those who wish to leave prostitution and to reintegrate them into society. This pillar, however, has been chronically under-funded, and it has been left to civil society associations to carry out these functions.

Penalties for the exploitation of prostitution were increased as part of the major overhaul of criminal law that resulted in the new Penal Code (1994). Pimping was reclassified as a serious offence when it takes place within an organised gang and when it is accompanied by torture or acts of barbarism. There are straightforward, aggravated and serious forms of pimping, attracting increasingly large fines and prison sentences of between five years and life. In the Penal Code (1994), the client was mentioned only in relation to prostitutes under the age of 15. Sex tourism entered the law in 1998: Article 227-27-1 of the Penal Code criminalises sexual offences towards minors committed outside France by French nationals or French residents (Derycke, 2001, p 20).

A series of international assertions of the French position on prostitution were made in the late 1990s, in the context of pressure by some countries and international organisations (notably the Netherlands[6] and the International Labour Organisation: Lim, 1998) to recognise prostitution as a legitimate occupation and prostitutes as sex workers. The foreign minister, Hubert Védrine, reaffirmed the French commitment to abolitionism in various international negotiations on trafficking and child prostitution and pornography[7]; and the minister for women's rights, Nicole Péry, included prostitution in her department's high-profile campaign against violence towards women, referring to it as a form of violence at the UN Beijing +5 Conference in New York in 2000 (Péry, 2000). In these statements, France reaffirmed its commitment to the 1949 Convention, which states that 'prostitution and the accompanying evil of the traffic in persons' are 'incompatible with the dignity and worth of the human person' and condemns any person who exploits the prostitution of another with or without their consent.

In the international and European arena, France represented itself during this period as the epitome of abolitionism. It opposed, in particular, the reopening of brothels in the Netherlands and the accompanying entry into international discourse of terms such as 'free' and 'forced' prostitution. It also insisted that public policy must focus on prostitution, not on trafficking, which, according to the 1949 Convention, is an 'accompanying evil' rather than a discrete issue.

The detailed and critical report on prostitution and public policy produced by Dinah Derycke in 2000 for the Senate's Delegation for Women's Rights supported the principle of abolitionist state policies, but argued that they were inconsistently and inadequately implemented. The report was well received by parliament, but was pushed into the background by a combination of factors. Firstly, Derycke herself retired on the grounds of ill health. Secondly, international and European measures demanded parliamentary debates on transnational organised crime, modern slavery and trafficking. These were framed as both a priority over 'mere' prostitution and, at the same time, similar enough for it to appear that prostitution no longer needed attention. Finally, in 2002, the presidential and parliamentary elections brought to power a right-wing president and parliamentary majority, at the end of a campaign focused almost exclusively on law and order. Prostitution suddenly found itself redefined as a law and order issue.

Nicolas Sarkozy's Domestic Security Law came into force in March 2003. Intended as a response to growing feelings of insecurity, it aimed to combat certain types of behaviour, including soliciting, exploitation of begging, aggressive begging, occupying someone else's land and assembling in the entrance or the stairwell of blocks of flats (Sarkozy, 2002). It reintroduced the offence of 'passive soliciting' (Article 50), which had been removed from the Penal Code in 1994. Soliciting, previously a minor offence, was redefined as a more serious offence (*un délit*), punishable by a larger fine and by imprisonment for up to two months. In the case of foreign women, the penalty for soliciting (whether active or passive) includes deportation (even those with the right to residence in France can have their permits removed). It criminalised (Article 50) the purchase of sex with a prostitute who is 'particularly vulnerable', 'due to illness, disability, physical or mental deficiency or pregnancy'. The law also introduced into the Penal Code a definition of trafficking and of the penalties attached to it. Some elements of protection for women in prostitution, who are represented as victims of exploitation and/or trafficking, are also included in the text of the law (Article 42)[8] and in statements by the minister for parity and equality at work, Nicole Ameline. Foreign women are to be given temporary permission to remain in the country and to work in exchange for denouncing their pimp or trafficker. This applies until the case has been heard, and in the event of a conviction, will be made permanent (Article 76).

At the municipal level, mayors had already begun to introduce by-laws preventing prostitution in particular residential and business areas in early 2002. This was in response to complaints by residents about the presence of prostitutes in their neighbourhoods. In the summer of 2002, Françoise de Panafieu, UMP deputy for the 17th arrondissement in Paris, led a high-profile campaign against street prostitution. As the state's commitment to abolitionism prevented it from passing legislation aimed specifically at prostitutes, these mayors initially took pains to circumvent the restrictions by introducing traffic and parking by-laws to drive prostitution out of certain areas. This meant that prostitutes were forced to leave well-lit busy streets and move into car parks, lay-bys and wasteland, where they work in far less safe conditions. However, with the rise of law and order discourse, in particular since the run-up to the 2002 presidential elections, an increasing number of local authorities have introduced more explicit by-laws aimed at preventing prostitution in designated areas.

Operation of laws and policies on prostitution

The Office central pour la répression de la traite des êtres humains (OCRTEH) was created in 1958 to fight pimping within France and to cooperate with Interpol and European organisations in the fight against trafficking. It is located in the central directorate of the judicial police under the authority of the minister of the interior (Mazur, 2004, p 124). In spring 2000, a new central office was created in the central directorate of the judicial police to fight criminal activity that uses information technology, including networks of pimps and traffickers. In 1999, 137 of the 189 pimps whose cases were heard received prison sentences. Derycke (2001, p 21) reports that the judiciary was satisfied with legislation and procedure on pimping, although there were problems when pimps fled the country or worked from outside the national borders.

A single position in the Department of Social Services oversees rehabilitation and prevention, and distributes government funds to prostitution aid groups (Mazur, 2004, p 124). At the departmental level, it was intended that Prevention and Rehabilitation Services (SPR) would be established in order to identify and help people in danger of prostitution and to give social and medical assistance to prostitutes. However, only 12 were set up in response to the 1960 Ordinance, and in 1999 there were only five, all run by associations (Derycke, 2001, p 28). The women's rights administration – periodic cabinet-level offices, the permanent women's rights services and its regional and departmental field offices – has also been periodically given formal responsibility for prostitution policy (Mazur, 2004, p 124). The ministries of health, finance, justice, interior, foreign affairs and education are also sometimes involved in prostitution policy.

Article 52 of the Domestic Security Law states that, from 2004, the government will present an annual report to parliament on changes in the demography, health and social conditions of those in prostitution and on the means that have been made available to organisations that work with them. The first such report had still not been published by the end of January 2006.

Although the state feminist definition of prostitution, which became high profile in the last years of the Jospin government (1997-2002), has been attenuated since the change of government, it has nevertheless left a legacy. Marie-Jo Zimmermann (of the right-wing majority coalition, UMP), in her report for the National Assembly's Delegation for women's rights on prostitution (Zimmermann, 2002, p 29) calls for public awareness campaigns to encourage people to think about 'the violence that the purchase of sexual services constitutes'. Although, on the whole, her report accepts Sarkozy's framing of prostitution, with only minor criticisms and regrets, she nevertheless writes, 'Information should be disseminated through mass public information campaigns on the reality of prostitution, its infringement of women's rights and dignity, of equality between the sexes, and of respect for others' (Zimmermann, 2002, p 33). It is noticeable that the framing of prostitution as a form of violence towards women has entered the mainstream of government thinking, expressed, for example, in the Gender Budget attached to the Finance Bill 2004 (Projet de loi des finances, 2004).

Analysis of policies and interventions

When it proposed the Domestic Security Bill, the government claimed that clamping down on particular activities would improve the quality of life, and especially the feeling of security, of the poorest members of society, who are most likely to become the victims of crime. Sarkozy claimed that the poor support a tougher stance on crime, that law and order is the main concern of the general public, and that 80% of people on the minimum wage approve of his Bill. An Ipsos poll, cited by the national press, demonstrated that the lower the income and education, the greater the support for the Bill (*Le Monde*, 23 October 2002).

The Bill provoked petitions, demonstrations and calls for action by parties of the left, trade unions and associations concerned with human rights, poverty and social justice. They accused Sarkozy of exploiting the climate of insecurity and rejected the plans to criminalise beggars, prostitutes, travellers and young people, arguing that 'no one chooses to be a beggar or a prostitute, to live in neighbourhoods with no facilities and no public services' (Ligue des droits de l'Homme, 2002). Claude Boucher from Bus des femmes, a support service in Paris run by prostitutes and former prostitutes, insists that many women she meets work as prostitutes in order to preserve their dignity, since neither social security benefits nor the minimum wage are enough to live on (Délégation de l'assemblée nationale aux droits des femmes et à l'égalité des chances entre les hommes et les femmes, 2002).

The criminalisation of passive soliciting was particularly contentious, not least because it is so hard to define. Sarkozy's original version of the Bill proposed the insertion of a new article in the Penal Code (Article 225-10-1) creating a serious offence of soliciting by any means including 'dress or posture'. It was the reference to 'dress', which caused an outcry, on the grounds that this would empower the police to determine whether or not someone was dressed 'like a prostitute'. It was removed by a government amendment during the Senate debate. The version that was eventually passed by the Senate refers to 'a posture, even passive'. Judges are unhappy with the creation of an offence for which the only evidence is police testimony, and early studies of the impact of this clause suggest that they are reluctant to convict (Colas, 2003).

Sarkozy justified the criminalisation of passive soliciting on the grounds that it protects prostitutes, and helps them to escape from the mafia networks that exploit them (*Le Monde*, 23 October 2002).

Critics argue, however, that if his concern with targeting traffickers were sincere, he would devote greater resources to this, rather than arresting their victims. The law does not focus on the fight against transnational organised crime, but rather on the policing of national borders. The new measures are disproportionately aimed at foreign prostitutes, who can be deported for soliciting, whether this is active or passive. They are constructed both as criminals and as victims, and both punished and, at the same time, 'rescued' from their exploiters. The fact that deporting them puts them straight back into the trafficking circuit is not addressed. All prostitution is collapsed into trafficking, making it difficult to propose policy solutions that respond to a diversity of situations and needs within the sex industry.

There have been many calls for measures aimed directly at trafficking rings, rather than claiming that arresting prostitutes will have significant impact on their activities. These calls have come from the Senate's Law Commission, the Delegations for women's rights in the Senate and the National Assembly, and opposition members of both houses. Some changes have been made in response: trafficking has now been defined as an offence and penalties set, although this was at least partly a response to international and European requirements. Trafficking legislation introduced in January 2003 gives victims of trafficking the right to remain while giving evidence against the trafficker and permanently in the case of a conviction, but critics remain sceptical about the practicalities of women testifying against traffickers and about the uneven balance of benefits to them and to the authorities. There are still contradictions here, deriving from the tension between security and human rights.

Sarkozy did not adopt a fully coherent position on prostitution; this is not what he set out to do. Instead, he aimed to satisfy voters concerned about the visible signs of prostitution that cause them anxiety (Sarkozy, 2002). He intended to clean up the streets, and, in this respect, he has succeeded. The Paris police report a 40% drop in the number of prostitutes on the streets (Zappi, 2004a). But, in so doing, Sarkozy has transformed the terms of the debate and redefined street prostitutes not as victims, but as criminals. The prostitution debate is now framed in terms of public nuisance and law and order, and is closely entwined with the control of immigration. It creates a narrow view of prostitution as taking place only on the streets, thus exonerating middle-class men who have become consumers of other forms of commercial sex, rather than the clients of prostitution who, although not targeted explicitly by this law, have finally been recognised in public debate as participants in prostitution. 'Independent', 'traditional', 'French' prostitutes have also to a large extent survived the worst effects of the law, with reassurances from the ministerial office that it was never intended to affect them. The targets, then, are those who, paradoxically, are more likely to be perceived as victims than any other women in prostitution: migrant women who, in the government's eyes, if not in reality, have all been trafficked and are all being exploited, often viciously, by foreign pimps. Of the 5,619 individuals charged with passive soliciting between March 2003 and July 2004, 90% were women. Of these, most came from Romania, Bulgaria and Albania (39.5%) and Nigeria, Sierra Leone and Cameroon (34.5%). Fifteen per cent were French, 6% were from South Africa, 3% from North Africa and 2% from Asia (*Le Monde*, 4 September 2004).

There has been an increase in the number of foreign prostitutes held in detention, notably in Paris, Nice, Bordeaux and Toulouse (Cimade, 2004). Between January 2003 and January 2004, the number of Romanian women being deported increased ten-fold. Of these 90% admitted to working as prostitutes. Those who denounce their trafficker are entitled to temporary permission to remain and to permission to work. In the first eight months of 2004, the police dismantled 32 networks: 17 from Eastern Europe and 13 from Africa (Agence France Presse, 2004). The law also mentions protection, lodging and reintegration, but there is no organised provision on the ground. The NGO Cimade (2004) claims that protection for victims of trafficking would mean: recognised victim status; clearer procedures removing the arbitrary nature of police decision-making; residents' permits for victims; access to the labour market, professional training and education; medical, social, legal and language assistance for victims; institutional networks; and secure emergency accommodation, none of which is consistently available in a coordinated fashion.

Lilian Mathieu (2003) claims that 'the consequences [of a return to repression] are disastrous for prostitutes: it has made them more secretive, vulnerable, insecure, exposed to HIV, and dependent on pimps'. Janine Mossuz-Lavau states that 'Far from protecting prostitutes, the law puts them in danger' (Chartier, 2004).

A preliminary study of the impact of the new legislation in Paris suggests that prostitution has not been reduced; it has simply moved to more isolated areas and more 'discreet' hours (3am-7am)[9]. The study suggests that this makes it more difficult for community health and prostitutes' rights groups to provide services and that it exposes prostitutes to greater risks of violence. It also reports a degradation in relations between French and foreign prostitutes, with increased evidence of racism. The newspapers report increased insecurity since the change in the law. In Toulouse and Lyon, there are reports of years of good relations built up with the police being destroyed overnight (Grosjean, 2003). There are some claims that young African and Slav girls are not being arrested, on the grounds that, as minors, they would have to be given accommodation and a visitor's permit. Blandine Grosjean (2004) writes, 'In March 2002, France nonetheless passed some of the most protective laws on minors and some of the most punitive on clients of minors'. Judges are reluctant to convict for soliciting. Of the 230 cases brought by the police in Bordeaux, for example, fewer than ten have resulted in a conviction. The Syndicat de la Magistrature disputes the concept of passive soliciting as an offence, when prostitution is legal (Colas, 2003; Tabet, 2003).

Debates on legalisation and decriminalisation

A tradition of respect for individual rights, a popular discourse that associates French national identity with liberal sexual mores, and the influence of social Catholicism in the construction of prostitutes as victims who need to be saved, all contribute to a widespread opposition to outright prohibition. However, although prostitution itself is not explicitly criminalised, the introduction into the criminal law of the offence of passive soliciting makes it very difficult to exercise this civil liberty. There is also widespread and deeply rooted opposition to the legalisation of brothels. However, there has been a noticeable growth in the number of sex clubs, bars and middle-class and up-market escort services.

Some prostitutes' groups and individuals, often financially well-off 'traditional' (French) prostitutes, call for the recognition of prostitution as a proper occupation, thus giving access to social security and pension rights, from which they are currently excluded, despite the fact that they are taxed on their earnings. Abolitionists are passionately opposed to this, on the grounds that prostitution is a violation of human rights, and cannot possibly be a form of work.

The criminalisation of the client in Swedish law in 1999 has brought the client into French prostitution debates for the first time. Prior to 1994, the client was absent from laws on prostitution. The New Penal Code made it an offence to purchase sex with a prostitute under the age of 15. This has now been raised to 18 and also applies to prostitutes who are 'particularly vulnerable'. There is no consensus on whether or not this should be extended to all clients. Members of parliament seemed rather reluctant to give this serious attention during the debates on the Domestic Security Bill, although a number of amendments on the subject were tabled by individuals. Feminist abolitionist activist and theorist Marie-Victoire Louis argues that it would lay down the principle that men do not have the right to buy sex. Others (for example, L'Amicale du Nid and Cabiria) argue that it would push prostitution underground, making it more difficult to provide support services to women in prostitution.

Key issue faced

Reasons for entry into prostitution

It is difficult to obtain reliable data on entry into prostitution, not least because of the hostility and polarisation of the surrounding debates, which has led to significant distortion of reported data. The main source of data is the OCRTEH, which bases its statistics on police checks. The OCRTEH estimates that there are 15,000 to 18,000 people in street prostitution in France, 7,000 of them in Paris. Most of the women prostitutes on the street are foreign (56%), with the majority of these from Eastern Europe, the Balkans and West Africa. Either they are trafficked explicitly, or the degradation of rights for new arrivals increases the chances of entering prostitution (Projet de loi des finances, 2004). Asylum seekers, for example, have no automatic right to work while their claim is being processed (www.service-public.fr/).

It is believed that 80% of women working as prostitutes in cities are controlled by pimps (Projet de loi des finances, 2004). In 2003, 700 pimps were arrested, the majority from sub-Saharan Africa and Eastern Europe. Of the 900 'victims', 98% were women. Many were from Eastern Europe (44%) and from sub-Saharan Africa (27.5%). In the same year, 2,400 people were arrested for soliciting. Of these, 31% were from sub-Saharan Africa; 36% from Eastern Europe; and 16% from France (Gbadamassi, 2004).

In her report, Dinah Derycke finds that entry into prostitution varies, but there are a number of trigger factors, including childhood abuse. She states that prostitution is rarely chosen: it is much more likely to result from 'family, social or economic violence' (Derycke, 2001, p 17).

The abolitionist Mouvement du Nid tends to emphasise the victimhood of those in prostitution, excluding the possibility of any agency. Writing for this organisation, Claudine Legardinier (1996, pp 32-3) lists traumatic childhood experiences, sexual abuse, and drug use as individual factors that increase the risk of entering prostitution. She claims, however, that 'lack of money is never the only or sufficient reason for entry'. She does not explain entry in terms of individual factors alone, however, mentioning structural reasons such as cultural representations of gender relations and sexuality; consumer culture; north/south inequalities, social exclusion and unemployment.

Claude Boucher from the Bus des femmes sees lack of money as an important causal factor, perhaps especially in the case of 'occasional prostitutes': women who prostitute themselves at the end of the month to make ends meet. These women, she argues, did not choose prostitution, but it was the only way they could maintain any sense of dignity in a climate of job insecurity. She states that 'some used to work in factories and prefer prostitution to an awful job' (Boucher, 2001, p 29).

Lilian Mathieu (2003) cites a study that found that in a sample of 241 male and female prostitutes in Paris, 41% came from 'modest, very modest or marginal social backgrounds'. A 1995 study of 355 male and female prostitutes in French cities found that 61% had no social security, only half had steady accommodation, and 2% were homeless. One-third had been assaulted during the five months prior to the survey. For Mathieu, prostitution 'is a last resort when legitimate sources of income are denied'. He argues that no one chooses to enter prostitution – it is the result of constraint or a resigned adaptation to distress, need or violence. Constraint may be economic, or in the form of the violence of the new mafia networks of pimps.

Conclusions

By 2002, public debate on prostitution, whether in institutional politics, the media, the organisations that work with prostitutes or against prostitution, was starkly polarised. Relations between the two poles were hostile, there was little, if any, dialogue, and the policy solutions that seemed to follow from their arguments were incomplete. Since the arrival in power of a right-wing government in 2002, prostitution has been reframed as a law and order issue. This has brought into question France's continued position as a leading abolitionist country, which is how it has often presented itself externally. The contradictions that were exposed by the Derycke report in 2001 have not been resolved. Outside political institutions, battles between abolitionists and prostitutes' rights advocates have been replaced temporarily by concerns with the impact of the new law on women in prostitution. However, they have not completely disappeared. French prostitution debates have been paralysed by hostile opposition between abolitionists and prostitutes' rights advocates. If women in prostitution are going to be placed at the centre of policy, activist and academic debates, there needs to be dialogue between these two poles.

There are three main areas in which work is likely to develop. The first is the question of the client, largely ignored until recently, but making its way onto the agenda since the criminalisation of clients in Sweden in 1999. Secondly, there is likely to be continued interest in links between prostitution and migration. Finally, future debates could lose the current exclusive focus on street prostitution, which can be explained by the fact that other forms were made illegal in 1946/60, that current prostitution debates are so closely tied to law and order discourse, and by the visibility of foreign women working on the streets.

Notes

[1] The highly malleable term *la sécurité* (security, or law and order) has become a dominant theme in French political discourse and can refer to a broad range of undefined threats or fears.

[2] For example, the right to work without the permission of their husband (1965), parental authority replaced paternal authority in 1970, the right to apply for a passport without the permission of their husband (1975), divorce by mutual consent (1975).

[3] 46.2% of the working population are women (EU average is 44%). The figures for France are comparable with Germany, Denmark and Portugal. They are lower than Finland and Sweden, and higher than Austria, Belgium, Spain, Greece, Ireland, Italy, Luxembourg, Netherlands and the UK (INSEE, 2004).

[4] See for example, *Le Nouvel Observateur*, 22 August 2002, with contributions by Claude Boucher, 'Défendre les travailleuses du sexe', Elisabeth Badinter, 'Si c'est leur choix', Wassila Tamzali,

'Le devoir d'interdire' and Françoise de Panafieu, 'Pourquoi j'ai tapé le poing sur la table'.

[5] For a full discussion of these debates, see Mazur (2004).

[6] The Netherlands was the first country to recognise prostitution as sex work (in 1999), making the distinction between free and forced prostitution (see Outshoorn, 2000).

[7] Such as the additional protocol to the Convention on the Rights of the Child on the sale and prostitution of children and child pornography, passed by the UN on 25 May 2000 and signed by 69 states, including all the member states of the EU, and the Convention on transnational organised crime with the additional protocol on trafficking, negotiated in Vienna and signed in December 2000 in Palermo.

[8] 'Any person victim of the exploitation of prostitution should benefit from a system of protection and aid, assured and coordinated by the administration in collaboration with the various social services.'

[9] A study by Janine Mossuz-Lavau and Marie-Elisabeth Handman, commissioned by the Mairie de Paris, submitted 27 November 2003, and widely reported in the press, for example, Zappi (2004a) and Grosjean (2004).

Recommended further reading

Allwood, G. (2004) 'Prostitution debates in France', *Contemporary Politics*, vol 10, no 2, pp 145-57.

Mathieu, L. (2003) 'The emergence and uncertain outcomes of prostitutes' social movements', *European Journal of Women's Studies*, vol 10, no 1 (February), pp 29-50.

Mathieu, L. (2004) 'The debate on prostitution in France: a conflict between abolitionism, regulation and prohibition', *Journal of Contemporary European Studies*, vol 12, no 2 (August), pp 153-63.

Mazur, A. (2004) 'Prostitute movements face elite apathy and gender-biased universalism in France', in J. Outshoorn (ed) *The politics of prostitution: Women's movements, democratic states and the globalisation of sex commerce*, Cambridge: Cambridge University Press, pp 123-43.

References

Agence France Presse (2004) 'En France, huit personnes prostituées sur dix sont étrangères', 1 October, (http://web.lexis-nexis.com/executive).

Bissuel, B. and Guélaud, C. (2004) 'La pauvreté touche d'abord les femmes, les jeunes et les étrangers', *Le Monde*, 18 October.

Borillo, D. (2002a) 'La liberté de se prostituer', *Libération*, 5 July.

Borillo, D. (2002b) 'Conférence', in Cabiria, *Rapport de synthèse 2002*, available at www.cabiria.asso.fr, accessed 2 December 2004.

Boucher, C. (2001) 'Le point de vue du bus des femmes', *Pro-Choix*, no 17 (February-March), pp 28-30.

Boucher, C. (2002a) 'Défendre les travailleuses du sexe', *Le Nouvel Observateur*, 22 August, no 1272.

Boucher, C. (2002b) 'Evidence to Délégation aux droits des femmes et à l'égalité des chances entre les hommes et les femmes, Compte rendu no 2, Mardi, 15 octobre' (available at www.assemblee-nationale.fr).

Bruckner, P., Fleury, C., Roudinesco, E. and Laguiller, A. (2000) 'Prostitution: le débat indispensable', *Le Nouvel Observateur*, 8 June, no 1857, (available at http://archives.nouvelobs.com, accessed 10 December 2004).

Cabiria (2000) *Annual report*, (available at www.cabiria.asso.fr).

Chartier, C. (2004) 'Le coup de la loi', *L'Express*, 15 March, (available at www.lexpress.presse.fr).

Cimade (2004) 'Les prostituées en détention' (available at www.cimade.org/actus/prostitue%20retention.htm).

Colas, H. (2003) 'A Bordeaux, la justice distanciée par la police', *L'Humanité*, 17 December.

Coquart, E. and Huet, P. (2000) *Le Livre noir de la prostitution*, Paris: Albin Michel.

Délégation de l'assemblée nationale aux droits des femmes et à l'égalité des chances entre les hommes et les femmes, 'Compte rendu no. 2', 15 October 2002, under the presidency of Marie-Jo Zimmermann (available at www.assemblee_nationale.fr/12/cr-delf/02-03/c0203002.asp).

Derycke, D. (2001) 'Rapport d'activité 2000: les politiques publiques et la prostitution, délégation du Sénat aux droits des femmes et à l'égalité des chances entre les hommes et les femmes, 31 January' (available at www.senat.fr).

Ferrand, M. (2004) 'La Place des femmes: grandes tendances', in Cordellier, S. and Lau, E., *L'Etat de la France*, Paris: La Découverte, pp 61–6.

Gbadamassi, F. (2004) 'De plus en plus de prostituées africaines en France', available at www.afrik.com, accessed 12 October 2004.

Grosjean, B. (2003) 'Des filles de joie bien à la peine', *Libération*, 13 June, (available at www.liberation.fr).

Grosjean, B. (2004) 'Prostitution: contre enquête de la Mairie de Paris', *Libération*, 14 January, (available at www.liberation.fr).

INSEE (2004) 'Taux d'activité des femmes et des hommes, Chiffres-lés concernant les femmes/La Parité: thème Travail-Emploi-Population active', (available at www.insee.fr).

Legardinier, C. (1996) *La Prostitution*, Toulouse: Les Editions Milan.

Ligue des droits de l'Homme, Syndicat des Avocats de France, Syndicat de la Magistrature (2002)'Lettre ouverte à Monsieur Sarkozy', (available at www.ldh-france.asso.fr/actu).

Lim, L.L. (1998) (ed) *The sex sector: The economic and social bases of prostitution in Southeast Asia*, Geneva: International Labour Office.

Loi no 2003-239 du 18 mars 2003 pour la sécurité intérieure, (available at www.legifrance.gouv.fr/WAspad/UnTexteDeJorf?numjo=INTX0200145L).

Louis, M.-V. (2001) 'Pour une critique de la politique pro-prostitution de Cabiria', (available at www.penelopes.org), August.

Mathieu, L. (2001) *Mobilisations de prostituées*, Paris: Belin.

Mathieu, L. (2003) 'Women beyond the pale', *Le Monde diplomatique*, (available at www.lemondediplomatique.fr), October.

Mazur, A. (2004) 'Prostitute movements face elite apathy and gender-biased universalism in France', in J. Outshoorn (ed), *The politics of prostitution: Women's movements, democratic states and the globalisation of sex commerce*, Cambridge: Cambridge University Press, pp 123-43.

Outshoorn, J. (2000) 'Legalizing prostitution as sexual service: the case of the Netherlands', Copenhagen ECPR Joint Sessions Workshop 12, April, (www.essex.ac.uk/ecpr).

Péry, N. (2000) *Dossier Prostitution*, (available at www.social.gouv.fr/femmes/actu/doss).

Projet de loi des finances (2004) *Projet de loi des finances pour 2004 Etats des crédits qui concourent aux actions en faveur des droits des femmes*, (available at http://alize.finances.gouv.fr/budget/plf2004/jaunes04/811pdf).

Sarkozy, N. (2002) 'Exposé des motifs, projet de loi pour la sécurité intérieure, no. 30, 2002-3', paper presented to the Senate, 23 October, (available at www.senat.fr).

Tabet, M.-C. (2003) 'Justice: la loi Sarkozy du 18 mars sur la prostitution', *Le Figaro*, 6 May.

UNDP (2004) *Human development report: Country fact sheets. France*, (available at http://hdr.undp.org/statistics/data/country_fact_sheets/cty_fs_FRA.html).

UNESCO (2000) 'Peuple de l'Abîme: la prostitution aujourd'hui', conference 16 May, (available at www.fondationscelles.org).

UNIFEM (2004) 'Gender responsive budgets', (available at www.unifem.org).

United Nations Office of the High Commissioner for Human Rights, *Convention for the Suppression of the Traffic in Persons and of the Exploitation of the Prostitution of Others*, 2 December 1949, (www.unhchr.ch).

World Bank (2004) 'World development indicators database, September', available at www.worldbank.org/data/, accessed 14 December 2004.

Zappi, S. (2004a) 'La Mairie de Paris doute d'une baisse spectaculaire de la prostitution', *Le Monde*, 15 January.

Zappi, S. (2004b) 'Les inégalités hommes–femmes persistent dans le monde du travail', *Le Monde*, 8 March.

Zimmermann, M.-J., *Rapport d'information fait au nom de la Délégation aux droits des femmes et à l'égalité des chances entre les hommes et les femmes sur le projet de loi pour la sécurité intérieure*, no 459, 5 December 2002, (available at www.assemblee-nationale.fr/12/rap-info/i0459.asp).

FOUR

Prostitution in Sweden: debates and policies 1980-2004

Yvonne Svanström

Introduction

Discussion around whether prostitution should be regulated, legalised or criminalised has had a long history in Sweden (Svanström, 2000 and 2005). In 1999 a new and unique law was introduced that criminalised only the 'buyers' of prostitution (1999 Act Prohibiting the Purchase of Sexual Services). Challenging the traditional view that those (generally women) who 'sell' sex are the greatest problem, the new law also hoped to see a reduction in the level of prostitution:

> The Swedish government has explicitly noted that the female body cannot be looked upon as merchandise which can be bought or sold.... All trade is based on the fact that there are customers and demand. If there were no customers looking upon women's bodies as objects, there would be no market where the victims for this trade could be offered and exploited ... (Ministry of Gender Equality, Margaretha Winberg, Riksdagsprotokoll 2000/01:67, 15 February, section 1)[1]

The law was promoted as a 'feminist law' where prostitution is seen as a form of violence against women (Proposition 1997/98: 55); this chapter outlines the discussions that led to this unique policy change and the impact that it has had.

The national context

Since the 1960s the Swedish state has partly integrated what has been called a 'Swedish gender equality discourse' in its politics.

This has led to a number of changes, including: the development of a Ministry of Equal Status in 1976; a parliamentary commission on equal status in the same year; and the creation of an Equal Opportunities Ombudsman in 1980 (Florin and Nilsson, 1999). The gender equality policy has mainly focused on women's right to work and to equal pay however, work life is still organised traditionally. Women work mostly in the care and education professions or in offices, and a large majority work part time (Florin and Nilsson, 1999). In spite of its 'gender equal' image, there are still substantial income differences between women and men in equivalent occupations in Sweden (Nyberg, 2005).

Comparatively, Sweden is financially well off. In indexes measuring welfare such as the UN Human Poverty Index (HPI-2), or the ZUMA welfare index for EU countries (rather than a crude GDP index), Sweden is situated at the top (Vogel and Wolf, 2004, pp 10-11). However, the retrenchment of the welfare state has seen a new polarisation between classes, although the gender gap seems to have decreased. With the Law on Women's Peace that was established in 1999 (which also criminalised the purchase of sexual services) came a number of changes in current laws, but also the new offence of breaking women's peace. This crime suggests that the total picture of the violation of a woman should be considered when deciding on the severity of a crime. If certain non-punishable acts (such as hiding the woman's keys or the telephone to keep her isolated) could be seen as part of the whole picture of violation and harassment that the woman had endured, the crime should be considered to be more severe. Since 1998 the number of reported crimes of violence against women has increased from 198 to 2,068 in 2004. As political scientist Maud Eduards suggests, men's violence against women does not follow the desired state gender equality political logic (Eduards, forthcoming).

A recent official commission is very harsh in its criticism against the new Law on Women's Peace. It states that men's violence against women has not been prioritised in the work of concerned authorities; that it has not received adequate funding, has not been fully incorporated into the current agenda and that personnel are not given special training on the subject. Thus, the commission concludes, work on men's violence against women lacks continuity, institutionalisation and politicisation (SOU, 2004: 121, p 17).

Different perspectives on prostitution within Sweden

Research on prostitution in Sweden has been undertaken since the late 1970s and early 1980s when a number of studies were produced, mainly within the sociology, social work and psychology disciplines (Larsson and Månsson, 1976; Månsson, 1981; Larsson, 1983). These studies connected prostitution to a commercialisation of society and of human values, and to the subjection of women. These studies viewed prostitution from what was called a 'gender role perspective' with a long patriarchal tradition:

> Heterosexual prostitution with men as buyers and women as prostitutes can be seen as an extreme expression of the sexual meaning of traditional gender roles. The fundamental idea of prostitution through the ages has been that a group of women should be available for men's sexual purposes. (Borg et al, 1981, p 579)

In the 1950s, monogamy, marriage and the nuclear family was still the most common form of living together, which came into conflict with the sexual liberation of the 1960s. When this, in turn, led to a commercialisation of sexuality in the 1970s it was argued that a repressed Puritan sexual moral was replaced by '... a pseudo-liberal attitude, where the right to sexual intercourse is money and where thousands of women are humiliated and damaged in the commercial dealings of sex' (Larsson and Månsson, 1976, p 135).

A state commission on prostitution was appointed in 1977. Researchers participated in the commission as experts. After a schism between the politically appointed female commissioner and the appointed experts (all except one left the commission), the experts published their own study before the commissioner's report (Borg et al, 1981). The remaining expert also published his own study (Persson, 1981), where he argued that the conflict within the commission came from political differences: where the official commissioner held 'classical liberal views on humans' – female prostitutes were prostituted as a result of exercising their free will – the other experts viewed prostitution as an exploitation of women (Persson, 1981; cf Brunnberg et al, 1981).

However, prostitution was not only seen as patriarchal exploitation of women, the commercialisation of society was also used as an explanation for the existence of prostitution: 'What this [prostitution] is ultimately about is very simple. The right to buy other people. This is still a fact even if the person buying sometimes can be worse off than the person selling' (Persson, 1981, p 210). In 1988, sociologist Sven-Axel Månsson wrote that to look upon prostitution from a gender role perspective and to connect prostitution to certain societal sexual patterns 'has now become the model for the relatively comprehensive Scandinavian research done in this area' (Månsson, 1988, p 4). Thus, there seems to have been consensus regarding questions on prostitution within the academic community during the 1980s.

Research in the 1990s and current research on prostitution in Sweden has a broader disciplinary scope. Research is now conducted within economic history, business economics, criminology, social work, social psychology, social anthropology and the history of ideas. Research topics include state policies and discourse on prostitution, trafficking, sexploitation industries and sex buyers. There is also a wider theoretical approach, which has led to some debate. Whereas some have a more radical feminist perspective and discuss prostitution as an exploitation of women (Westerstrand, 2000; Pettersson and Tiby, 2003; Holgersson and Svanström, 2004; Månsson and Söderlind, 2004; Svanström, 2004a and 2004b), others focus their research on prostitution as a sexual service and a possible trade (Gould, 2001; Kulick, 2003; Dodillet, 2004; Kulick, 2005; Ljung and Lennartsson, 2004). This latter approach was absent in research on prostitution during the 1970s and 1980s.

The consensus among Swedish feminists, within the autonomous movement and among 'state feminists' and academic feminists, to look upon prostitution as oppression rather than as work was more or less unanimous until the last decade. In parliament both left and liberal women's federations have supported Bills that proposed the criminalisation of the purchase of sexual services. In the 1970s, for instance, the autonomous women's movement and the party-organised women's federations together questioned a state commission report on sexual violence that suggested that more evidence would be needed to accuse someone of rape and also that the penalties should be lowered. It was also suggested in the report that the behaviour of the woman and the way she had dressed prior to the alleged rape should be taken into account when deciding on the severity of the crime. Thirteen different women's organisations with different political ideologies protested against the report, something that resulted in a new state commission and an additional commission investigating prostitution (Thomsson, 2000)[2]. During the 1970s citizens' action groups such as The Action

Fight against Pornography and Prostitution (Aktionen kamp mot porr och prostitution) drew together such dissimilar organisations as the Swedish Baptists' Youth Organisation and the Swedish Left Women's Organisation (Gentele, 1979; cf Fredelius, 1978). At the same time the Sexual Political Front (Sexualpolitisk front) was also active, with a programme that, among other things, demanded a liberalised law on procuring, and that the clampdown on visible prostitution should be stopped. Alongside this, the organisation also wanted to stop the recruiting of prostitutes, and one of the proposed ways was 'women's right to work with a good pay' (Sexualpolitisk front, 1977, pp 128-9)[3].

In the 1990s the question of whether prostitution should be regarded as exploitation of women or as a trade dominated the debate. This debate has in turn been linked to the discussion that emerged in connection with the Swedish law criminalising the purchase of sexual services, where critics of the law argued that it prevented women from exercising their trade. To a large extent the debate has taken place in newspapers. The pro-prostitution organisation ROSEA (Riksorganisationen för Sex- och Erotikarbetare [the National Organisation for Sex and Erotic Workers]) was established in 2003, but has not really been active in the debate (www.rosea.se). The People's Organisation against Pornography (Folkaktionen mot porr och pornografi) existed between 1985 and 1999, and presently, the most well-known network against prostitution is probably the Network against Prostitution (Nätverket mot prostitution).

Laws and policies

Existing laws and policies on prostitution

Swedish law states that it is illegal to purchase casual sexual services, and this is under penalty of fines or imprisonment for up to six months. So far, however, no men have been sentenced to jail. In November 2004 a government Bill suggested revisions of the current law. As well as certain technical changes, the Bill recommends adding that it is criminal to make use of casual sexual services that somebody else pays or has paid for. This would more effectively make it impossible to be on the receiving end of 'escort services', paid for by a large corporation, for instance (Proposition 2004/05: 45, pp 103-7).

As a response to the EU decision to intensify and increase

international cooperation on trafficking, the 1998 Swedish commission on sexual crime and certain surrounding issues was to investigate whether the Swedish law needed complementary additions. A government Bill was presented in 2002 proposing a new law on trafficking human beings. The law was passed in May 2002 (Riksdagsprotokoll 01/02:115, May 29). However, the Bill and the subsequent law were criticised. The law stated that a crime of trafficking had only taken place if it could be proven that the trafficking had been conducted through some sort of force, or that the victim's situation was especially vulnerable, and that she had no other possible option than to submit to the traffickers' will. Critics pointed out that the situations that led to trafficking had usually taken place abroad, and in court the victim would find herself in a situation where she had to prove that she was forced, or, if she had agreed to be trafficked, that she had no other viable options. In different party Bills it was also observed that this law did not correspond to the law criminalising the purchase of sexual services, since that law criminalised the buyer in spite of the realisation of the person selling sexual services (Svanström, 2004b)[4].

A new government Bill on trafficking was presented in March 2004 and passed in parliament in May the same year (Proposition 2003/04: 111, Justitieutskottets betänkande 2003/04: JUU20, Riksdagsprotokoll 2003/04: 122). It suggested the ratification of the UN Protocol to prevent, suppress and punish trafficking in persons, especially women and children, supplementing the UN Convention against Transnational Organized Crime. Furthermore, the Bill proposed a new law on the trafficking of human beings, where the trafficking crime would be widened. The report from the Justice Department supported the ratification of the UN protocol and the suggestions for a new law. The formulation of a new law on trafficking stated that a certain amount of force had to be used in order for a crime of trafficking having been committed. In the government Bill itself it was pointed out that requiring evidence of force shifted the focus from the actions of the accused trafficker to the background and situation of the victim of trafficking – had she really been forced or travelled voluntarily? Furthermore, the principles behind the Swedish Act Prohibiting the Purchase of Sexual Services stated that a crime had been committed even if the woman selling sexual services did so voluntarily. Thus, existing Swedish laws already supported that the use of force did not need to be a part of the definition of trafficking. However, the proposal claimed that the wording of such a law was complicated, but it stated that it was the government's intent to appoint a special commissioner to investigate this issue (Ett utvidgat straffansvar för människohandel 2003/04: 111, pp 58-9). At the time of writing (early 2005) there was still no commissioner. However, 150 million SEK has been allocated to different projects, run by the Swedish Agency for International Development Cooperation in 2004 and 2005. This is supposed to finance international cooperation against trafficking (speech by Laila Freivalds, Foreign Minister, 19 October 2005, Brussels, International Conference on Trafficking: see www.regeringen.se/sb/d/5003/a/51865).

Operation of laws and policies

The police from different districts in the country differ in their opinions of the prostitution law. In a 2001 report the Skåne police authorities (in the southern district in Sweden) criticised the law on a number of aspects. The report stated that visible prostitution had decreased. However, the declining customer base and declining price, and, thus, increased competition had forced women in prostitution to perform sexual services without condoms in return for a higher price. This, in turn, they claimed, had meant an increase in sexually transmitted diseases (STDs). On the whole, the price for sexual services had declined by 50%, which meant that women also had to take on more customers. Moreover, the number of reported crimes of violence against women in prostitution had increased, according to the report. The fact that the crime of purchasing sexual services merited the same penalty as shoplifting meant that the observance of the law was modest.

However, the will of the police force itself actually to enforce the law was criticised in a report from the National Criminal Investigation Department (Rikskriminalpolisstyrelsen). The report argued that there was a split between the political will and the priorities of the police. In some cases the gap between the political will and police practice could be observed in a reluctance to grant resources for police work against trafficking in women for sexual exploitation. The victims were 'just prostitutes' and 'they want this anyway', some police departments stated (Handel med kvinnor, 2003, p 25). Furthermore, the report stated, special consideration was shown to sex buyers in the judicial system. Public prosecutors, bringing sex buyers to court at the same time as prosecuting people accused of pimping, had been criticised by certain judges. These judges held the opinion that sex buyers should not be pilloried together with main proceedings in cases on procuring (Handel med kvinnor, 2003). When interviewed, the National Criminal Investigation Department's expert on trafficking in women said that '... while abused women are forced to describe what they have experienced in detail, the court seems almost uncomfortable when having to embarrass a man who has bought sexual services ... Men seem to have a far greater understanding of why men buy sexual services, and may still not see this as a crime' (Wierup, 2003, p 6).

Different district courts (particularly in Malmö and Stockholm) also ruled differently: the Malmö court demanded stronger evidence and generally sentenced convicted sex buyers to lower penalties than in Stockholm. This meant that the sex buyer had to be caught in flagrante for the evidence to be sufficient in court. The problem with county courts demanding high levels of evidence also went against the police's duty to prevent crime, since in order to secure evidence the police officers had to wait until the crime was being committed (Nord and Rosenberg, 2001). Critics of the law concluded that if the purpose of the law were to limit prostitution, this would not be fully realised; especially since some prostitution moved indoors (or that the business was conducted by mobile phone). The law could thus only be applied to street prostitution, and since the penalty was fairly mild, it could not merit the use of police resources to trace escort services, for instance, or internet prostitution (Nord and Rosenberg, 2001).

Further criticism of the judicial system came in 2003 in connection with a large, high-profile case when, after substantial police investigation, an illegal brothel was uncovered in Stockholm. For three years a brothel had been kept in an ordinary apartment building, and many of the women in the brothel were victims of trafficking. Thus, the case also brought the government's ongoing work on a trafficking law to the fore. The woman running the brothel was prosecuted for procuring, and a number of the men who had bought sexual services at the brothel could be traced through a detailed register of customers. The computer evidence showed the name of the woman in the brothel, time and date, where the 'sexual transaction' had taken place (at the brothel or in the sex buyer's home or elsewhere), the sum paid and then a final 'OK' when business had been done. There were 571 registered customers, and a well-known Swedish financier was among them, something that was given coverage in the media. In the late summer of 2003 news headlines reported: 'Financier not prosecuted for sex crime' (Ålstig, 2003). One of the morning papers described in critical terms how the writ-server had failed to serve the financier his summons before the period for prosecution had expired. The article also noted that both the financier's home and office addresses were known and to get there could hardly have been a problem, since there was '… less than a couple of kilometres between the police who were looking, and the financier who hid' (Billger, 2003, p 8). The district prosecutor was interviewed and said: 'He admitted just like that. But this will be a deed exempt from punishment. To hide after actually admitting to an offence is pitiful' (Billger, 2003, p 8; cf Holgersson and Svanström, 2004, pp 52-4).

The same district prosecutor used the information in the brothel's registers to identify 73 men as sex buyers, and brought 40 of them to court. Twenty-five were sentenced to fines in 2004. Of those that pleaded not guilty, eight were sentenced in spite of their denial. However, in later cases this type of evidence was not seen as sufficient, since it could not be ascertained that it was the accused that had bought the sexual services (Nilsson, 2004). Nonetheless, the same kind of digital evidence was enough to sentence the brothel keeper, a Finnish woman, to four years' imprisonment and deportation for serious procurement. In a later interview, the prosecutor, Hans Ihrman, stated that the fact that the judicial system demands such comprehensive evidence boded ill and sent out the wrong signals. While stating that the law had changed the attitude among people towards prostitution, his explanation for the strictness of the courts was that the crime is seen as most reproachable and stigmatising, and thus the evidence in the cases needs to be very strong for courts to want to sentence these men (Tures, 2004).

Analysis of policies and interventions

Since the law was passed on 1 January 1999 there has been an increasing number of reported crimes but, with the exception of the first year, the number of convictions has remained more or less the same. As shown in Table 4.1 (below), the number of guilty verdicts has been more or less stable, at around 20 convictions, with a peak in 2003 when there were 23. However, at the same time the number of reported crimes is far higher, with an increase from 94 in 1999 to 300 in 2003. It has to be observed that the large number of reported crimes in 2003 is connected to the case discussed above, where an illegal brothel was uncovered in Stockholm. The number of cases discontinued by the prosecution (nolle prosequi) was very small (two cases, both in 2002).

Table 4.1: Crime of purchase of sexual services (numbers reported, 1999-2003)

Year	Reported crimes	Summary fine issued by police (strafförelägganden)	Discontinued by prosecutor (åtalsunderlåtelse)	Fined at court
1999	94	5	0	5
2000	92	7	0	22
2001	86	18	0	20
2002	110	21	2	14
2003	300	49	0	23
Total	682	100	2	84

Sources: Brottsförebyggande rådet (BRÅ), table 420, Lagförda för brott [persons found guilty of offences] 1999, 2000, 2001, 2002, 2003 (www.bra.se/extra/pod/?module_instance=8/), and for reported crimes (statistik.bra.se/solwebb/action/anmalda/urval/sok).

When the new law was introduced in 1999 very large decreases in prostitution were reported in Sweden's three largest cities, as estimated by social services and police departments. Gothenburg reported the largest decrease, where it was estimated the number of women involved in street prostitution had diminished by over two-thirds compared with the previous year. While more recent estimates (in 2003) show a slight increase on 1999, the figures are still far lower than they had been in 1998. This pattern is shown below in Table 4.2.

Estimates of the number of women involved in street prostitution have therefore greatly reduced since the introduction of the new law. However, and as mentioned earlier, the law applied only to street prostitution. It is not known how many of the women who were involved in street prostitution in 1998 subsequently become involved in off-street prostitution.

Table 4.2: Estimates of number of women in street prostitution in Sweden's three largest cities

City	1998	1999	2003
Stockholm (population 750,348)	280	170	200[a]
Gothenburg (population 466,990)	286	90	100
Malmö (population 259,579)	160	80	135
Total	726	340	435

Note: [a] There was a high level of discrepancy in Stockholm between estimates in 2003. Social services estimated the number of women to between 180 and 200, and the police estimated 50-60 women. The report (Kännedom om prostitution, 2004) suggests the discrepancies may derive from groups of women being in the street at different hours and on different weekdays. I have chosen to use the highest estimates in this table.

Source: Kännedom om prostitution, 2004, pp 22, 24, Statistiska centralbyrån, befolkningsstatistik 2001.

The first prostitution project was initiated in Malmö, Sweden's third-largest city, in 1977, after a report revealed increased criminality, including prostitution. The report received wide media attention (Larsson and Månsson, 1976). The Malmö prostitution project was designed to work with the social problems of prostitution (SOU, 1995: 16, pp 11-12). There had been no similar work previously undertaken in Sweden, and this project became a model for future social work against prostitution. A number of characteristics have been used to describe the approach of the project: the group was the first organisation doing this kind of work, and the participants (the authorities, the social workers, the researchers, the police etc) had a feeling of being pioneers, which increased their sense of involvement. Although there were some differences of opinion, the social workers agreed on a mutual perspective towards the women involved in prostitution; a perspective they also shared with the involved police officers. It was formulated as 'the simple goal of helping the prostitutes away from prostitution to a better life' (SOU 1995: 16, p 13). The project did not have to follow traditional administrative procedure and could concentrate on the needs of the women in prostitution and, together with the high level of involvement and a shared perspective on prostitution, it gave an opening to develop a method adapted to the situation. Finally, the project has been described as a total commitment towards one specific problem within one particular city, including involvement in different areas from different authorities. The number of women in prostitution decreased from over 300 in 1974 to 60 women in 1981 (SOU, 1995:16). The ensuing work in Malmö was less successful. The social workers now had to go through ordinary channels when processing paperwork concerning women in prostitution, and there was none of the cooperation with researchers that had been an important part of the original project (SOU, 1995: 16).

In Stockholm the police initiated a special surveillance team on prostitution in 1978 and, at a later stage, cooperation with social workers. Visiting work (where the social worker approached women in the street or elsewhere – work in the UK that would be called 'outreach work') was prioritised, and was also directed towards the sex buyers but without much success. A conflict within the group led to its dissolution in 1990, and a new group, with less independence, was organised, called the City Section (Citysektionen), mainly working in the field of street prostitution (SOU, 1995: 16)[5].

The prostitution group in Gothenburg was established in 1981. The group has had the opportunity (through additional funds) to organise certain research projects, and among those was a project focusing on sex buyers and their reasons for buying sexual services. The Gothenburg group focuses on visiting work in street prostitution, together with support and treatment (SOU, 1995: 16). Its research projects have added to the knowledge base on prostitution as a whole. In that sense the Gothenburg organisation is different from the current organisations in Malmö and Stockholm.

In 2004 the so-called prostitution groups in the three largest cities in Sweden were organised under the cities' social services. Social workers conduct visiting work mainly directed towards street prostitution (but also through the internet to some extent, where emails with information on how to get in contact with the prostitution groups are sent to internet addresses where sexual services are being offered), support work, advisory work treatment and also the spreading of information. In Stockholm the Prostitution Centre (Prostitutions Centrum) is another unit within the social services, working in individual support, crisis therapy and the spreading of information. The centre works with clients both individually and in groups, but does not conduct visiting work (Kännedom om prostitution 2003, 2004).

Debates on legalisation and decriminalisation

Since the mid 1990s, prostitution in Sweden has been debated in terms of how it should be handled legally, whether neither, both or only one of the parties involved in prostitution should be criminalised, rather than discussing what prostitution as such represents, and whether it is desirable in society or not. In essence, since 1998, the discussion has focused on the current Act Prohibiting the Purchase of Sexual Services, and its possible advantages and disadvantages. One starting point for the debate was when the second commission on prostitution delivered its report in 1995 (SOU, 1995: 15-17)[6]. Soon after the commission had been appointed, a Bill was presented in parliament. This Bill was signed only by women from different parties: the Social Democrats, the Left Party and the Liberals (Motion 1992/93: Ju622). It demanded the criminalisation of the sex buyer, and argued that there was no need for a new commission on this issue[7]. After two years the commission's report came, recommending that both selling and buying sexual services should be prohibited. In the name of what was called gender equality, it argued that both parties had to be criminalised, since it would be 'peculiar' if only one party was seen as guilty of crime, while the other was considered innocent. Although the woman in a prostitution transaction traditionally had been seen as the victim, one could ask oneself if a man buying sex was not also victimised in this trade, the report stated. The effect of criminalisation would also be greater if both parties were included (SOU, 1995: 15).

The results from the commission were presented on 14 March 1995 and on the same day two prominent experts attacked the results in an article in the liberal morning paper *Dagens Nyheter*. Both experts had a long history of studying prostitution; both had been involved in the 1977 commission, and one of them had been part of the commission that now came with its report. He had, however, left the commission in 1994 in protest against the expected report and its recommendation. In their article they claimed that to criminalise both parties in order to distribute the punishment equally between the sex buyer and the woman in prostitution, obscured what prostitution was really about – men's power and men's sexuality. If a law should be introduced, it should be directed towards the buyer (Månsson and Olsson, 1995). The next day the same paper's editorial criticised the commission's result: 'to punish them [the women] is to punish the victims. If criminalisation is seen as necessary to make a social "imprint", it would be enough to penalise the purchase' (Höök, 1995).

The following year, 1996, another Bill was presented in parliament. It demanded that the purchase of sexual services should be prohibited, and it was signed by all political parties' women's federations except the Conservatives (Motion 1996/97:Ju718). Thus, when the government Bill was proposed in 1998, there was already substantial parliamentary support among women MPs. The proposal for a Violence Against Women Act came in February 1998 and was debated in parliament at the end of May that same year. The Bill contained suggestions to counteract violence against women and sexual harassment in work life and suggested the criminalisation of the purchase of sexual services, thus going against the recommendation of the 1995 commission on prostitution (Proposition 1997/98: 55). The Bill received much media attention, and one of the conservative editorials stated that the government 'adhered to radical feminism' (Popova, 1998; cf Gould, 2001).

When the proposal was presented in parliament the consensus among the parties concerning suggestions on how to work against violence against women was paramount, but the issue of criminalising the client in prostitution caused considerable debate (Riksdagsprotokoll 1997/98: 114). The Conservatives and the Liberals were against criminalisation. The Christian Democrats supported criminalisation of both parties in prostitution. The Social Democrats, the Left, the Green and the Centre parties were all in favour of the Bill. The arguments used against supporting the government proposal were that prostitution would go underground, leading to an increase in violence, more power to procurers, and less potential for the police to discover prostitution. It was also argued that the proposal was symbolic rather than motivated from a realistic point of view. Furthermore, prostitution was seen as a social policy problem rather than as a problem for the criminal justice system. Those in support of the proposal used (radical) feminist arguments and stated that women's bodies should not be bought and that prostitution was oppression of all women. It was stated that two-thirds of the ongoing prostitution business had already gone underground, and that the new law would decrease the demand for sexual services. (Riksdagsprotokoll 1997/98: 114). When voting on the Bill, 181 MPs voted for and 92 against, 13 abstained, while 63 were absent. The majority of those voting against the proposal belonged to the Conservative or Liberal parties (89 votes). The Christian Democrats abstained from voting (Riksdagsprotokoll 1997/98: 115).

One debate took place in the social democratic paper *Aftonbladet*. A well-known sex liberal debater wrote an article together with a sex worker, stating that the coming law meant a stigmatisation of a workgroup, that is, sex workers. They criticised what they saw as the foundation for the law: women did not sell their bodies; they sold sexual services. Moreover, the group of sex workers was heterogeneous, and not all women were drug addicts or abused – a statement generally heard in the debate. Sexuality in prostitution could be affirmative and positive for both the client and the sex worker. They were also very critical of what they saw as the victim's role given to the sex workers, and that they themselves as a workgroup in society had not been invited to participate in formulating a law that would affect their trade (Andersson and Östergren, 1998). In response, two women from the Left party wrote an article stating that verdicts from other women in prostitution gave another picture. However, there were reasons to take the 'prostitution lobby' seriously, since to see prostitution as exploitation of women was unusual south of Sweden, that is, on the continent

(Eriksson and Lindroth, 1998). In another article a former prostitute stated that the law would be supportive. She herself had been raped and filmed against her will while prostituting herself. 'Perhaps we will not be disbelieved about having been abused when prostitution in itself is seen as abuse' (Günay, 1998, p 4).

Key issues faced

Reasons for entry into prostitution

In a report in 2004 the National Board on Health and Welfare (Socialstyrelsen) discussed different types of entry into prostitution for women selling sexual services[8]. The report identified a number of possible ways of entering into prostitution, but stated that in both Malmö and Stockholm most women in street prostitution were drug users, sometimes as well as being homeless. Nevertheless, some of these women may be long-time drug abusers, but it is not until they start using more expensive drugs such as amphetamine or heroin that they also enter into prostitution. Both the police and the social workers mention a 'vicious circle', where prostitution finances drug abuse, and drugs are necessary for the women to be able to deal emotionally with prostitution. In Gothenburg, however, the numbers of drug-using women in prostitution are lower than in Malmö and Stockholm, and the Gothenburg police claim that there are somewhat older women, between the ages of 40 and 50, active in prostitution. For these women, prostitution is said to be a way out of social isolation, and some of them are supposedly opposed to the new law on prostitution. Some women were said to finance a gambling addiction through prostitution, many of them are also heavily in debt. A few women are reported as having mental health difficulties and according to the informants, these women have been lured into prostitution under the assumption that they would meet a man to spend their life with (Kännedom om prostitution 2003, 2004).

There are also fairly well-established women in prostitution, according to therapists at the Swedish Association for Sexuality Education (RFSU) and the Prostitution Centre in Stockholm. Economic reasons can be one motive for entry, but according to these informants, there are often other psychological motives behind the rational economic reasons. The money is often used to finance over-consumption (eg the purchase of new clothes instead of doing laundry), and the purchase of things the women do not really need (eg buying expensive fur coats that are 'forgotten' or 'lost') (Kännedom om prostitution 2003, 2004).

Regarding young girls' entry into prostitution, according to the same report, the majority of those that start selling sexual services apparently by chance are sexually traumatised. Some of the young girls have been sexually abused; others have been bullied at school. The first prostitution contacts are often made through the internet on 'neutral' chat sites, and the girls are often approached themselves and offered money for sexual services. Most of these young girls are also said to alternate between periods of prostitution and self-mutilation. Most of them have also prostituted themselves in smaller cities (Kännedom om prostitution 2003, 2004)

Reasons for buying sex

In a population-based survey from 1998, questions on sexuality were posed, and among these were questions on commercial sex[9]. The findings showed that one in eight men (12.7%) in Sweden had paid for commercial sex on one or more occasions. Close to 80% of these had entered into prostitution contacts abroad, in connection with work or on vacation (Månsson, 1998, pp 236 and 241). Unfortunately, questions on why these men had bought sexual services were not asked, and the report referred to other research on this issue.

Research that investigates the sex buyers' reasons for involvement in prostitution are mostly based on interviews, either personal interviews or telephone interviews, and the number of interviewees is often rather small. The first study that focused on sex buyers was conducted in 1984 with interviews of 66 sex buyers. Regarding their first encounter with prostitution, the sex buyers' stated reasons were mainly motives such as adventure and curiosity or that the woman 'flaunted herself' (Månsson and Linders, 1984). Another report (based on interviews with 72 men) argues that men's encounter with prostitution happened by chance, as a result of an active search, or as a part of ritual during a period in life when they tried to establish contacts with women. All of the men looked upon prostitution as an economic transaction (Hydén, 1990). Based on the same interviews, a further report states that the majority of the first contacts were made with women in Sweden (contradicted by the results from the later population-based study mentioned above, which may be a result of increased sex tourism), and that the majority of the first contacts were planned events (Andersson-Collins, 1990)[10].

The latest study investigating men's reasons for buying sexual services came out in 1996. Its main purpose was to ascertain 'why men "really" visit women in prostitution', while also trying to find methods and strategies to reach and offer support to sex buyers (Sandell et al, 1996). Thus, the question of why these men entered the prostitution scene in the first place was not discussed. The people in the research group were a combination of social workers, psychotherapists and had conducted research in social work. Three of them worked in the prostitution group in Gothenburg. Through what was called a 'helicopter perspective', the group analysed the 40 interviews with sex buyers and categorised them into five different types of buyers: 'the all-consumers' who lived in steady relationships while buying sexual services and 'those avoiding relationships' who could not hold on to a steady relationship, are characterised as egocentrics choosing to buy sex as a part of a lifestyle, where life was 'a market where everything can be bought or sold' (Sandell et al, 1996). These men accounted for the majority of the sample (14 men). 'The relationship seekers' (11 men) and 'the refused' (six men) are understood as men who have a romantic notion of women, looking for the right one. However, they have such low self-esteem that they cannot get close to 'real women' and the only way is to buy sexual services (Sandell et al, 1996). Finally, the 'complementary buyers' were seen as men lacking something in their ordinary life; unfulfilled in their relationships but still wanting to keep and shelter their families. Thus, their only solution was to buy sexual services (Sandell et al, 1996). This study was severely criticised by feminist scholars (Westerstrand, 1996; Wendt Höjer, 1996). It was criticised for being tendencious, and through taking the individual perspective of the buyer, losing sight of the structural inequalities of women and men in society. Later studies on sex buyers have not included qualitative questions regarding their reasons for entering into prostitution (Månsson, 1998; SoS-rapport, 2000: 5, pp 23 and 41-3; Holgersson and Svanström, 2004).

Conclusions

Since the beginning of the 1980s an interesting change has taken place concerning prostitution in Sweden. In the 1980s there was more or less a consensus among academics and activists that prostitution had to be seen as exploitation of women. Appointed commissioners and the Swedish government, however, did not look upon prostitution from this feminist perspective, but applied a gender equality framework that led to the recommendation in 1995 to criminalise both the seller and the buyer in prostitution.

At the beginning of the 2000s the scene looks quite different. There are much wider academic theoretical positions concerning prostitution/sex work, and some activist groups look upon prostitution as exploitation of women while others see the same phenomenon as sex work. At the same time, the Swedish state has taken a radical feminist stance, looking upon prostitution as the exploitation of women. To understand this change in state politics we have to acknowledge the change in the make-up of parliament, with an increased number of women members of parliament. The issue of prostitution has been a question that has united women MPs across party lines and this unified political action led to the Act Prohibiting the Purchase of Sexual Services. The Act also has support among the Swedish citizens. According to figures from institutions involved in crime prevention and social services, prostitution decreased after the establishment of the Act, but the number of women in prostitution has now increased again according to recent reports.

Yet, the Swedish state is at the same time contradictory in its attitude towards prostitution where trafficking is concerned. The current law on trafficking in human beings is more in line with countries liberal to prostitution. Furthermore, the offence of buying sexual services merits the same punishment as shoplifting, sending the message that the offence is not too serious after all. Furthermore, the attitudes to women in prostitution and to the Act Prohibiting the Purchase of Sexual Services within certain parts of the police force and the judicial system are still characterised by patriarchal values, and the sex buyers receive unjustified consideration. In Sweden today the discussion on prostitution has come to a standstill as far as debating the issue is concerned. Rather than discussing prostitution as a phenomenon – unwanted or wanted in a modern society – the discussion is focusing on the advantages or disadvantages of the law.

This chapter has focused on academic, activist and state perspectives on prostitution during a period of 25 years. Further, it has discussed the current policies of the Swedish state, where the purchase of sexual services has been criminalised since 1999. It has discussed how some of the different institutions involved in upholding the law are still reluctant to do so, and how at times they seem to look upon prostitution as sex work rather than exploitation.

Notes

[1] All translations in this article have been made by the author. I wish to thank the editors of this volume for their invaluable help and constructive comments on earlier versions of this text.

[2] In the 1970s there were two other debates, one concerned a party member's Bill that suggested the introduction of state brothels, something which was severely criticised by the women's movement (Motion 1972: 59). The other concerned the alleged involvement of members of parliament and the government in buying sexual services at an illegal brothel in 1976 (Rauscher and Mattsson, 2004).

[3] Research on this period with particular focus on the debates on prostitution is still to be done.

[4] Sweden had been criticised for not ratifying the 1949 UN Convention on the suppression of the traffic in persons and of the exploitation of the prostitution of others, thus placing itself together with countries with a more liberal view of prostitution such as Germany, the Netherlands and Thailand (Månsson, 2000).

[5] When the group was dissolved and the staff resigned all the documentation of the group's work during 12 years was destroyed (SOU, 1995: 16, p 35).

[6] The first commission presented its report in 1910, recommending that the then regulation of communal prostitution should be revised.

[7] During the period 1983-93 more than 50 party and member Bills concerning prostitution were proposed, and of those about 30 proposed the criminalisation of the purchase of sexual services. These came from representatives of all parties, sometimes both men and women from the same party, sometimes only women, but never groups of men only (Svanström, 2004a).

[8] In the government Bill in 1998 it was stated that the National Board of Health and Welfare had the responsibility to report continuously on the extent of prostitution and the social work that is undertaken on a local level.

[9] The survey was sent to 5,200 people between the ages of 18 and 74. Of these, 469 individuals did not belong to the population group (for instance, they were deceased, in prison, abroad, had emigrated, etc), and thus, the original population was 4,781 individuals, of whom 2,810 answered the questionnaire. The fallings-off were thus rather large, and an analysis of missing cases show that the number of older women in the survey is proportionally small.

[10] A report from the City Section in Stockholm from 1994, based on interviews with 50 sex buyers, stated that the majority also had had their sexual debut with a woman in prostitution (Lantz, 1994, p 34).

Recommended further reading

Gould, A. (2002) 'Sweden's law on prostitution: feminism, drugs and the foreign threat', in S. Thorbek and B. Pattanaik (eds) *Transnational prostitution: Changing patterns in a global context*, New York: Zed Books, pp 201-15.

Kilvington, J., Day, S. and Ward, H. (2001) 'Prostitution policy in Europe: a time of change?', *Feminist Review*, vol 67, pp 78-93.

Kulick, D. (2005) 'Four hundred Swedish Perverts', *GLQ*, vol 11, no 2, pp 205-35.

Svanström, Y (2004) 'Criminalising the john: a Swedish gender model?', in J. Outshoorn (ed) *The politics of prostitution: Women's movements, democratic states, and the globalisation of sex commerce*, Cambridge: Cambridge University Press, pp 225-44.

References

'Starkt stöd för skärpt sexlag' (2002) *Svenska Dagbladet*, 7 February.

Ålstig, C. (2003) 'Finansman slipper åtal för sexbrott', *Aftonbladet*, 12 August.

Andersson, L. and Östergren, P. (1998a), 'Ny lag förvärrar för sexarbetare', *Aftonbladet*, 11 May.

Andersson-Collins, G. (1990), *Solitärer: en rapport om prostitutionskunder*, Stockholm: Socialförvaltningen.

Billger, O. (2003) 'Inget åtal för erkänt sexköp', *Svenska Dagbladet*, 12 August.

Borelius, U. and Nordin, K. (1991), *Sex för pengar på mäns vis – om homosexuell mansprostitution i Göteborg*, Lägesrapport från Projektgruppen hs mansprostitution, Gothenburg.

Borg, A., Elwien, F., Frühling, M., Grönwall. L., Liljeström, R., Månsson, S.-A., Nelin, A., Olsson, H., Sjöberg, T. (1981), *Prostitution: Beskrivning, analys, förslag till åtgärder*, Stockholm: Liber.

Brunnberg, E., Olsson, H. and Widerberg, K. (1981), 'Samtal kring prostitutionsutredningen', *Kvinnovetenskaplig tidskrift*, no 3, pp 26-31.

Dodillet, S. (2004) 'Visionen av det prostitutionsfria samhället: om tankarna bakom sexköpslagen', in E. Ahlstedt (ed) *Vision och verklighet: populärvetenskapliga föreläsningar hållna under Humanistdagarna den 9-10 oktober 2004*, Gothenburg: Gothenburg University.

Eduards, M. (forthcoming), *Till kvinnors försvar. En svensk kroppspolitisk historia*, Stockholm: Atlas Akademi.

Eriksson M. and Lindroth, I. (1998) 'Repliken Underskatta inte prostitutionslobbyn', *Aftonbladet*, 30 May.

Florin, C. and Nilsson, B. (1999), *'Något som liknar en oblodig revolution ...': Jämställdhetens politisering under 1960- och 70-talen*, Umeå: Jämställdhetskommittén, Umea University.

Fredelius, G. (1978) *Ett onödigt ont : en antologi mot porr och prostitution*, Stockholm: Ordfront.

Gentele, J. (1979) *Ta strid för kärleken – kamp mot porr och prostitution: En antologi utgiven av Aktionen kamp mot porr och prostitution*, Stockholm: Ordfront.

Gould, A. (2001) 'The criminalisation of buying sex: the politics of prostitution in Sweden', *Journal of Social Politics*, vol 30, no 3, pp 437-56.

Günay, J. (1998) 'Nya lagen hjälper oss prostituerade', *Dagens Nyheter*, 6 August.

Handel med kvinnor (2003), lägesrapport 5, 31 December 2002, Rikskriminalpolisen, Kriminalunderrättelsetjänsten, Illegal invandring.

Holgersson, C. and Svanström, Y. (2004) *Lagliga och olagliga affärer: Om sexköp och organisationer*, Stockholm: ref no 020513, NorFa-rapportering.

Hydén, L. (1990) *De osynliga männen: En socialpsykologisk studie av manliga prostitutionskunder*. Stockholm: Stockholms socialförvaltning.

Höök, A. (1995) 'Tvivelaktigt prostitutionsförslag. Lagstiftning är ingen universalmetod för att bli av med det vi ogillar', *Dagens Nyheter*, 15 March.

Justitieutskottets betänkande 2003/04 JUU20.

Kännedom om prostitution 1998-1999 (2000), Stockholm: Socialstyrelsen.

Kännedom om prostitution 2003 (2004), Stockholm: Socialstyrelsen.

Kulick, D. (2003), 'Sex in the new Europe: the criminalization of clients and Swedish fear of penetration', *Anthropological Theory*, vol 3, no 2, pp 199-218.

Kulick, D. (2005), 'Four hundred Swedish Perverts', *GLQ*, vol 11, no 2, pp 205-35.

Lantz, I. (1994), *'Torsken i flickstimme': om prostitutionskunder i Stockholm*, Stockholm: Socialtjänsten, Citysektionen.

Larsson, S. (1983), *Könshandeln – om prostituterades villkor*, Stockholm: Gotab.

Larsson, S. and Månsson, S. (1976), *Svarta affärer: utredning om vissa klubbars och näringsställens sociala betydelse och struktur*, Malmö: Socialförvaltningen.

Lewin, B. (ed) (1998), *Sex i Sverige: Om sexuallivet i Sverige 1996*. Stockholm: Folkhälso-institutet.

Ljung, A. and Lennartsson, R. (2004), 'Mannen utan egenskaper. Kulturella perspektiv på maskulinitet i vardande', *Kvinnovetenskaplig tidskrift*, no 1-2, pp 113-32.

Människohandel för sexuella ändamål (2004) lägesrapport 6, 1 January-31 December 2003, KUT Rapport 2004: 2, Rikskriminalpolisen.

Månsson, S. (1981), *Könshandelns framjare och profitörer: om förhållandet mellan hallick och prostituerad*, Lund: Doxa.

Månsson, S. (1988), 'The man in sexual commerce', *Meddelanden från socialhögskolan*, no 2.

Månsson, S. (1998), 'Den köpta sexualiteten', in B. Lewin, (ed), *Sex i Sverige: om sexuallivet i Sverige 1996*. Stockholm: Folkhälsoinstitutet, pp 167-82.

Månsson, S. (2000), 'Sverige och den globala könshandeln', *Social politik*, no 4-5, pp 5-7.

Månsson, S. and Linders, A. (1984) *Sexualitet utan ansikte: könsköparna*, Stockholm: Carlsson & Jönsson.

Månsson, S.-A. and Olsson, H. (1995) 'Den röda horluvan tillbaka', *Dagens Nyheter*, 14 March.

Månsson, S. and Söderlind, P. (2004), *Sexindustrin på nätet: Aktörer, innehåll, relationer och ekonomiska flöden*, Stockholm, Égalité.

Motion 1972: 59 Om statlig bordellverksamhet.

Motion 1992/93: Ju622 Prostitution.

Motion 1996/97: Ju718 Kriminalisering av könsköp.

Nilsson, K. (2004) 'Sexköpare slipper åtal', *Dagens Nyheter*, 5 February.

Nord, A. and Rosenberg, T. (2001), 'Rapport: Lag (1998:408) om förbud mot köp av sexuella tjänster. Metodutveckling avseende åtgärder mot prostitution', ALM 429-14044/99, Polismyndigheten i Skåne, unpublished report.

Nyberg, A. (2005) 'Har den ekonomiska jämställdheten ökat sedan början av 1990-talet?', Forskarrapporter till Jämställdhetspolitiska utredningen 2005:66, Stockholm: Fritzes.

Persson, L. (1981), *Horor, hallickar och torskar: En kartläggning av prostitutionen i Stockholm*, Stockholm: Norstedts.

Pettersson, T. and Tiby, E. (2003) 'The production and reproduction of prostitution', *Journal of Scandinavian Studies in Criminology and Crime Prevention*, vol 3, no 2, pp 154-72.

Popova, S. (1998) 'Jämställdhetspolitik Persson - den överordnade', *Svenska Dagbladet*, 8 March.

Proposition 1997/98: 55 Kvinnofrid.

Proposition 2003/04: 111 Ett utvidgat straffansvar för människohandel.

Proposition 2004/05: 45, En ny sexualbrottslagstiftning.

Rauscher, D. and Mattsson, J. (2004), *Makten, männen, mörkläggningen: Historien om bordellhärvan 1976*, Stockholm: Vertigo.

Riksdagsprotokoll (Protocol from the Swedish Parliament) 1997/98:115.

Riksdagsprotokoll (Protocol from the Swedish Parliament) 2003/04:122.

Riksdagsprotokoll (Protocol from the Swedish Parliament) 1997/98: 114.

Riksdagsprotokoll (Protocol from the Swedish Parliament) 2000/01:67.

Sandell, G., Petterrsson, E., Larsson, J. and Kuosmanen, J. (1996) *Könsköparna: varför går män egentligen till prostituerade?: Djupanalys av män som köper sex*, Stockholm: Natur och kultur.

Sexualpolitisk front (1977) 'Detta är Sexualpolitisk front: förbundet presenterar sitt program' *Pockettidningen R*, vol 7, no 4, pp 129-35.

SOU 1981:71 *Prostitutionen i Sverige*, Stockhom: Fritzes.

SOU 1995:15 *Könshandeln*, Stockholm: Fritzes.

SOU 1995:16 *Socialt arbete mot prostitution i Sverige*, Stockholm: Fritzes.

SOU 1995:60 *Kvinnofrid*, Stockholm: Fritzes.

SOU 2004:121 *Ett slag i luften: en utredning om myndigheter, mansvåld och makt. Betänkande av utredningen om kvinnofridsuppdragen*, Stockholm: Fritzes.

Svanström, Y. (2000) 'Policing public women. The regulation of prostitution in Stockholm 1812-1880', unpublished dissertation, Stockholm, Atlas Akademi.

Svanström, Y. (2004a) 'Criminalising the john: a Swedish gender model?', in J. Outshoorn (ed) *The politics of prostitution: Women's movements, democratic states, and the globalisation of sex commerce*, Cambridge: Cambridge University Press, pp 225-64.

Svanström, Y. (2004b) 'Handel med kvinnor: debatten i Sverige och Nederländerna om prostitution och trafficking', in C. Florin and C. Bergqvist (eds) *Framtiden i samtiden: könsrelationer i förändring i Sverige och omvärlden*, Stockholm: Institutet för framtidsstudier, pp 290-323.

Svanström, Y. (2005) 'Through the prism of prostitution: Attitudes to women and sexuality in Sweden at two fins-de-siècle', *NORA – Nordic Journal of Women's Studies*, no 1, pp 48-58.

Thomsson, U. (2000), "Rätten till våra kroppar': Kvinnorörelsen och våldtäktsdebatten.' *Kvinnovetenskaplig tidskrift*, no 4, pp 51-64.

Tures, E. (2004) 'Åklagare vill sänka kraven för sexköpsåtal', *Göteborgsposten*, 4 March.

Vogel, J. and Wolf, M. (2004), 'Index för internationella välfärdsjämförelser: Sverige i täten', *Välfärd*, no 1, pp 7-15.

Wendt Höjer, M. (1996), 'Var finns den gode mannen?', *Göteborgsposten*, 3 June.

Westerstrand, J. (1996), 'Vem har rätt att må bra?', *Kvinnovetenskaplig tidskrift*, no 2, pp 72-4.

Westerstrand, J. (2000), 'En främmande fågel? Lagen om förbud mot köp av sexuella tjänster ur ett feministiskt rättsligt perspektiv', examensarbete i rättshistoria, unpublished master thesis in law, Uppsala: Uppsala University, Department of Law.

Wierup, L. (2003) 'Polisen prioriterar inte sexhandeln', *Dagens Nyheter*, 14 February.

FIVE

The Republic of Moldova: prostitution and trafficking in women

Kristina Abiala

Introduction

To understand prostitution in Moldova we have to trace it back to the Soviet period from 1940, through the years following its independence in 1991 and up to the beginning of the twenty-first century. From being seen as alien to the state and not officially discussed to being considered a dangerous social vice, prostitution is now discussed mainly within the sexual trafficking agenda. Within this agenda are a number of questions, such as: can prostitution be justified? Why does it exist, and will it stop? Why are young women leaving Moldova? Are they deceived or forced? Do they know what they are getting into? The socio-economic position of Moldovan citizens and the attitudes of the general population towards prostitution and trafficking also form important parts of the current context wherein discourses are handled and reconstructed.

The national context

The Federal Republic of Moldova (hereafter Moldova) has a population of 4.3 million (UNDP, 2004)[1]. Approximately the same size as Belgium, Moldova is situated in Central Europe between Ukraine and Romania. Until August 1991 Moldova was the Moldovan Soviet Socialist Republic, a part of the USSR, and had been so since 1940 (UNDP, 2004).[2] The historiography on gender relations and sexuality must therefore be contextualised by taking the conditions in the former Soviet Union into consideration. The country suffered hard from the demise of the Soviet Union, a series of natural disasters and the 1998 financial crisis in Russia (UNHCR, 2004, p 4).

Following independence, the economy was prioritised at the cost of social reforms: '[a]s economic reforms stall or are either wrongly constructed or implemented, the cost the Moldovan people has had to pay is great' (Johansson, 2003, p 23). This process of transition to a market economy is thought to have contributed to the phenomenon of trafficking: 'Sudden political change, economic collapse, civil unrest, internal armed conflict ... greatly increase the likelihood that a country will become a source of trafficking ... the victims may be one of the few resources of marketable wealth' (US State Department, 2003, p 8).

Moldova was ranked[3] number 122 according to its production in 2000, in between India and Honduras, with $2,672 per capita, which can be compared with Belgium's $281,590.[4] Corruption is widespread and this is acknowledged by the Council of Europe[5], which states that, 'the Republic of Moldova is without any doubt one of the countries deeply affected by corruption' (European Commission, 2004, p 7). This is attributed to the way the judiciary system functions, to politicians, to the poor performance of governmental agencies, and also to poverty.

Do citizens have a long and healthy life, knowledge and decent standard of living, and are there any gender differences? The Human Development Index (HDI) and Gender Related Development Index (GDI), constructed by UNDP, measure life expectancy at birth, literacy rate and estimated earned income. Moldova is HDI-ranked number 113 (of 177 countries) and GDI-ranked number 91[6] (of 144 countries). This indicates that women in Moldova have a very difficult situation, compared both with men in Moldova and with women in many other countries.

Moldova remains the poorest country in Europe. The International Monetary Fund (IMF) estimated in 2001 that poverty affected between 55% and 70% of the population, especially in the southern part of the country, in small rural towns (IMF, 2002, p 7). In a survey 75% of the respondents declared that their family income allows them to buy only the essentials, or not even that (IPP, 2003; n=1,153). Families with many children, single-parent families (often mothers with children), young families and the unemployed, especially in rural areas, are groups that are particularly affected by poverty (UNICEF, 2000, p 13). Poverty, together with the absence of parental care and increasing family instability, can lead to higher incidences of abuse, neglect, exploitation and homelessness.

At the beginning of the 21st century between 10% and 20% of the labour force was not working. There has been an alarming increase in poverty and unemployment, and Moldovans, especially women, are desperate to find employment. Many see jobs abroad as the only answer to an impossible economic situation (Minnesota Advocates for Human Rights, 2000a, p 11). Women in the former Soviet republics, with lower educational status, living in rural areas, and older women are often said to represent an 'underclass' (Domanski, 2002, p 393). The general social situation is critical. Pensions and salaries are not always paid; many schools are not functioning and hospitals lack resources (Johansson, 2003, p 23). SIDA (2003, p 18) highlights the extent of this problem: 'Poor families have little access to health services, fear bad health and are often unable to treat serious or chronic illnesses. The mix of formal and informal payments puts care out of reach ...'. Reliance on informal networks and the informal economy often become the only available strategies left for survival.

A Moldovan study recently found that 71% of young people in 2003 expressed a wish to move abroad, either forever or for a short time (IPP, 2003). In total, between 600,000 and 1 million Moldovans are believed to have migrated to earn a living (UNOHCHR, 2002, p 25). This means that up to 25% of the population has left the country. Of these 58% have left for Russia and 70% migrate outside the regular system of laws on migration and trafficking in persons.

Among other things, migration leads to money being sent back to the emigrants' families in Moldova. Such money is estimated to add up to twice the size of the country's GDP (Scanlan, 2002, p 7). The Moldova Remittance Study 2005 estimates that over half a billion was transferred in 2004 (UNDP, 2005, p 118). Moldova's economy is remittance based, and in a country where emigrants send aid, can authorities be counted upon to counteract the activity behind it?

Patriarchal patterns in society and families were endemic in the Soviet times. The Soviet constitution granted women equality officially, but in practice women were not treated as equals: 'Soviet law always regarded women as a "specific labour force" because of their maternity function' (Posadskaya, 1993; cf Minnesota Advocates for Human Rights, 2000b, p 8). The Soviet law provided benefits, such as paid maternity leave, but the approach can be described as paternalistic. It involved a shift of function from the private to the public, but not a redefinition of male and female roles. Now there has been a re-emergence of traditional values towards women that restrict their opportunities (Posadskaya, 1993; Kay, 1997; Katz, 2001).

At the same time, a mythology of 'the strong Moldovan women' has developed, seeing her as the provider for the family, the keeper of traditions, and a person to be revered and respected. This mythology is in stark contrast with the reality of women's lives (Minnesota Advocates for Human Rights, 2000b, p 7). Over 70% of female respondents to a survey by the UNDP in 1999 said that they felt the female was not respected and that the rights of women were not observed. They claimed that they did not occupy their well-deserved position in society and did not express a confidence that there would be change in the future (UNDP, 2000, p 65).

Domestic violence is common in Moldova. There seems to be some belief in the proverb 'A woman who is not beaten is like a room that has not been swept' (Minnesota Advocates for Human Rights, 2000a, p 12)[7]. The government of Moldova has taken very few steps to address the problem of domestic violence. The Criminal Code does not specifically address crimes of domestic assault; the government rarely prosecutes domestic assault crimes; and penalties are generally insignificant. Rather, the police view domestic violence as a personal and social problem that should be settled within the family. According to the International Organisation for Migration (IOM), more than 80% of trafficking victims had been subjected to domestic violence before they were trafficked (UNDP, 2003, p 72).

Different perspectives on prostitution or trafficking

> In Moldova street prostitution does not exist – who would afford it? – but a lot of people come here to help us to combat trafficking in women.[8]

So, did Communism in the former Soviet Union actually mean an end to prostitution? In 1939 in the publication *Women in the USSR*, M. Pichugina affirms that: '[I]n tsarist Russia, prostitution was widespread and legalized by the government. Prostitution has been completely wiped out in the USSR. Nor has it been abolished by means of police legislation, but by life itself, by the economic security and complete independence of the Soviet woman' (Pichugina, 1939 [2000], p 22).

However, a study of prostitution in post-war Lithuania suggests that '[t]he subject of prostitution in the Soviet era forms a blank space ... such a silence is common to all areas that share a Soviet past' (Marcinkeviciene and Praspaliauskiene, 2003, p 651). Prostitution became an openly discussed issue only with the perestroika (restructuring) from the middle of the 1980s. Before that the Communist government made it a goal to eradicate prostitution as a phenomenon. Besides deporting women to Siberia, it attempted to eliminate the very word 'prostitution' from public discourse. If mentioned, women in prostitution were denominated 'women with impudent behaviour or with light-minded behaviour'. 'In this façade of "reality" there were no prostitutes: all women were Komsomol[9] members, whether they were milkmaids or builders' (Marcinkeviciene and Praspaliauskiene, 2003, p 652).

Prostitution was not eradicated in Moldova. Both within the country and abroad, rates of Moldovan women in prostitution are probably increasing. A doctor interviewed in Moldova stated: 'Everyone knows about prostitution throughout Moldova. Anyone can find a woman to buy at any time' (Minnesota Advocates for Human Rights, 2000b, p 12). The participants in prostitution are seen differently according to their role. Clients may be viewed as 'respectable', while women in prostitution are held in disdain. But prostitution is currently not an issue for much debate in Moldova.

Trafficking in women, on the other hand, is a very hot topic on the agenda of numerous national and international actors in Moldova. The relationship between prostitution and trafficking is a complicated one. Trafficking in women can be seen as one aspect of prostitution, although not all prostitution involves trafficking. This relationship is rarely discussed in Moldova. From the beginning of the 21st century there has been a shift in the discourse from the concept of prostitution to one of trafficking. The result is that prostitution per se is often missing from the official agenda.

We can notice this shift in the debate, from prostitution to trafficking in women, in relation to the UN Convention on the Elimination of Discrimination Against Women (CEDAW) that was signed by Moldova in 1994. Article 6 states that '[s]tate parties shall take all appropriate measures, including legislation, to suppress all forms of traffic in women and exploitation of prostitution of women'. In an initial report (CEDAW, 1998) Moldovan officials describe female drug addiction and exploitation with the aim of prostitution as '[a] dangerous social vice that has been extended throughout the Republic'. Exploitation of prostitution and trafficking in women constitute a new problem, the report says. 'These social weaknesses have spread rapidly ...'; 'mobile groups of prostitution' are also mentioned[10]. The Ministry of Internal Affairs submitted amendments to the legislation covering penalties for offences in 'the sphere of social morality, for example prostitution and procurement'.

In 2002 the UN CEDAW committee considered this report.

Article 6 is only briefly commented on, and it is discussed in terms of trafficking in women. The committee was concerned with the increase in trafficking in women and girls 'for a variety of purposes including sexual exploitation, often under false pretences'. It urges the Moldovan government to implement a holistic approach to combat trafficking in women for commercial or sexual purposes, including punishment for traffickers (United Nations, 2000). With a little help from the international community, this phenomenon is now most often discussed in terms of 'trafficking'.

Laws and policies

Existing laws and policies on prostitution

In the new Criminal Code of the Republic of Moldova that came into force in June 2003, two Articles are applicable for prostitution and trafficking in women: Article 220 on 'Pandering', and Article 165 on 'Trafficking in human beings'. In the Code on Administrative Offences, Article 171, prostitution and propagation of prostitution is punished by a fine.

In Article 220 on 'pandering', the 'pimp' is addressed. The inducement or inclination towards prostitution, the recruitment of a person for practising prostitution, the assistance to prostitution, and receiving benefits as a result of practising prostitution by another shall be punished by a fine (in the amount of 200 to 800 times the minimum wage) or imprisonment for a period of two to five years. The punishment is four to seven years if the crime is (a) committed against a minor, (b) committed by an organised criminal group or a criminal association, or (c) followed by grave consequences.

In Article 171 on prostitution in the Code on Administrative Offences, practising prostitution is punished by a fine in the amount of 15 to 75 times the minimum wage, or administrative arrest of up to 20 days. Some actions, committed repeatedly within one year after administrative sanction, are punished by a fine in the amount of 75 to 100 times the minimum wage. In Article 171/2 the propagation of prostitution through editorials, audiovisual means, or any other way is punished by a fine in the amount of 100 to 150 times the minimum wage.[11] At the time of writing (late 2005), there were no proposals from the Ministry of Interior or general prosecutor's office to legalise prostitution in Moldova.[12]

The country has *not* signed the UN Protocol to prevent, suppress and punish trafficking in persons, especially women and children that came into force in December 2003[13]. Article 165 on 'trafficking in human beings' in the Moldovan Criminal Code both resembles and differs from the protocol. The Moldovan code makes a distinction between non-dangerous violence, dangerous violence and serious bodily injury or permanent psychological damage. Instead of using the concepts of coercion, abduction and fraud, as in the protocol, the code targets debt bondage by including 'abduction, confiscation of documents and servitude for the repayment of a debt whose limits are not reasonably defined'[14]. The code also focuses more on organised crime and serious violence (eg crime against two or more persons or by two or more persons and the use of torture, rape, physical bondage and weapons). Trafficking in persons is, by the code, defined with reference to the purpose of the activity in terms of force and slavery-like conditions, and by means of threat and deception, not with reference to the woman's consent.

What is missing from the Moldovan code, as compared to the protocol, is the question of consent, and a discussion on what measures are needed to provide for the physical, psychological and social recovery of the women. The questions of prevention, cooperation with other state parties, border measures and investigation or prosecution of the offences are also not regulated.

Operation of laws and policies

In 2004, the Ministry of Interior's Anti-Trafficking Unit opened 274 investigations (as compared to 189 in 2003). Sixteen individuals were convicted for trafficking in persons and seven for trafficking in children. Thirteen received prison sentences (six in 2003), ranging from two to 16 years (US State Department, the Office to Monitor and Combat Trafficking in Persons, 2005, p 158).

Anti-trafficking courses were instituted at the police academy. The Ministry of Interior hired a new female police officer (on the one hand this could be seen as beneficial to the trafficked women; however, if corruption is widespread (including within the police), the female officer risks getting the role of an alibi, making her role a difficult one) (US State Department, the Office to Monitor and Combat Trafficking in Persons, 2005). According to the data of the Moldovan Ministry of Interior, 437 crimes that are directly or indirectly linked with trafficking were registered in the country in 2003 (UN Office of Belarus, 2004)[15]. Committees have been formed and plans made to combat trafficking in Moldova. A National Plan of Actions was adopted in 2001 to address the problem. The same year the National Committee of Counter-Trafficking was established with representatives from 15 governmental agencies (IOM, 2004, p 107). Moldova participates in the South-Eastern European Cooperative Initiative Human Trafficking Task Force, which is intended to coordinate regional efforts by governments to combat trafficking in persons. In December 2002, the government signed a joint declaration with other south-eastern European nations to assist victims of trafficking (US Department of Labor, 2005). Since 2003, 37 regional offices of the Organised Crime Department have been set up, with units for counter-trafficking activities. The government has established and trained an anti-trafficking unit in the police force.

The criticism of the actions of the government in this area is, however, strong. In 2004, the IOM recognised government officials as a new channel of corruption in Moldova (IOM, 2004, p 106). An evaluator of one of the other main foreign donors is also very critical of the Moldovan government:

> An important issue that needs to be addressed is co-operation with the Government, which has been identified as an obstacle to successful project implementation. ... Many officials seem to profit in one way or another from trafficking. The fight against corruption, presently supported through a UNDP project, is still a tentative endeavour. (SDC, 2004, p 5)

Representatives of the US State Department claim that the Moldovan government has failed to sponsor protection for victims, but continued to rely on NGOs and international organisations, both often funded by foreign donors. Victims who refuse to cooperate may be investigated and punished for criminal offences and although police encourage most victims to testify against their traffickers they do not provide any protection (US State Department, Office to Monitor and Combat Trafficking in Persons, 2005).

In its 2004 annual report on human rights violations the International Helsinki Federation for Human Rights (IHF-HR) commented that the state had failed to adopt special measures to fight trafficking in women and children. The authorities treated the problem superficially – which was also proved by the fact that Moldova has not ratified the UN Protocol on trafficking (IHF-HR, 2004).

A feminist network has presented an NGO country report,

Moldovian alternative report (ENAWA, 2000)[16]. The report comments on the implementation of the UN CEDAW, and on deficiencies. It says that there are no clear concepts, analyses or descriptions, no correct facts or proposals, and '[t]here are cases when the State prevents the activity of the women's NGO' (ENAWA, 2000, p 1). A woman from the NGO organisation La Strada Moldova reported to the press that a police officer told her '[y]ou would quit your job tomorrow if you knew which powerful and important people were involved in this' (Basa Press, 5 February 2002).

The US State Department's Office to Monitor and Combat Trafficking in Persons released a *Trafficking in persons report* in 2004. It stated that '[t]he Government of Moldova does not fully comply with minimum standards for the elimination of trafficking, however, it is making significant efforts to do so.... Law enforcement efforts and regional cooperation improved as well, but government prevention and protection efforts continued to lag behind' (US State Department, 2004, p 158). The government's activity in the area of *prevention* of trafficking is one exception. Both the president and the chairman of the National Committee are active. The Moldovan president's focus on trafficking greatly increased, and he directed the chairman of the National Committee, a deputy prime minister, to invigorate its efforts. The committee sponsored an international conference with foreign missions, and various ministries directly promoted several showings of the film *Lilya 4-Ever* throughout Moldova (US State Department, Office to Monitor and Combat Trafficking in Persons, 2004).

Due to a lack of funds at the national level, as well as corruption and links between government officials and organised crime, the majority of trafficking protection and awareness-raising measures are being implemented by Moldovan NGOs. Some important rehabilitation of women is done by these NGOs.

Since 2001 counter-trafficking activities have mushroomed in Moldova. An evaluator remarked in 2004 'there is a plethora of CT [counter-trafficking] projects in Moldova' (SDC, 2004, p 19). This rapid growth of the NGO sector even leads to some overlapping in the public awareness-raising segment. In 2001 the British Helsinki Human Rights Group analysed the NGO community in Chisinau. They complain that the NGOs are a means by which people could receive a lot of money for doing very little. Very considerable grants can be obtained (tens of thousands of dollars) for organising a few seminars:

> There are already literally hundreds of such NGOs in Moldova, no doubt for this very reason. A similar reproach can be made of the numerous other international organizations that, they remark, take an interest in the tragedy of trafficking in human being. These initiatives make little real difference to the fates of those actually trapped in this trade. (BHHRG, 2003, p 5)

Analysis of policies and interventions

Within the area of feminist policy formation (Mazur, 2002),[17] the focus is on the process of policy representation, the language, actors, power and effects. With the 'What's the problem? approach' (Bacchi, 2001) the social construction of subjects, the closure of a space for normative debates, and the ability of different actors to put issues on the governmental agenda take precedence. How are women in prostitution/trafficking in or from Moldova constituted as actors? What is discussed, and what is not? By which words and concepts? Which actors are involved, and how is power distributed?

In Moldova NGOs (local as well as international), intergovernmental organisations, regional intergovernmental and international bodies are often the advocates of policies and laws on trafficking in women. They implement them, often with the help of money from abroad. They bring experts from abroad, and they employ local experts. Since there are obvious obstacles to implementation in terms of national economy, the government is somewhat at the mercy of donors. Women in this context are most often portrayed as victims of the national socio-economic circumstances that make them vulnerable to the criminal actors, as if the awareness of the degrading treatment these women face does not allow room for an image of a woman who makes decisions. The decision to enter prostitution or to be trafficked is not made as a free choice inside a vacuum, but is conditioned by the societal circumstances. She is more or less uninformed of the circumstances she is about to encounter, but still she makes some kind of a decision meant to improve her life. But, the image of a naive victim is perhaps an image that is useful when raising funds for the social work that is done to prevent such women from leaving the country uninformed of the dangers they probably will face.

An analysis of the functioning of the government, public administration, police and others reveals that, although there are honest, hardworking and capable functionaries, corruption and indifference seem to impede implementation. In many cases laws and policies form no more than a discourse on prostitution and trafficking in women, to which practice forms a glaring contrast. As a discourse on prostitution, the Moldovan law on pandering/ pimping and the administrative fine for prostitution enhances an image of the dangers of 'organised crime'[18]. Women in prostitution are constituted both as the 'immoral Other' and at the same time as naive victims. These images are something all Moldovan women, and men, will have to relate to.

Debates on legislation and decriminalisation

Prostitution per se is not often the topic of public debate in Moldova. Decriminalisation of prostitution has been discussed in the parliament, and by important parts of the NGO community. These two parties were in agreement that prostitution in Moldova should not be legalised. An international conference was held in Chisinau, the capital of Moldova, in October 2004, where the participating representatives of 12 European countries and the US made an appeal containing a statement against the legalisation of prostitution due to its believed impact on trafficking in women and girls (Soroptimist International, 2005).

The members of parliament that proposed an amendment of the laws to legalise prostitution build some of their arguments on questions related to public revenues. In a news article in 2002 a woman offers the same kind of arguments. She complains that 'honest citizens' struggle to survive on the brink of poverty and still pay national taxes. 'Porno dealers', on the other hand, do not make payments into the state. The proposal was not passed and she regrets that prostitution remains an unofficial business[19]. There are also instances when government officials reveal an opinion that prostitution should not be criminalised. When a foreign prosecutor at a conference suggested a law against those who pay for prostitution, the men present laughed in response (Minnesota Advocates for Human Rights, 2000b, p 12); the suggestion was not well received.

Key issue faced

Reasons for entry into prostitution

Reasons for entry into prostitution as well as trafficking into prostitution often referred to are generally identified at the level of the state, the socio-economic level, and sometimes at the level of the individual (Demleiter, 2001; UNICEF, 2002; US State Department, 2003; UK Home Office, 2004). Moldova is an example of a former Soviet republic that has not yet been able to balance its economy or to take care of the social needs of its population. Poverty and debt are believed to make people vulnerable to prostitution and trafficking, and so is unemployment and poor educational attainment. The level of corruption, which is an indication of the inability of the state to control its population, is also thought to facilitate the development of criminal activity, such as trafficking in women. Traditional assumptions about gender relationships, domestic violence, drug and alcohol abuse, and break-up of families are also believed to make people vulnerable. At the same time, at least for some parts of the population, a growing consumer culture and media coverage of life in 'Western' Europe probably inspire young people to want to go abroad to earn a living and to get access to consumer goods.

There are few examples of a public debate on prostitution and trafficking in women in Moldova. One exception is the debate in the parliament when a proposal to legitimise prostitution was rejected. An external evaluator on counter-trafficking activities noticed that the views of the Moldovan government on the reason for trafficking, the role of the victims and the measures that need to be taken to combat it, differ significantly from the views of the donor and NGO community. The government sees victims as immoral youths who have no one else but themselves to blame for their predicament (SDC, 2004, p 5). This could indicate that the discourse is built on traditional morality.

The NGOs' views on entry are often based on a rhetoric built around an image of young women deceived into trafficking and prostitution, hence the emphasis on public-awareness campaigns and prevention interventions. A moral order discourse with a preoccupation with the 'innocent victim' seems to be prevalent (cf Kantola and Squires, 2004).

The attitudes of the population are part of the context wherein discourses are handled and reconstructed. What are the attitudes of the Moldovan population on prostitution and trafficking? In a survey in April 2003, 1,100 individuals in Moldova were asked questions on attitudes to prostitution and trafficking in women[20]. The survey found that:

- 74% of the respondents claim that prostitution cannot be justified;
- 59% do not believe that prostitution offers a way of becoming independent;
- 48% fully agree to, or assume that it could be true, that prostitution is always going to be there because men seem to need it (there are significant differences depending on factors such as income, residence and education, but not gender);
- 46% do not think that prostitution is needed for the families to survive;
- 44% do not think that prostitution is going to stop when Moldova gets richer;
- 75% believe that young women move abroad because there is no possibility of finding a job in Moldova;
- 23% think that trafficked women were offered work as au pairs, domestic workers, nurses etc;
- 22% think that trafficked women were offered marriage to foreigners;
- 73% think that (very many/many) women are trafficked by deception, with a suggestion of other jobs (eg au pair, waitress);
- 53% think that (very many/many) women migrate voluntarily, knowing that they will be engaged in prostitution;
- 42% think that (very many/many) women are trafficked by force.

The results from our study thus indicate that prostitution more often is not seen as necessary for the families to survive, and it is not expected to stop when Moldova gets richer. An explanation that gets support is that prostitution is always going to be there because men seem to need it. This could indicate the prevalence of an essentialist view on male sexuality as a natural force that cannot/should not be stopped. Many in the survey connect trafficking to unemployment. The job offers they imagine abroad are service work in the informal sector, or women might have been offered to marry a foreigner. The conditions that embed trafficking are thought to be a question of (a) deception, (b) voluntary engagement in prostitution, and (c) trafficking by force. Traditional values on gender relations and a stress on the image of an innocent victim seem to permeate the views of the Moldovan population, as measured in this survey.

Conclusion

Today Moldova remains the poorest country in Europe, and at the same time is affected by corruption. Since independence in 1991 the government has emphasised the economy at the cost of social reforms. Between 10% and 20% of the population are unemployed, and women in particular are desperate to find a job; up to 25% of the population has migrated to earn a living abroad. Moldovan women face a very difficult situation, both compared to men in Moldova and to women in many other countries. There has been a re-emergence of traditional patriarchal patterns and at the same time the mythology of 'the strong Moldovan women' starkly contrasts with the reality of many women's lives, where domestic violence is one of several problems. To understand prostitution and trafficking in women in the Republic of Moldova, it is important also to consider the effects of the conditions in the former Soviet Union, of which Moldova was a part.

Factors on the level of the nation-state in terms of socio-economics, for example economic imbalance and corruption, are believed to contribute to activity in prostitution and trafficking in Moldovan women. Poverty, debt and unemployment are driving forces for migration, and thereby increase the risk of getting involved in trafficking. Traditional patriarchal patterns and domestic violence make women vulnerable for entry into prostitution/trafficking.

Recruitment to, assistance in, and receiving benefits from prostitution are regulated in the Criminal Code's article on 'pandering' or pimping. Prostitution per se is regulated in the Code of Administrative Offences, and punished by a fine or 'administrative arrest'. 'Trafficking in persons, especially women and children' is included in the Criminal Code, but the operations of the government in this area are strongly criticised. Due to lack of funds at the national level, as well as corruption, the majority of the counter-trafficking activities are implemented by national and international NGOs. Although since 2001 counter-trafficking activities in Moldova have increased sharply, NGOs have occasionally been criticised for receiving large sums of money for doing little.

Although prostitution does exist in Moldova, it is not often a subject for debate. This silence is probably common for areas that share a Soviet past. At the beginning of the 21st century there was a shift in discourse from 'prostitution as a social vice and social weakness' to one of 'trafficking in women'. There was some discussion of the issue in the parliament, where a proposal to legalise prostitution was rejected. NGOs are sometimes involved in the perception of women in sexual trafficking as deceived and naive victims. This can be compared to attitudes of the Moldovan population towards prostitution and trafficking. The survey illuminates an essentialist view of male sexuality: prostitution is always going to exist because men seem to need it. In the survey, unemployment is often emphasised as a reason for entry into prostitution. The conditions surrounding trafficking are most often imagined as a question of deception.

A pessimistic view of future developments contains the possibility that international actors will continue to mastermind the construction of the discourses on prostitution and trafficking in women, as well as the implementation of the laws and policies for Moldova. Thereby these actors will have a great influence on both discourse formation and implementation, without any guarantees that they are firmly rooted in this country with deep knowledge about its inhabitants. The external actors have agenda of their own that will be difficult for the recipient country to react against since it comes with a filled wallet. So, an important part of the image of the women and other actors involved in prostitution and sexual trafficking will be created in a foreign context and will not have grown out of a sufficient consideration of the country's history or the current situation of its women.

The Moldovan government might amend new laws and policies without having the will or the resources to implement them. The social construction of women will still be based on traditional patriarchal values, and added to that, the image of Moldovan women in terms of a dichotomy: the strong women as a 'natural' preserver of the family and nation, and also as the naive victim of crime and sexual exploitation.

A more positive outlook embraces a phase of coordination and cooperation between the Moldovan government and the international donors with the result that the Moldovan government will analyse the 'root causes' of prostitution and trafficking. It will prioritise the development of women's situations and evaluate what long-term investments could be made. The NGOs active in counter-trafficking activities in Moldova will work with long-term rehabilitation to get women back into society; and all the different actors working to improve the situation for women in Moldova will coordinate their work to avoid overlap in activities. Other nation-states will also be more ready to permit migrant Moldovans at least temporary work permits, which will enable people to earn a living in the formal work sectors abroad.

Notes

[1] In Moldova a census was carried out in 1989, when the population size was estimated at 4.2 million.The next census was held in October 2004 (net of the Transnistrian region/self-proclaimed republic, which held a census of its own a month later). Some preliminary data were published in January 2004 in Moldovian (available at www.statistica.md/recensamint/Data_prel_din2004.doc). According to the Head of Office at the Embassy of Sweden in Chisinau, Moldova, the results were to be published in English in March 2006 (personal mail 20 February 2006), The preliminary results indicate that the size of the population is 3.4 million (net of 'raionaelor de East', Transnistria, which has a population of approximately 0.5 million). Added to that are the 0.3 million who were not at home at the time of the census, but were reported by others.

[2] The Russian Empire annexed Moldova, from the Turks, in 1812. Romania seceded in an intervention in 1917. In 1924 Russia established the Moldovian Autonomous Soviet Socialist Republic in the eastern part of the country (now known as Transnistria). In 1940 the whole of Moldova became a republic in the Soviet Union.

[3] Measured in GDP-PPP. Gross domestic product (GDP) is a crude measure of a country's economic strength commonly used. The figures should be interpreted with caution; they do not measure 'black market' activity, or the distribution of resources within the country. GDP-PPP makes the 'price yardstick' more comparable across countries, giving a better picture of the relative sizes of the economies. (Estimates of GDP per capita in 2000 are presented at http://aol.countrywatch.com.)

[4] Belgium is chosen for comparison on size and GDP-PPP only.

[5] The CE Group of States Against Corruption (GRECO).

[6] With Tajikistan, the 'worst performer' in Central and Eastern Europe and the CIS, at number 93.

[7] Beating a woman is here compared to keeping a clean house – both are everyday household acts.

[8] Author interview of a staff member of an NGO in Chisinau, Moldova, September 2003.

[9] Komsomol, or the All-Union Leninist Communist League of the Soviet Union for people aged 14 to 28.

[10] It is not clear from the text what this signifies, but this could indicate the occurrence of intranational sexual trafficking already by 1998, before the concept 'sexual trafficking' was used.

[11] Information and translation by email from OSCE Mission to Moldova, Ludmila Shargov, Human Rights Assistant in Chisinau, Moldova, 20 January 2005.

[12] Information from the IOM Moldova.

[13] Supplementing the UN Convention against Transnational Organized Crime.

[14] www.legislationline.org/index.php?country=28&org=0&eu=0&topic=14

[15] Basic data are not reported so comparisons are not easy to make.

[16] European and North American Women Action (ENAWA) is a network of media, ICT, information and advocacy organisations strengthening and integrating a feminist analysis in the information and media landscape in relation to social movements and the women's movement in our region and the world (see www.enawa.org).

[17] One area of interest for Feminist Comparative Policy (FCP) analysis developed by Mazur (2002).

[18] Organised crime is an ambiguous and conflated concept, see Paoli (2002). Criminal networks is probably a better phrase to use.

[19] www.welcome-moldova.com/articles/prostitution.shtml (March 2002).

[20] A survey *Democracy and Social Transition in the Republic of Moldova* of 1,100 individuals in Moldova, was conducted in April 2003 by a research group at Södertörn university college in Sweden, led by professor Elfar Loftsson. This is the first publication of this data analysis.

Recommended further reading

Buckley, M. (ed) (1997) *Post-Soviet women: From the Baltic to Central Asia*, Cambridge: Cambridge University Press.

Ehrenreich, B. and Hochschild, A.R. (2002) *Global woman: Nannies, maids, and sex workers in the new economy*, New York: Metropolitan Books.

Štuhlhofer, A. and Sandfort, T. (eds) (2005) *Sexuality and gender in postcommunist Eastern Europe and Russia*, New York: Haworth Press.

Williams, P. (1999) *Illegal immigration and commercial sex, the new slave trade*, London: Frank Cass.

References

Bacchi, C.L. (2001) *Women, policy and politics. The construction of policy problems*, London: Sage Publications.

British Helsinki Human Rights Group (BHHRG) (2003) *Human rights in the OSCE region: Europe, Central Asia and North America, report 2003* (Events of 2002) (available at www.bhhrg.org/CountryReport.asp?ReportID=160&CountryID=16).

Committee on the Elimination of Discrimination Against Women (CEDAW) (1998) *Consideration of report submitted by state parties under Article 18 of the convention on the elimination of all forms of discrimination against women. Initial report of states parties. Republic of Moldova* (available at www.hri.ca/fortherecord2000/documentation/tbodies/cedaw-c-mda-1.htm).

Demleiter, N. (2001) 'The law at crossroads: the construction of migrant woman trafficked into prostitution', in R. Koslowski and D. Kule (eds) *Global smuggling: comparative perspectives*, Baltimore: Johns Hopkins University Press, pp 257–93.

Domanski, H. (2002) 'Is the East European "underclass" feminized?', *Communist and Post-Communist Studies*, vol 35, no 4, pp 383-94.

European and North American Women Action (ENAWA) (2000) *Moldovian alternative report* (available at www.enawa.org/NGO/moldova1.html).

European Commission (2004) *Commission staff working paper, European neighbourhood policy, country report, Moldova* (available at http://europa.eu.int/comm/world/enp/pdf/country/Moldova_11_May_EN.pdf).

Institute for Public Policy (IPP) (2003) *Barometer of public opinion – May 2003*, available at (www.ipp.md).

International Helsinki Federation for Human Rights (IHF-HR) (2004) *Human rights in the OSCE region: Europe, Central Asia and North America, report 2004* (Events of 2003) available at http://www.ihf-hr.org/documents/doc_summary.php?sec_id=3&d_id=1322).

International Monetary Fund (IMF) (2002) *Republic of Moldova*, Washington: IMF.

International Organization for Migration (IOM) (2004) *Counter-trafficking service. Changing patterns and trends of trafficking in persons in the Balkan region*, available at (www.iom.int/DOCUMENTS/PUBLICATION/EN/balkans_trafficking.pdf).

Johansson, A. (2003) *Whither Moldova? Conflicts and dangers in a post-Soviet Republic*, Stockholm: Swedish Defence Research Agency, Division of Defence Analysis.

Kantola, J. and Squires, J. (2004) 'Discourses surrounding prostitution policies in the UK', *European Journal of Women's Studies*, vol 11, no 1, pp 77-101.

Katz, K. (2001) *Gender, Work and Wages in the Soviet Union: a Soviet legacy of discrimination*, Basingstoke: Palgrave.

Kay, R. (1997) 'Images of an ideal woman: perceptions of Russian womanhood through the media, education and women's own eyes', in M. Buckley (ed) *Post-Soviet women: From the Baltic to Central Asia*, Cambridge: Cambridge University Press, pp 77–91.

Marcinkeviciene, D. and Praspaliauskiene, R. (2003) 'Prostitution in post-war Lithuania', *Women's History Review*, vol 12, no 4, pp 651-60.

Mazur, A.G. (2002) *Theorizing feminist policy*, Oxford: Oxford University Press.

Minnesota Advocates for Human Rights (2000a) *Domestic violence in Moldova* (available at www.mnadvocates.org/sites/608a3887-dd53-4796-8904-997a0131ca54/uploads/MoldovaReport_10-11-2002.pdf).

Minnesota Advocates for Human Rights (2000b) *Trafficking in women: Moldova and Ukraine* (available at www.mnadvocates.org/sites/608a3887-dd53-4796-8904-997a0131ca54/uploads/TraffickingReport.pdf).

Paoli, L. (2002) 'The paradoxes of organized crime', *Crime, Law & Social Change*, vol 37, no 1, pp 51-97.

Pichugina, M. (1939 [2002]) *Women in the USSR*, Moscow: Foreign Languages Publishing House, (available at www.marxists.org/subject/women/authors/pichugina/women.html).

Posadskaya, A. (1993) 'Changes in gender discourse and politics in the former Soviet Union', in V.M. Moghadam (ed) *Democratic reform and the position of women in transitional economies*, Oxford: Clarendon Press, pp 162–79.

Scanlan, S. (2002) *Report on trafficking from Moldova: Irregular labour markets and restrictive migration policies in Western Europe* (available at www.lio.org/public/english/protection/migrant/download/moldova.pdf).

Soroptimist International (2005) *Soroptimists uniting to combat trafficking of women and girls*, Cambridge: Soroptimist International.

Swedish International Development Cooperation Agency (SIDA) (2003) *Moldova country review – An overview of social, political and economic conditions and development cooperation activities*, Stockholm: SIDA.

Swiss Agency for Development and Cooperation (SDC) (2004) *External evaluation of SDC's counter-trafficking program in Moldova*, Bern: Swiss Ministry of Foreign Affairs (available at www.sdc.admin.ch/ressources/deza_product_en_1119.pdf).

United Nations (2000) *Report of the committee on the elimination of discrimination against women*, (available at www.hri.ca/fortherecord2000/documentation/genassembly/a-55-38.htm).

United Nations Children's Fund (UNICEF) (2000) *Poverty and welfare over the 1990s in the Republic of Moldova indicators of status and trends* (available at www.unicef-icdc.org/research/ESP/CountryReports2000_01/Moldova00.pdf).

UNICEF (2002) *Trafficking in human beings in Southeastern Europe*, (available at www.unhchr.ch/women/trafficking.pdf).

United Nations Development Programme (UNDP) (2000) *National human development report, Republic of Moldova*, (available at www.undp.md/keypubdocument/HUMAN_2000.pdf).

UNDP (2003) *Trafficking in human beings in South Eastern Europe*, (available at www.osce.org/documents/odihr/2003/12/1645_en.pdf).

UNDP (2005) *Country statistics*, (available at http://hdr.undp.org/statistics/data/cty/cty_f_MDA.html).

United Nations Development Programme Moldova (2005) *Republic of Moldova: Economic politics for growth, employment and poverty reduction* (available at www.undp.md/publications/doc/UNDP_ENGL-pdf).

United Nations High Commissioner for Refugees (UNHCR) (2004) *Moldova: Situation analysis and trend assessment* (available at www.unhcr.ch/cgi-bin/texis/vtx/publ/opendoc.pdf?tbl=RSDCOI&id=418f804a4&page=publ).

United Nations Office of Belarus (2004) *Belarusian and Moldavian experts discussed problems of trafficking* (available at www.un.minsk.by/en/bulletin/2004-1/un-works/belmold.html).

United Nations Office of the High Commissioner for Human Rights (UNOHCHR) (2002) *Trafficking in human beings in Southeastern Europe* (available at www.unhchr.ch/women/trafficking.pdf).

UK Home Office (2004) *Paying the price: A consultation paper on prostitution* (available at www.homeoffice.gov.uk/docs3/paying_the_price.html).

US Department of Labor (2005) *Moldova* (available at www.dol.gov/ilab/media/reports/iclp/tda2003/moldova.htm).

US State Department, the Office to Monitor and Combat Trafficking in Persons (2004) *Trafficking in persons report* (available at www.state.gov/documents/organization/33614.pdf).

US State Department, the Office to Monitor and Combat Trafficking in Persons (2005) *Trafficking in persons report* (available at www.state.gov/documents/organization/47255.pdf).

Part Two
Asia

SIX

Prostitution in India: laws, debates and responses

Geetanjali Gangoli

Introduction

India plays a central role today in the economic, social and political infrastructure of South Asia. However, it is a land of contrasts, where great wealth coexists with grinding and devastating poverty; where violence against women is rampant even though a vital and active feminist movement fights for women's rights; where sexuality is celebrated in the erotic temple sculptures of Konark, and in ancient texts such as the Kamasutra (Art of Love) and there is widespread sexual repression and control over women's sexuality.

Prostitution in India has taken myriad forms historically, and in the current contemporary context. In the pre-colonial period, India experienced different forms of prostitution. These included: religious prostitution or the devadası system, where young girls entered in a symbolic marriage with god, but were considered sexually available to men; and the tawaif or courtesan system, where young girls were trained in classical dance and music but also engaged in sexual services with their clients. It was only in the colonial period, however, that prostitution and 'red-light areas', as we know them today, were created. The British army in India had a policy of supporting the creation of such regulated zones around cantonments, railway stations and working-class areas in urban centres where young single men lived. Prostitution was conceived of as a necessary evil, to meet the sexual needs of young men (Ballhatchet, 1980, p 79).

Many of these red-light areas have survived in urban centres, including Mumbai, Kolkata and New Delhi, and here prostitution takes the form of a highly organised and internally regulated brothel system. In other parts of the country, including rural India, the sex trade is more informal and unregulated. The pre-colonial forms of prostitution, including the devadasi and tawaif systems still survive, though are much amended, and are often difficult to distinguish from the brothel systems. At the upper end of the sex trade are 'call girls', who are in many cases educated and middle-class women, who operate independently or through a mediator.

The national context

Scholars agree that it is very difficult to measure the 'status of women', especially in the context of a large and diverse country such as India (Radha Devi, 1993; Kishor and Gupta, 2004). While women in India theoretically enjoy a number of legal rights, in practice these are denied to them. The fundamental rights incorporated in the Indian Constitution include equality under the law for men and women (Article 14), equal accessibility to public spaces (Article 15), equal opportunity in matters of public employment (Article 16) and equal pay for equal work (Article 39). In addition there are statutory provisions that guarantee these rights, such as the 1976 Equal Remuneration Act and the 1976 Maternity Benefit Act. The 1961 Dowry Prohibition Act prohibits the giving and taking of dowry, and Section 498A of the 1983 Indian Penal Code criminalises physical and mental cruelty to a married woman by her husband or his relatives. Hindu women have equal succession rights under the 1955 Hindu Succession Act.

Recent studies, however, have suggested that variables, including women's access to education, the media and paid employment, are some financial indicators of women's status, while participation in decision making, age at marriage, extent of and social and personal acceptance of domestic violence, and women's mobility are social indicators (Kishor and Gupta, 2004). National data demonstrate that the proportion of women working for cash is low in most states in India (ranging from 49% in some states to 10% in others), as is women's freedom of movement more generally. Only one in three women can go to the market without permission from their family, and one in four visit friends and relatives without permission. Women have less education than men, with only just over 50% of the female population in India being literate, as compared to 75% of the male population. Not surprisingly, therefore, women enter marriage much earlier than men, and marry men who are both older and more educated than themselves (Kishor and Gupta, 2004).

Most women have limited participation in decisions about their lives, including visiting their natal families, health care and making expensive purchases. National data also reveal that one in five women have experienced some form of violence from their husbands, or other members of their families since the age of 15. There is a high degree of acceptance of domestic violence among women, with 57% of ever-married women aged between 15 and 49 accepting that a man is justified in beating his wife if she does not fulfil accepted gender roles including cooking and caring for the home, or if her natal family do not provide the expected dowry (Kishor and Gupta, 2004). Dowry demands at marriage are a part of Indian marriages. While dowry was once a Hindu upper-caste custom, it has become a part of the marriage customs of different religious communities. Dowry demands are also considered one of the causes for preferences for sons (Sunder Rajan, 2003).

Thus we see that Indian women have many rights and privileges in law, but these are often denied to them in practice. In addition there are other structural factors such as caste oppression and poverty that also lead to a removal of women's rights in practice. Many of these factors – caste, poverty, dowry demands and the low status of women within the family and community – can be seen as factors that may push women into the sex trade.

Laws and policies

In this section, I look at existing national laws and policy regarding prostitution and trafficking for prostitution. What do anti-prostitution laws aim to do? What do they tell us about perceptions and constructs of women in prostitution, and more generally, of all women? Existing Indian laws 'tolerate' prostitution, but do not address violence within prostitution or ways to redress it (D'Cunha, 1991; Gangoli, 1998). Next, I analyse the implementation of the laws by the police and judicial pronouncements looking at the extent to which women in the profession have access to rights under the law. The police combine legal and extra-legal powers that enable them to harass women in the profession, while being complicit with the worst excesses within prostitution. The judiciary combines harshness with regard to women in prostitution, legitimising rights abuse. Simultaneously, legal attitudes to prostitution impact upon non-prostituted women. The following section examines proposals to legalise prostitution in one state in India and investigates the extent to which patriarchal assumptions about prostitution are challenged or strengthened by the proposed laws. Legalisation as envisaged increases the control of the state over the bodies of women in prostitution. Next, I probe the policy suggestions made by the central government that seek to combine politically correct language and feminist rhetoric with conservative notions of prostitution and women in prostitution.

Existing laws

In colonial India, prostitution was seen as a 'necessary evil': the concern was to keep women in the sex trade 'clean' and free from sexually transmitted diseases, as the fear was that they would infect single men and, later, their families. Hence, a system of licensing was evolved; the 1864, 1866 and 1869 Contagious Diseases Acts were passed. These were applicable to garrison and port towns and were enacted to prevent venereal disease among soldiers and sailors. These laws mandated registration, periodical medical examination and treatment. Women found suffering from sexually transmitted diseases (STDs) were confined to 'lock' hospitals until they were cured. Many women tried to escape the law by not registering themselves. The Acts were repealed in 1871 after the women's movement in Britain agitated against them on the grounds that they violated the Magna Carta (National Commission for Women, 1996). The licensing system, however, was not formally abolished in India until 1929 (Punekar and Rao, 1962).

After independence, India adopted the toleration system under the 1956 Suppression of Immoral Traffic Act (henceforth SITA) later amended to the 1986 Immoral Traffic in Women and Girls (Prevention) Act (henceforth PITA). SITA was adopted, but not as an outcome of a sustained feminist or moral movement against prostitution. It was framed because India is a signatory to the UN Convention for the suppression of traffic in persons and the exploitation of others passed in 1950. SITA follows the provisions of the UN Convention, focusing on trafficking, which sees any entry into prostitution as trafficking, irrespective of age, gender or consent. Unlike the UN Convention, however, SITA focused only on women practitioners of prostitution.

Under SITA, prostitution is defined as: '... the act of a female who offers her body for promiscuous sexual intercourse for hire, whether in money or in kind, and whether offered immediately or otherwise, the expression prostitute will be construed accordingly' (SITA, 1956, Section 2(f)). Sections 7(i) and 8(b) penalise the practice of prostitution in or near a public place, including soliciting or seduction for prostitution. In addition, SITA penalises brothel keeping, abetment to brothel keeping, living off the earnings of a prostitute (Section 4), procuring, inducing or trafficking for prostitution (Section 5). Section 10 provides for the release of offenders on probation or after admonition. These provisions are aimed at making it difficult, though not impossible, for women to practise prostitution. In 1986, SITA was amended. The Bill introduced in the Lok Sabha was not fundamentally different in character from SITA, although the stated objectives of the Bill were to move the focus from suppression (of prostitution) to prevention, and it was passed in a single sitting in the Lok Sabha, following little effective debate. What debate took place, however, gives us some insights into the ambivalence displayed by lawmakers on the issue.

The ambivalent attitude is clear in the relief displayed by one MP about the change in the name of the existing law on prostitution from the Suppression of Immoral Traffic Act (abbreviated to SITA) to the Immoral Traffic in Women and Children (Prevention) Act (abbreviated to PITA).

> Another feature of the Bill is that the nomenclature ... which was very ridiculous has been changed. The Suppression of Immoral Traffic Act, which was popularly known as SITA has been changed. I remember in courts of law so many hundreds of Sitas used to stand and we used to refer to them as Sita No. 1, Sita No. 2 and Sita No. 3. It is very rightful that this name has been changed. (Mr Naik, Lok Sabha Debates, 1986, p 158)

For this MP, calling a prostitute by the name of the hallowed Sita, the consort of Lord Rama, and the icon of virtuous wife-hood and womanhood, was irreligious and degrading.

Legislative responses to prostitution and prostitutes ranged from patronising sympathy to downright condemnation. In the first response, prostitutes were treated as victims of a crime against women and hence considered unfortunate. 'Unfortunate' though they may be, prostitutes were also projected as erring women, simultaneously as sinners and as victims.

> Lastly, I would like to say that unless and until our society changes its attitude, both men and women, at least the majority, it will be very difficult to eradicate prostitution from our country ... prostitutes ... are victims of the

> circumstances. Many of the prostitutes do not want to carry on their lives in those circumstances. But *since they have done wrong once*, they are rejected by the society. (Dr Guha, Lok Sabha Debates, 1986, p 150, my emphasis)

The method of rehabilitation most favoured is not to introduce new skills and resources to women within prostitution, but to marry them off. In a somewhat strange reversal of priorities, land, jobs and loans are offered to men who are ready to marry prostitutes. Margaret Alva, the then minister of state in the Department of Youth Affairs and Sports and Women and Child Development, spoke of the difficulties faced while marrying off prostitutes, and states that; '... there are powerful forces who are prepared to fight any effort at rehabilitating these *girls*' (Mrs Alva, Lok Sabha Debates, 1986, p 174, my emphasis).

Many provisions remain unchanged from SITA to PITA, including the penal provisions for soliciting, seducing, activity in the vicinity of public places, procuring, detaining, brothel keeping, abetment to brothel keeping, renting premises for the purposes of prostitution and living off the earnings of a prostitute. Under PITA, a brothel is defined broadly as 'any place where sexual abuse occurs'. Significantly, the burden of proof is placed on the owner or the landlord of the brothel. This aims to remove the loopholes in the earlier Act.

Under PITA, criminal provisions with regard to children in prostitution were increased and the new law attempted to define childhood in the context of prostitution. Living on the earnings of prostitution of a child or minor is a more serious offence under Section 4 than living off the prostitution of an adult[1]. Under PITA, the police refer children and minors in prostitution for rehabilitation, most often to a protective home or institution. The law is, however, weighted against adult women. In what seems a violation of civil liberties, the burden of proof is reversed for adult women arrested for soliciting, brothel keeping or any other provision under PITA. This is contrary to the protection available in international law and in criminal law in India.

PITA recognises male prostitution by including male prostitutes in the category of soliciting or seduction for prostitution. However, while women can be convicted for up to six months under this offence, male offenders face imprisonment for between seven days to three months. The law therefore has an inbuilt gender bias.

Under PITA, the powers of the police to prevent trafficking were expanded. While SITA empowered a special police officer to conduct a search of any premises without a warrant; PITA extends these powers to the trafficking police officers accompanying the special police officer. Trafficking for prostitution is subjected to provisions other than PITA. Indian Penal Code (IPC) Section 366A prohibits procurement of minor girls for illicit intercourse, while Section 366B bans importing minors from another country for the purpose of prostitution. Selling and buying of minors for the purpose of prostitution is proscribed under Sections 372 and 373.

In addition to these provisions, women in prostitution are subjected to provisions in the Police Acts in different states of India that aim to control 'indecent behaviour' and 'public nuisance'. Women can also be arrested under IPC Section 292 for obscenity. The laws against publicly visible prostitution reveal a deep discomfort with uncontrolled sexuality – sexuality that is not confined to the private, and controllable, domain. An adult woman found guilty of prostitution can therefore be arrested for indecent exposure or soliciting under three different laws: PITA, IPC and the relevant Police Acts.

Discrimination against sex workers is implicit in other sections of the law. Under the 1986 Juvenile Justice Act the state is empowered to evolve a system for the protection, development and rehabilitation of what are defined as 'neglected juveniles'. Under the Act, a distinction is made between other children and children of prostitutes, and more generally children found in a brothel. While for all other children, there needs to be actual neglect, physical or sexual abuse or exploitation before a child may be separated from his or her parents or guardians, in the case of children of prostitutes or those seen as living a 'depraved' life, these provisions do not have to be met. The latter, by virtue of their parentage, are deemed 'neglected juveniles' (1986 Juvenile Justice Act, Section 2(1)).

The judiciary and policy making

A 1997 judgment on prostitution (*Jain v Union of India*, 1997) has been influential in shaping public policy. It responds to a public-interest litigation seeking improvements in the plight of prostitutes and their children. It issues directions for the prevention of induction of women into prostitution, rescue and rehabilitation and schemes for the welfare of prostitutes' children and of child prostitutes. Significantly, the judgment bases itself on two attitudes: one that prostitutes are 'fallen women' and second, that their children are best separated from them. Interestingly, this is seen as protecting the rights of women in prostitution. The following excerpt makes this clear:

> The primary question in this case is: what are the rights of the children of fallen women, the modules to segregate them from their mothers and others to give them protection, care and rehabilitation in the mainstream of the national life. And as a facet of it, what should be the scheme to be evolved to eradicate prostitution, i.e., the source itself; and what succour and sustenance can be provided to the fallen victims of flesh trade? (*Jain v Union of India*, 1997, pp 3026-7)

The judgment quotes extensively from the UN Convention on the Rights of the Child, and fundamental rights in the Constitution of India. It suggests that, in the best interests of the child, women in prostitution should be separated from their children using 'three C's, viz. counselling, cajoling and coercion'. The judgment at this point makes no distinction between child prostitutes and children of prostitutes, and focuses on 'rehabilitation' of prostitutes, as a state duty:

> Therefore, it is the duty of the State and all voluntary non-government organisations and public spirited persons to come in to their aid to retrieve them from prostitution, rehabilitate them with a helping hand to lead a life of dignity of person, self employment through provisions of education, financial support, developed marketing facilities. … Marriage is another object to give them real status in society. Acceptance by the family is another important input to rekindle the faith of self respect and self confidence. (*Jain v Union of India*, 1997, p 3035)

Significantly, the judgment also recognises elsewhere that a majority of women in prostitution have been married[2]. Marriage per se does not prevent women from entering prostitution, although it may lend them status during the course of their marriage. The judgment, however, draws a sharp parallel between women in prostitution and in marriage, seeing the former as victims of coercion and force or immoral. Given this, women choosing prostitution as a lifestyle are greedy and immoral:

> … prostitution is primarily due to ignorance, illiteracy, coercive trapping or scare of social stigma. … Recent trend is that ladies from higher levels of income are initiated into the prostitution to sustain sufficient day-to-day luxurious style of life so as to ensure continuous economic support for their well-being. (*Jain v Union of India*, 1997, p 3035)

This judgment brings together many strands that have been noticed so far in official policy. It displays a prurient interest in the lives of prostitutes, combines equal measures of pity, contempt and a disregard for the choices made by women in prostitution, veering between victimisation and condemnation.

Efforts to legalise: the Maharashtra experience

Efforts to approximate the legalisation model have been made in the state of Maharashtra. Two Bills dealing with issues relating to prostitution have been introduced between 1989 and 1994 in the Maharashtra Legislative Assembly. Although they have not been passed, they indicate the legislative bent regarding this issue.

In 1988, the Maharashtra Legislative Assembly saw the introduction of 'A Bill to provide for the regulation and control of activities of prostitutes and brothels with a view to prevent the growth of disease known as Acquired Immunity Deficiency Syndrome (AIDS)'. The statement of objects of the Bill held unambiguously that:

> The object in bringing this legislation is to prevent and control the growth of the Acquired Immunity Deficiency Syndrome (AIDS) disease. The medical experts have opined that the main cause of this disease is common prostitution. About 90% of prostitutes are suffering from venereal diseases. It is also reported that about 1 lakh[3] common prostitutes are found in Bombay and they are the major cause of worry for medical authorities.… In view of imminent danger of the spread of AIDS, it has become very important and necessary to have such legislation. Hence this Bill. (Legislative Assembly Bill VIII, 1988)

To meet the objectives of the Bill, the provisions laid out are: compulsory registration of all prostitutes in the state with the state authority; a minimum-age clause of 21 years; that the person in charge of the brothel should display a list of the prostitutes in the brothel with their ages. Every woman registered will be medically examined once every three months. If these clauses are not met, offenders are liable to prosecution. Prostitution as defined under the Bill 'means and includes the profession carried out by a woman to have a sexual intercourse with a man with or without consideration with the knowledge that such person is not her husband'. The definition is so wide that it can include sexual activity outside marital sex. Implicit in the definition is the notion that non-marital sexual activity is tantamount to prostitution, promiscuity and immorality.

The provisions in the Bill violate the most basic human rights. Women in prostitution are to be registered and subjected to compulsory medical examination. The Bill does not spell out what the tests will constitute, nor does it spell out who will bear the expense of the tests. The very ambiguity makes it possible for the state to subject women in prostitution to any kind of medical examination or experiment.

Another Bill introduced in 1994 is a more sophisticated version of this. Called the 1994 Maharashtra Protection of Commercial Sex Workers Bill, it is supported by the Maharashtra State Commission for Women, and the Women and Child Welfare Department, State of Maharashtra. It combines politically correct language with policy suggestions slanted against the interests of women in prostitution. Section 5 recognises commercial sex work as a legitimate commercial activity. However, the purpose of the Bill is apparent in the preamble that states:

> ... whereas various venereal diseases, sexually transmitted diseases including AIDS involving such persons and their customers are spreading the said and other diseases in geometric progression, endangering public health at large.
>
> And whereas urgent measures are called for to check the spread of the disease and to protect the health of the commercial sex workers and their customers and innocent persons having sexual relations with such customers. (Maharashtra Protection of Commercial Sex Workers Bill, 1994)

The Bill adopts a carrot-and-stick policy with prostitutes, making it mandatory for them to register with a board constituted by the government. The board is to be responsible for welfare schemes for the benefit of the sex workers, and shall be the consenting authority in civil and criminal cases filed against the sex worker. (Section 4) Failure to register with the board is liable to imprisonment up to seven years. The board will ensure that women in prostitution will be subjected to periodical and compulsory medical tests for STDs. Completely violating human rights is this proviso:

> All the persons suffering from Sexually Transmitted Disease shall be liable to be branded with indelible ink on their persons to indicate the presence of Sexually Transmitted Disease and the Board shall have authority to decide from time to time, the manner of markings, subject to the instructions of the Government in this regard. (Maharashtra Protection of Commercial Sex Workers Bill, 1994, Section 4(i))

Further, women in prostitution suffering from STDs are liable to quarantine until cured and a fine. The board is not liable for any responsibility with regard to women found suffering from STDs, except to notify the next of kin of the person (Maharashtra Protection of Commercial Sex Workers Bill, 1994, Section 17, Section 4d).

The Bill stigmatises women in prostitution, rather than protecting them; thus its title is a misnomer. Further, it violates WHO guidelines regarding HIV testing that take a stand against compulsory testing of any section of the population, especially sex workers, on the grounds that it is counterproductive[4]. The proposed Bill, however, attempts to legalise some of the rights violations that are already being unleashed on prostitutes. The Bill itself has not been passed following an organised demonstration and protests against it by human rights organisations in the state, and more to the point, a change in the ruling party in the state of Maharasthra. However, the 1989 Bill and the 1994 Bill together represent the political will of the state on the issue of sex work.

Proposals for change: the central authority

Academics and policy makers drafted new laws on prostitution in the early 1990s that are still under discussion. Called the Law Reform Project, it was coordinated by Professor N.R. Madhava Menon and sponsored by the Department of Women and Child Development, Government of India. The introduction to the proposed changes by Professor Menon makes his concerns clear:

> While the law intended to prevent commercial exploitation of sex, what actually resulted is corruption in the enforcement machinery and wider exploitation in more surreptitious ways often with the protection of the so called law enforcement apparatus! The problem now is with law and the manner of its enforcement, than with prostitution and its related vices. At the same time, manifestations of prostitution in contemporary times are posing serious threats to human dignity, public health and morality and to women's rights. This is the agenda which this project in legislative reforms aims to address. (Menon, 1994, p 14)

While the report displays an awareness of contemporary debates on prostitution, including issues of work, labour and decriminalisation and legalisation, the actual law displays conventional notions of morality. This is apparent from the title of the proposed laws – the first is named the 1993 Prevention of Immoral Traffic and Rehabilitation of Prostituted Persons Bill, and the second is the 1993 Prohibition of Immoral Traffic and Empowerment of Sexual Workers Bill. The proposed Bills therefore continue to operate from the parameters of socially defined morality, within which prostitution, even if seen as work, is designated as immoral. The significant departure from existing laws is that prostitutes are seen in gender-neutral terms: as workers and persons.

Politically correct language does not detract, however, from the regressive content of the proposal. The statement of objects and reasons of one of the laws drafted makes this aspect abundantly clear.

> Immoral traffic ... is continuing unabated ... it has led to the spread of dreaded disease including AIDS threatening public health generally and the life of prostituted persons in particular. ... While voluntary sexual relations is the right of every adult citizen, it cannot be commercialised to the detriment of innocent victims, immature children, destitute women, and at the cost of social hygiene and public health. (Prevention of Immoral

> Traffic and Rehabilitation of Prostituted Persons Bill, 1993, Statement of objects and reasons)

The Bill is, however, not completely against the interests of sex workers. Some aspects of it could well benefit them. Under the Bill, sex workers can file for compensation in cases of violence, coercion or refusal of the client to use 'medically advised hygienic procedures'. In addition, prostitution involving children is punishable with imprisonment extending to five years and a fine of at least Rs. 1 lakh[5]. What may not be equally beneficial is that all those seen as abetting prostitution, including clients, are liable to fines and correctional or compensatory work. The names of clients are liable to be circulated by the government (Sections 4 and 5).

The latter clause, while acting on conservative, moralist (and some feminist) notions, that men going to prostitutes must be publicly humiliated, could well work against the interests of women in the profession. It could potentially reduce the number of men who would visit prostitutes. The moral outrage seemingly shifts from the woman in prostitution to her client. Isolating and humiliating clients may serve the interests of some patriarchies that seek to preserve marriage and the conventional family. The very knowledge that a man uses the services of a prostitute is shameful in this discourse. The division between the prostitute and the wife/mother stands preserved. Ultimately, the shame and humiliation is vested in the prostitute, as she is considered so stigmatised that, by association, the client is stigmatised and degraded.

The proposed Bill allows scope for mandatory testing for HIV, not only on women in prostitution, but on their children and spouses. Section 7 states that:

> The appropriate Government shall conduct with the help of social action groups working for the welfare of women in the area, a survey every five years, of prostitution and the nature of problems prostituted women suffer from. Special effort should be taken to identify in such surveys the extent of HIV/AIDS cases among them, their children and their spouses. (Prevention of Immoral Traffic and Rehabilitation of Prostituted Persons Bill, 1993)

The rights violations so far restricted to sex workers are extended to their children and husbands. In a similar vein is the second Bill, the 1993 Prohibition of Immoral Traffic and Empowerment of Sexual

Workers Bill. The statements of objects and reasons of the Bill discuss the issue of decriminalisation and the pros and cons of treating prostitution as work. The ambivalence of the drafters is captured in this statement:

> While law should severely punish people involved with immoral trafficking and those indulging in child prostitution, it should decriminalise totally the voluntary sexual work of prostitutes ... equating it with any other manual labour. This view, though apparently obnoxious to contemporary public morals, is said to be the only sensible position that law can adopt if it intends to empower the women involved and to effectively regulate the health risks of prostitutes, the customers and the public at large. (Prohibition of Immoral Traffic and Empowerment of Sexual Workers Bill, 1993, Statement of objects and reasons)

This statement attempts to display a concern for prostitutes and a respect for their choices, but what comes through strongly in my reading is an implicit moralism and the concern for public health, that is, the sexual health of the male client and his marital family.

The Bill provides for sex workers to be extended the right to safe conditions of work from the client and the brothel keeper. In addition, they are entitled to refuse a client on grounds of health, safety and hygiene. The brothel keeper is expected to provide medical treatment and a monthly medical check-up from a registered medical practitioner. Since the nature of the check-up is not laid down, it is not unreasonable to fear that it could well include mandatory testing for HIV (Sections 3, 4, 7 and 10).

Provisions for setting up a welfare fund for the children of prostitutes at the state level are created, to entitle children to receive free medical and educational services up to the age of 18 (Sections 15 and 16).

The implicit moral agenda of the Bill is revealed in its definition of 'immoral trafficking':

> Immoral Trafficking means and includes buying, selling or procuring women and children for sexual abuse, prostitution or such forms of sexual exploitation.
>
> Explanation:
>
> Causing a child or woman to be so abused prostituted

> or exploited by force, fraud, deceit, undue influence, or misrepresentation is trafficking within the meaning of this section.
>
> Fake marriages and dedication of girls which compel them to give up their dignity even if done ostensibly for religious purposes would amount to trafficking under this section. (Prohibition of Immoral Traffic and Empowerment of Sexual Workers Bill, 1993, Section 2a)

Little distinction is made between adult women and children in this section. Besides, the words 'immoral' and 'dignity' bring to the fore the agenda of the law, which sees prostitution in terms of loss of morality and dignity. Given this, the following definition of 'sex worker' is not as innocent or well meaning as it seems: 'Sex Worker means a woman who has taken to prostitution voluntarily and is doing the activity as an occupation' (Section 2b). If indeed immorality and loss of dignity is attached to prostitution, defining it as work or accepting that some women may choose it voluntarily and see it as an occupation does not lend prostitution any additional value. Rather it may stigmatise such women further, as they are seen to be voluntarily giving up their dignity and morality.

The real contradiction in these Bills is that they attempt to reconcile the conflicting claims of identity politics, a certain kind of conventional moralism that sees prostitution as promiscuity, and a concern for public health, a euphemism for the sexual health of male clients and their families. Any concern for women in prostitution is therefore spurious. Nor do the Bills attempt to address the problems articulated by sex workers, that is, problems of police brutality and excesses or social stigmatisation.

A plan of action by the central government recommends steps to improve the health status of women in prostitution. It also supports the rationale of the 1986 Juvenile Justice Act, which defines children of prostitutes as being 'neglected juveniles' and recommends their separation from their mothers. Regarding strategies to separate children from their mothers, the plan states:

> Coercion to remove the child and mother, wherever possible, would be more relevant in the context of the type of environment she lives in, for instance, in areas where brothels are located. Considering the fact that taking away a child from her mother by coercion would only add to her trauma and that of her mother and

> keeping in view the inadequacy of institutional facilities for sheltering the children, as far as possible, persuasion and motivation would be used to remove the child to a healthy environment. (WCD and HRD, 1998, Section VIII, p 1)

The section on rescue and rehabilitation states the concerns of the plan more blandly:

> All efforts will be made to persuade and motivate women and child victims of commercial sexual exploitation to recover and reintegrate them in society to lead a dignified life. Efforts would be made through awareness programmes, counselling, cajoling, and if necessary, by coercion to remove all children above 6 years of age, especially teenage boys and girl children of women victims to institutional care in boarding homes/hostels/ foster homes/residential schools etc. (WCD and HRD, 1998, Section IX, p 1)

Clearly, the plan recommends coercion in cases where persuasion fails. Even as the paucity of institutional support is admitted, the plan continues to recommend separation of children to a 'healthy' environment. As in the 1986 Juvenile Justice Act, the actual relationship between the parent and the child is not relevant when it comes to prostitutes and their children.

Significantly, the fear expressed by the authors of the plan is that children of prostitutes will end up as prostitutes themselves. There seems little evidence to support this fear or that children of prostitutes are neglected juveniles as the law suggests. Interviews with women in prostitution reveal that most of them are in the profession for the sake of their children and take steps to ensure that their children will not enter prostitution. Even if the fear were indeed justified, there would be little rationale for separating the children from their mothers.The Criminal Code allows for convicted criminals to keep their children with them in prison. Given that prostitution is not a criminal activity, separating the children against their will violates the rights of women and the children.

Debates around decriminalisation and legalisation

While NGOs and women's organisations working with women in prostitution may have different views about the merits of one system of law over another, there is a general consensus that existing law in India on prostitution is not effective and works against the interests of women in the sex trade (Sinha and Sleightholme, 1996). This is based on the experiences of women in prostitution, as this opinion of the criminal justice system from a woman in the trade brings out: 'They do not consider us as human beings.... They add to our harassment and humiliation.... They fail to understand the human aspects of the problem. They perceive it as a law and order problem' (CSWB, 1998, pp 86-7).

The Durbar Mahila Samanwaya Committee (DMSC), which works with women and men in the sex trade, suggests that the existing law does little to tackle the irregularities within the trade and believes it should be abolished. Rather, it makes a demand for self-regulation, not legalisation:

> We do not want any legalisation – we want our right to regulate our own lives, both within the profession and outside. This right should not be taken as 'immoral' and 'inhuman'. As the first step towards self regulation, we would like to form a board which will make rules and regulate the entry of new girls and also deliberate on the issues that may achieve the all round development of the sex workers and control all relevant activities. (DMSC, 1997a)

Women in the profession criticise the law and see a link between the lawmakers and the clients in very direct ways. As a Bombay-based sex worker and activist puts it: 'The law doesn't help. PITA is a useless law. Everyone knows about us, men come to use us, then they pass a law that says that prostitution should be stopped.'[6]

Some sex workers' organisations believe that legalisation can help to improve their lives and would prevent excesses by the police. The Delhi-based Centre for Feminist Legal Research (CFLR) has brought out an extensive memorandum on laws relating to prostitution in India, proposing certain legal amendments. It recommends the repeal of PITA on the grounds that the provisions regarding trafficking and procuring are vague and concerned with morality. Instead, it proposes that the definition of trafficking put forward by GAATW be adopted: 'All acts involved in the recruitment and/or transportation of a woman within and across national borders for work or services by means of violence or threat of violence, abuse of authority or dominant position, debt bondage, deception or other forms of coercion' (CFLR, 1999, pp 6-7).

The CFLR suggests that special laws be drafted to tackle trafficking of minors, as the question of consent is irrelevant for children. Simultaneously, rape and sexual assault laws should be amended so those women in prostitution can access these laws. CFLR also proposes a three-pronged law reform strategy: decriminalisation of voluntary sex work; extension of rights to sex workers and the setting up of a redressal machinery. It proposes that activities such as running brothels, living off the earnings of prostitution and soliciting be decriminalised. In addition, relevant provisions in the IPC and the Police Acts should be amended to prevent their being used against sex workers. CFLR feels that a mere repeal of criminal provisions will not help women in prostitution access other legal rights:

> The social marginalisation of women in sex work will not be overcome merely by decriminalising sex work. Statutory recognition of the fact that women in sex work have the same rights as other citizens is essential. Special laws must be enacted to recognise and redress the historical disadvantage women in sex work have suffered as a result of social stigma as well as a denial of legal rights. (CFLR, 1999, pp 17-18)

These proposed rights include: the right to work; the right to safe conditions of work; the right to worker status; the right to health; the right to education for the sex worker and her children; the right to association; the right to freedom of movement and residence in the place of her choice; the right to privacy and the amendment or repeal of laws inconsistent with these laws, such as the relevant provisions in the 1986 Juvenile Justice Act. Redressal mechanisms to ensure that these rights are extended include proposals to set up a special forum at the trial court level to deal with complaints or to use the existing legal system effectively by accessing the 1947 Industrial Disputes Act, the 1926 Trade Union Act and the 1923 Workmen's Compensation Act. These comprehensive and detailed proposals nevertheless do not address issues of citizenship and access of rights to non-citizens, who form the most vulnerable section of women in prostitution. Sizeable proportions of women in prostitution in India belong to other South Asian countries, including Nepal and Bangladesh. Asserting citizenship rights therefore may be completely irrelevant to them, especially since their status in their country of residence is quasi-legal.

A statement of concern by Sanghli-based Sangram (a union of sex workers), GAATW and AWHRC in March 1999 similarly offers an alternative to existing anti-prostitution laws in South Asia. These include repealing all laws that victimise women in prostitution and do not recognise voluntary prostitution, a legal recognition of the families of prostitutes as a legitimate unit, and criminal law intervention in the case of rape, sexual abuse and coercion as for mainstream women. In addition, the statement says that prostitution of children should be treated as a criminal activity, but that the definition of 'child' needs to be made community and country specific (Sangram et al, 1999). What this statement argues for, therefore, is the removal of criminal provisions and an extension of rights, including protection against violence, to women in prostitution.

Unlike the proposals by CFLR, the Sanghli statement goes beyond a simple assertion of citizenship rights. It recommends, at a policy level, a total delinking of trafficking and prostitution, suggesting that the purpose of the final destination for trafficking is irrelevant. What are more important are issues of coercion, abuse and deception. To quote: 'The concerns and interests of trafficked women and the need to provide them support and security must take precedence over the citizenship concerns of member states regarding the legal identity of the woman. Eventual repatriation can not be the primary goal' (Sangram et al, 1999, pp 2–3).

Key issue faced

Reasons for entry into prostiution

As Table 6.1 demonstrates, in the Indian context, a range of complex reasons can lead to the entry of women into prostitution, and there are close connections between migration, poverty and entry into the sex trade.

Acute poverty is the single most important reason for joining sex work in Kolkata. Studies in Orissa similarly suggest that economic survival, lack of employment opportunities and poverty are central reasons for entering prostitution with over 30% of women entering sex work due to poverty. In addition, social and economic

Table 6.1: Reasons for entry into the sex trade

Reasons for joining	Total number	Total percentage
Acute poverty	221	49.10
Willingly	39	8.67
Family dispute	97	21.56
Misguided	70	15.56
Tradition	21	4.67
Kidnapped	2	0.44

Source: DMSC (1997b, p 12).

deprivation caused by natural calamities such as the 1999 cyclone led to an increase in migration and sex work. In some areas of Orissa, families sell their daughters into prostitution due to poverty. Other economic reasons are dowry demands, which lead to women entering prostitution to earn money for their dowry, or for their unmarried sisters (Pandey et al, 2003).

Coercion and force

Some media and academic discourse underscores the role of coercion and force in entry into sex work. It is suggested that in some parts of the country, criminalisation, and the power exercised by trafficking networks, force parents to sell their daughters into the sex trade (Pandey, Jena and Samal, 2003; Sinha and Sleightholme, 1996). During the course of my fieldwork, however, I found that while many women start off by telling stories of coercion and violence, once a relationship is established, the stories often change.

As a paper on sex workers in a South African mine points out, people's stories of being tricked into sex work were remarkably similar, almost a part of a script. However:

> … the objective veracity of people's accounts is not the most important or interesting feature of the life histories. What is more important is how people reconstruct and account for their life choices, given that these accounts reflect the social identities that play a key role in shaping people's sexual behavior. In this context, the main interest of these stories of origin lies in the role that they play as a strategy for coping with a spoiled identity … (Campbell, 2000, p 488)

In India, as in South Africa, social stigma may be a powerful factor pushing women in sex work to cast themselves as 'innocent victims'.

Once the researcher spends time and energy in the 'field', the stories often change. Women who started in the first instance recounting uncomplicated stories of 'innocent victimhood' later trusted me enough to recast themselves as agents. The following excerpts from my interviews make this clearer:

> I've been in India for the past 12-and-a-half years. I was brought here by my fate; nobody has kept me here by force ... I am in touch with my family. I send money and letters home regularly[7].

> I started working because I fought with my mother-in-law. She abused me and harassed me. My husband is an alcoholic. He pushed me to enter sex work and I realised that this is the only way I can earn some money and feed my family. I go to Bowbazaar in the morning and have rented a house there[8].

> Someone from my village who belongs to this line brought me here. I came because our family is too poor to look after me[9].

Migration

The links between the sex trade and migration are strong. This can be attributed to a number of causal factors: the relative anonymity of the new destination, limited options for employment and the need to survive in a new location without family support. Migrant women are seen as going against the traditional female role – of staying home and being looked after by the family – and are pushed into sex work by forces that see them as transgressive (Lin, 1999). Having stepped out of the normative 'female role', they are more amenable to opportunities that may not be acceptable in their place of origin.

Conclusions

While women in India theoretically enjoy a range of rights, in practice most women are denied them. Poverty, deprivation, caste and traditions lead to a situation where women are generally disempowered, and have few choices before them in terms of income generation. Entry into the sex trade therefore becomes, in some cases, an important subsistence activity. However, there are multiple and complex reasons for entry, which cannot easily be reduced to one or more factor (poverty, coercion etc). Therefore, it is important to look at multiple ways in which women and minors enter and negotiate entry into prostitution. Further, it is important to examine the compulsions pushing women into arranging their lives into simplified stories of force and coercion for the consumption of researchers and journalists.

At a general level, anti-prostitution laws in India are designed not so much to stop prostitution, but to regulate and control prostitutes and their bodies. The purpose is not to improve the working conditions of prostitutes. Nor is there any concern for their health, except in the one area where it would, in the perception of the lawmakers, affect the health of the public, which is sexual health. Simultaneously, the moral code that governs anti-prostitution laws regulating or prohibiting prostitution ends up being used to justify the harassment, arrest, imprisonment, rape and murder of prostitutes. Women in prostitution find that the existing laws and policies are less than helpful, either in preventing prostitution, or in improving the status and rights of women within prostitution.

There is little consensus, however, on whether legalisation or decriminalisation would benefit women and children in prostitution. Feminists and women in prostitution disagree, often vociferously, on the legal system that they find most important. What is needed, however, is more research on the nature of the sex trade in India, and the perceived needs of women and children in the sex trade, and to arrive at strategies based on these needs.

Based on current research these are the trends that may be apparent in the near future in the Indian context:

- increased poverty due to globalisation, and an increase in the numbers of women and girl children entering the sex trade;
- state policies increasingly centred on issues of health and HIV/ STD prevention; possibility of increased surveillance on women in the sex trade as a result;
- women in the sex trade continuing to experience stigma, which will continue to be one of the most important factors preventing women from exiting the sex trade, or preventing their daughters from entering it.

Notes

[1] A child is defined as a person below 16 years, a minor between 16 and 18 years and an adult above 18 years.

[2] The judgment quotes the VC Mahajan Committee on Prostitution that states that 16% enter prostitution due to family tradition and that 10.6% are married, 34.4% unmarried and 54.2% are divorced or widowed.

[3] 1 lakh equals 100,000, or 0.1 million.

[4] WHO guidelines state that:

> Prostitutes who can't escape testing and turn out to be HIV positive may be fined or lose their registration. But this doesn't protect the public health. Infected individuals will simply move on to another place. Where there is a system of registration, the infected sex workers will join the ranks of unofficial prostitutes, who generally have even less power to negotiate safe sex. Testing does not even protect the local clients. No matter how many 'condom only' signs are posted, any brothel owner (or government official) who insists on testing sex workers – and lets client know that they are HIV negative – is sending a clear message that if a client doesn't want to use a condom, he'll still be safe. Of course, the client may well be infected himself and infect the prostitute, who will then infect others who decide not to use a condom, and so on. (cited in Sakhrani, 1998)

[5] 1 lakh = 100,000, and 1 lakh rupees equals approximately £1,250.

[6] Author interview with health worker from BMC-HIV Cell, Bombay, 22 August 1998.

[7] Interview with Rekha Lamba, sex worker in Kolkata of Nepalese origin, 27 September 1998.

[8] Interview with 'Aloka, flying' sex worker from Garai, Kolkata, 20 September 2001.

[9] Interview with Joyati, sex worker in Malishahi, Bhubaneswar, 6 September 2001.

Recommended further reading

D'Cunha, J. (1991) *The legalisation of prostitution: A sociological inquiry into the laws relating to prostitution in India and the West*, Bangalore: Bookmakers.

Sinha, I. and Sleightholme, C. (1996) *Guilty without trial: Women in the sex trade in Calcutta*, Calcutta: Stree.

Gangoli, G. (1998) 'Prostitution, legalisation and decriminalisation – recent debates', *Economic and Political Weekly*, 7 March 1998, pp 504-5.

References

A Bill to provide for the regulation and control of activities of prostitutes and brothels with a view to prevent the growth of disease known as Acquired Immunity Deficiency Syndrome (AIDS) (1988), Mumbai: Maharashtra Legislative Assembly.

Ballhatchet, K. (1980) *Race, sex and class under the Raj: Imperial attitudes and policies and their critics*, London: Weidenfeld and Nicholson.

Campbell, C. (2000) 'Selling sex in the time of AIDS: identity, sexuality and commercial sex-work on a South African mine', *Social Science and Medicine*, vol 50, no 2, pp 479-94.

Central Social Welfare Board (CSWB) (1998) *Prostitution in metropolitan cities in India*, New Delhi: Government of India.

Centre for Feminist Legal Research (CFLR) (1999) *Memorandum on reform of laws relating to prostitution in India*, Delhi: CFLR.

Durbar Mahila Samanwaya Committee (DMSC) (1997a) *Sex workers' right to self determination*, Calcutta: on file with Sanlaap (File no. FF12), Documentation Centre, Kolkata.

DMSC (1997b) *The fallen learn to rise –The social impact of STD-HIV intervention programme*, Calcutta: DMSC.

Immoral Traffic in Women and Girls (Prevention) Act (1986), New Delhi (Amendment to SITA, 1956).

Jain v Union of India (1997) Supreme Court 3021.

Kishor, S. and Gupta, K. (2004) 'Women's empowerment in India and its states - evidence from the NFHS', *Economic and Political Weekly*, 14 February, pp 649-712.

Lin, C. (1999) 'Prostitution and migration: issues and approaches. Summary of network presentation, Calcutta, March 1998', *APSNET - Bulletin of the Asia-Pacific Network of Sex-workers*, vol 1, no 1, pp 13-16.

Lok Sabha Debates (1986) 22 August, Law Library, University of Delhi.

Maharashtra Protection of Sex Workers: A Bill (1994), Mumbai: Maharashtra Legislative Assembly.

Menon, N.R.M. (1994) *The problem, the concerns and the background - report on the law reform project*, New Delhi: Department of Women and Child Development, Government of India.

National Commission for Women (1996) *Societal violence on women and children in prostitution*, New Delhi: Government of India.

Pandey, B., Jena, D. and Samal, N. (2003) *Trafficking in women in Orissa*, Bhubaneswar: ISED, UNIFEM, USAID.

Prevention of Immoral Traffic and Rehabilitation of Prostituted Persons' Bill (1993), New Delhi: Department of Women and Child Development (WCD), Government of India.

Prohibition of Immoral Traffic and Empowerment of Sexual Workers Bill (1993), New Delhi: WCD: Government of India.

Punekar, S.D. and Rao, K. (1962) *A study of prostitutes in Bombay (with reference to family background)*, Bombay: Lalvani Publishing House.

Radha Devi, D. (1993) 'Status of women in India: a comparison by state', *Asia-Pacific Population Journal*, vol 8, no 4, pp 59-77.

Sakhrani, M. (1998) 'Maharashtra Protection of Commercial Sex Workers Act, 1994 – a critique', *The Lawyers*, May, issue 1994, pp 23–24.

Sangram, GAATW and AWHRC (1999) *A statement of concerns*, Sanghli: Sangram.

Sinha, I. and Sleightholme, C. (1996) *Guilty without trial: Women in the sex trade in Calcutta*, Calcutta: Stree.

Sunder Rajan, R. (2003) *The scandal of the state: Women, law and citizenship in postcolonial India*, New Delhi: Kali for Women.

Suppression of Immoral Traffic Act (1956), New Delhi (104 of 1956)

WCD (Women and Child Development) and HRD (Human Resource Department) (1998) *Child prostitutes and children of prostitutes and plan of action to combat trafficking and commercial sexual exploitation of women and children*, New Delhi: WCD and HRD.

SEVEN

Good women, bad women: prostitution in Pakistan

Fouzia Saeed

Introduction

Culturally and historically, Pakistan is very much a part of South Asia. Over the centuries, the subcontinent was divided, and re-divided, into several independent states by different invaders. It is only since 1947, however, that Pakistan has taken on a distinct identity as a separate country with its own distinct sovereignty. In these last 55 years it has evolved its own specific cultural features, firstly as a Muslim state and secondly because of its own distinct political and economic developments.

Although prostitution is a universal phenomenon, in the subcontinent it acquired a unique form. It comes closest to the geisha system of Japan (Golden, 1998). Prostitution was not seen as sex alone, but as part of an entertainment package that included enjoying music, poetry, witty conversation, female company, alcohol and sexual services with the service providers trained well in all of these skills (Madhur and Gupta, 1965; Punekar and Rao, 1967). In these communities there were also musicians of high calibre who provided only the music, while the dancing girls or the women singers additionally provided sexual services. Mostly these groups of entertainers had the patronage of those who could afford to nurture such communities, including the ruling class, royalty and the nobles. Communities of singers, dancers and entertainers evolved and became associated with the different courts of the rulers (Joardar, 1984). They resided close to the ruling estates to provide services to the rulers and their courtiers and travelled with the armies to provide services for the officers. Specific areas in settlements were designated for prostitutes, where they lived and provided their services. They were called to the palaces of the rulers to provide music and other services as needed and desired. This system is also known as the courtesan system (Saeed, 2001).

In South Asia, occupational castes evolved over time for people who provided specialised skills to a community. Thus blacksmiths, goldsmiths, shoemakers, gardeners and other such 'lower ranking' occupations became the hereditary professions of specific communities. A professional caste for prostitutes also evolved over time. This caste was given different names in different areas, but all of them basically meant that this community was one of prostitutes (Rao and Rao, 1967; Joardar, 1985). Their men and women belonged to the same group, even though men provided a support role while women were the main workers.

The non-elite had a parallel system of brothels where the trade went on sometimes with music and sometimes without. This system evolved much later when the tight control by the emperors and nobility was loosened. It coincided with the growth in sea trade, with sailors providing good clientele for the lower-ranking prostitutes. During the times of British rule in South Asia, the composition of the nobility changed as those who showed loyalty with them became the local leaders and were given land and riches. These newly rich did not have the same taste in music and could not provide the patronage that the earlier rajas and rulers of older native states had provided. The British to some extent took the role of the patron and started to regulate this profession (Ghosh, 1984).

After 1947, Pakistan inherited the historical red-light areas in Lahore and Multan. These were well developed, with a reputation that attracted not only rich clients, but also talent hunters looking for actors and singers. All other bigger and smaller cities also had a red-light area, such as Nipa Road in Karachi, and Qasai Gali in Rawalpindi.

In Pakistan the caste system was not as institutionalised as in India (Litvack et al, 1998)[1] and mostly served a social organisational role. It was not acknowledged as part of the religion, government policies or constitution; however, remnants of this hierarchical heritage remain a part of Pakistani culture. The castes diluted into ethnic groups or *zaat* (Rose, 1933). Brahmans were replaced by *Syeds* in status, but not in function. Only those that were at the very high levels or extremely low levels of the hierarchies rigorously reinforced these social legacies, either through pride or stigma. The middle classes essentially forgot about the hierarchy. As one of the lower-ranking castes, the communities of prostitutes retained the hereditary nature of their occupation as well as the stigma and the title of their occupational group. In Pakistan most of these communities are called *Kanjars*. The community of musicians, who associate very closely with them, are called *Mirasi* (Saeed, 2001). Before going into the details of these ethnic groups that associate with the profession of prostitution traditionally and think of it as their hereditary occupation, we should take a broader look at the general conditions of Pakistani women.

The national context

Looking at basic human and women's rights, Pakistani women have full rights of equal citizenship in the constitution of Pakistan. The Constitution states:

> Article 25: *Equality of Citizens*: All citizens are equal before law and are entitled to equal protection of law. There shall be no discrimination on the basis of sex alone and nothing in this article shall prevent the State from making special provisions for the protection of women and children.
>
> Article 26: *Non-Discrimination*: In respect of access to public places. In respect of access to places of public entertainment or resort, not intended for religious purposes only, there shall be no discrimination against any citizens. Nothing in this clause shall prevent the State from making any special provision for women and children.
>
> Article 27: *Non-Discrimination in Employment*: No citizen otherwise qualified for appointment in the services of Pakistan shall be discriminated against in respect of any such appointment on the ground only of race, religion, caste, sex, residence or place of birth. (Pakistan Constitution)

In addition to the above Articles the Constitution states that 'Steps shall be taken to ensure full participation of women in all spheres of national life'.

Despite the constitutional rights, the entire social fabric is based on patriarchal values, shared to some extent by the rest of South Asia. The economic and social issues that Pakistani women face are quite similar to those faced by their fellows right across the subcontinent, including: low literacy rates, high death-rate during childbirth, restricted access to education and employment and a general inferior status in society (ADB, 2000).

The Gender Development Index (GDI), developed by the United Nations Development Programme (UNDP), compares gender differences on critical dimensions of human development, specifically on life expectancy, adult literacy, enrolment ratios and estimated earned income. Similarly, the Gender Empowerment Measure (GEM) measures the percentage of women in decision-making and senior positions in the workforce combined with an estimate of relative income levels of men and women. Both of these measures are an indicator of women's position in society. Other than Sri Lanka, Pakistan stands with other South Asian countries among the lowest one fourth of all countries in the world in both the GDI and GEM measures.

To take a more specific look at Pakistan's basic socio-economic indicators one finds that the literacy rate for young women between the ages 15 to 24 is low at 42%, as compared to that for men, which is 64%. The female economic activity rate is 36.3%, most of which is associated with agriculture. Among the professions the most common are medical doctors, nurses, teachers and office workers. Among low-paid labour, women work as domestic helps, wage earners in brick kiln factories and, other textile factories. Most of the women work at home and with their families and in the informal sector, where their economic activity is not measured in economic surveys (Human Rights Commission of Pakistan, 2004).

On one hand, poverty has been increasing and is affecting women more than men, and on the other hand, the position of women in the political arena is being revolutionised. In 2001, the government provided 33% of seats in the local bodies for women nationwide, and 36,000 women were elected (Ministry of Women's Development, 2005). This appears to have expanded the ability of women to put forward their issues to their representatives. Similarly, there was an influx of women in the provincial and national assemblies. About 17% of seats were reserved for women and there was an increase in the number of women who successfully campaigned for the regular seats also. Women always have had the right to vote and own property in Pakistan. However, there is now a wide campaign to encourage women to make greater use of these rights.

Although one sees progress in the status and basic provisions for women, like education, health facilities, access to political decision-making and access to other opportunities (Ministry of Women's

Development, 2005), the centuries-old patriarchal social structure, entrenched in the local feudal systems, determines the parameters of women's lives and their freedom. Regardless of constitutional, legal and religious rights that go in favour of women, they are still trapped in the shackles of male dominance. Religious and legal rights are at times not fully given or are manipulated. Violence against women is prevalent and freedom of movement is limited (Hayward, 2000; Shaheed and Zaidi, 2005).

Men have the right of social and moral judgment, and women are left to prove their chastity. Women put up with the patriarchal system because there is little room for deviation. Deviation can be punished through any manner of responses, from rape and murder to never being asked to marry. Despite all these limitations, women of different strata have acquired varying degrees of freedom. Gradually, Pakistani society has moved from almost total social disapproval of female education to girls not only receiving an education, but getting jobs and, in the middle class, going abroad for education. One can see pockets of women who have carved out spaces for themselves and dispelled the prevailing myths and stereotypes.

The Pakistani women's movement has been quite brave and well organised for several decades (Nyrop, 1995). It has resisted discriminatory laws, joined other forces for restoration of democracy and raised critical women's issues in public and with policy makers. However, through most of its existence, the movement was restricted mostly to the middle urban classes as it was these women who had created relatively more space for themselves to take on collective issues.

Among the issues raised by them and the media, which is quite progressive, violence against women and discriminatory laws were the two highly prioritised issues. In both, the effects of patriarchy were attacked openly. Perhaps due to the urgency of other issues at hand, the movement never really took on the cause of prostitutes or the issue of prostitution. Similarly, prostitutes also never really organised themselves as women or joined the women's movement. The only groups who regularly raised issues related to prostitutes were the political leaders of the red-light districts. However, these leaders, mostly men, had their commercial interests in mind, not the welfare of the women.

Although organised research on prostitution had never been carried out in Pakistan until very recently, issues related to the perpetuation of prostitution or the vulnerability of prostitutes are directly connected to the general position of women in Pakistani society. These include the general inability of women to assert their rights without going through a man; the positions of earner, protector and moral judge being regarded as exclusively male; women's roles restricted to child bearer, nurturer of the family and someone who must prove herself to be good and chaste all her life; the notion that a woman who entertains men or asserts herself in any way is a bad woman; and, most importantly, that a man is a man, he is not good or bad, so he can do bad things and not lose his reputation or become stigmatised for his actions (Saeed, 2001).

However, it is important to look at the diversity and range of experiences of and attitudes towards women. One has to understand that it is the same Pakistani society that twice elected a woman as its prime minister and at the same time holds on to ancient feudal values and patriarchal norms.

Different perspectives on prostitution

In order to understand the perspectives on prostitution in Pakistan it is important to know first the different categories of this profession, as the reformatory efforts that can be proposed vary for each category. The state's role in undertaking action affecting these communities has been critical, so it is also very important to understand the positive or negative effects of state action as it attempted to 'deal with the problem'. In this section various efforts and views of different stakeholders have been given.

As far as systems of prostitution are concerned, there are two clear categories. One is a traditional system of prostitution and the other is the more modern brothel system. The call girls and streetwalkers can be included in the brothel system. It is important to describe the two systems to understand the perspectives and reform efforts that have been taken for both.

In the traditional system, prostitutes live in a family situation. They are brought up by their mothers and other family members and live in a household with their siblings. A household is headed by a *naika*, a woman manager who manages a few young dancing girls, mostly her daughters, but they could be her nieces or close relatives. The *naika* and other elder women in the family, sometimes with the help of male pimps, try to get good clients for the young prostitutes.

The communities involved traditionally with this trade usually think of it as their family occupation. In a typical traditional set-up, the management takes care of the dancers as their assets and also looks after their future. As a matter of routine a young dancing girl is trained into a management role to be sure that her future is secured. In the traditional system, the sexual services are coupled with music and dancing. The traditional way of entertaining a client has been to have music, singing and dancing in their *kothas* – little shops, or what they themselves call their *offices*. The other way was to go out to give private dance performances for clients or larger gatherings organised by a specific client. Now the trend is changing to performing in variety shows, which are more like stage entertainment programmes. In any case, although the form is changing, the coupling of musical entertainment with sexual services is still very much the same. Thus the self-image of these professional women is mostly that of an artist, and they take great pride in their work.

In sharp contrast with the family upbringing of the traditional prostitute, the girls in the brothel system in most cases enter the profession either through kidnapping or other forms of coercion. Here the focus is simply on providing sexual services; singing and dancing are not a part of it. The brothels are usually not placed in traditional red-light areas, but are spread around the city, even in residential areas. The main manager or the head pimp is a man, and most of the managers are men. The brothel managers are only interested in the 'prime years' of a prostitute, that is, when she is a young woman, and do not care about how she will survive in her old age. The women live without any family linkages and they are actively discouraged from creating any support system. To ensure they do not have any outside support, they are frequently transferred to different cities. These brothels are advertised secretly by the word of mouth of agents. In general, people are not familiar with their existence and precise locations, whereas the red-light areas are well known to all.

There is one category of these brothels that is more of a combination of the two systems. These brothels are set up by families from the red-light area communities. Over the years, the more successful families from the traditional communities have moved from their homes, out into the suburbs. In their effort not to be obvious, the first thing they drop is music, and they continue their occupation in a more subtle, quiet and discreet manner. Thus, at times, maintaining a facade of being regular residents of an area, they continue the business as well. These brothels, although qualifying to be in the second category, sometimes retain characteristics of the traditional system.

As far as society's approach towards prostitution is concerned, it focuses on the obvious. The red-light areas are the parts that come under attack; perhaps it is easy to overlook what the eye does not see. Red-light areas are seen as a big contradiction to the Islamic image that the state wants to project and are always seen as a dark spot that needs to be washed away. People in general are more accepting, but do consider this a bad business and these communities to be made up of bad people.

The state and the government

Ayub Khan was a military dictator and ruled for about ten years (1958-68). In his reform package he decided to dismantle the red-light areas. His government pushed the residents out in the hope of eradicating prostitution. Prostitution was clearly seen as an embarrassment and as evil, and eradication was seen as the only solution to this 'problem'. The community of prostitutes was seen as the 'problem', while those seeking their services never came under his scrutiny.

This was a difficult time for these communities as they moved out, settled into different communities in other residential areas and restarted their occupation. The resultant spread of the trade from one specific area in the cities into the general residential areas created an angry backlash from the families who did not want brothels next to their homes. The government had to change its policy. The residents of the red-light area were allowed to come back on specific conditions; however, one part of the red-light area in Lahore that had only provided low-class sexual services remained closed.

As a result of the backlash, the political leaders of the *Kanjar* community were able to negotiate successfully with the government to reclassify the dancers as performing artists. They obtained the right to perform through a High Court ruling that allowed them to perform in their *kothas* from 10pm to 1am. The government accepted them only as performers and looked the other way regarding their other activities. Anyone who was not a performer and did not indulge in music and only provided sexual services was considered a criminal. However, brothels that were outside the red-light areas were not really the focus. It is important to note that neither civil society nor academics were involved in this whole episode in any way.

In the time of Zulfiqar Ali Bhutto, in the early 1970s, the communities from the red-light area were more comfortable as the arts and artists both enjoyed a higher status. There was more protection from the police for them. The leaders of the community ensured that a client who wanted to take a dancing girl to his home for a performance had to register with the police. This protected the girl and her team in case the hosts became violent or refused to pay. There were other progressive policies that gave the community some protection and social status as artists.

During Zia-ul-Haq's regime (1977-88), which is considered to be the most repressive in the history of Pakistan, there was an effort to Islamise the country (Arif, 2001; Cohen, 2005). Music and dancing came under attack in every way. Prostitution was seen as an evil in society. The members of these communities were branded *bad* people as they not only were seen as being immoral due to their profession of providing sexual services, but were also into singing and dancing. The government's approach was to eradicate this phenomenon at any cost. The method used was to harass the residents to an extent that they would leave the occupation. Similarly, the clients and anyone who was seen during the performing hours were also harassed, with the idea that if they managed to scare the clients away, the decline in the clientele would discourage the *Kanjars* from pursuing this trade.

The government exercised this calculated harassment systematically through the police. The hours for performance of the dancing girls were reduced to two hours every evening. There was little flexibility in rehearsing or practising music. The police guarded the implementation of those hours. They had police checkpoints at all entrances of the red-light areas during those hours and they would record the names of visitors to the area in that time on a register. This scared the clients away. Straight after the hours finished there would be so much police presence on the narrow roads that it seemed that there was a continuous police raid.

During the Zia regime women in general suffered immensely because of discriminatory legislation introduced by the President (Weiss, 1986; Mazari, 2002). These ordinances met with heavy resistance from the feminist circles in spite of the marshal law restrictions on protest. One of the pieces of legislation, the Hadood Ordinances, covered adultery. Until then adultery in Pakistan had always been socially condemned, but it was not regulated by law. The Hadood Ordinances[2] had an extremely damaging impact on the red-light areas. More than a tool for checking adultery it became a licence to pick up any dancing girl whenever the police needed a bribe. Hadood, a stick for beating the red-light areas' residents, men and women, became a tool for extortion. The overt intimidation discouraged clients from coming to the marked areas. This, naturally, led to discreet arrangement between client and prostitute to meet elsewhere, where their clients felt safer. Thus, not only did the government's approach fail to eradicate prostitution, but it helped in spreading it to areas outside the more visible red-light areas.

Long after the Zia period ended, his policies continue to plague Pakistani society. The particular harassment of the red-light areas has increased, partly because no one has ever focused on articulating the rights of these individuals as citizens. As a result, residents who could afford to leave the red-light areas have established brothels with far less government supervision.

The communities of prostitutes

These communities are composed of the dancing girls and their management (who were dancing girls in their youth). The women of the musician community are not involved in prostitution and are kept in homes far away from the red-light areas. Still, the men are close partners with the prostitute community, providing the music for the clients and lessons for the girls. Prior to the Zia era, the leaders of the prostitute community were able to organise themselves and, from time to time, have been effective in taking the government to task. The senior musicians also organised themselves, but were not as effective as a group. During Bhutto's period, a well-known pimp in the city of Lahore, who was the son of a prostitute, gained high respect within his community and was elected as the legitimate political representative of his area in the city council.

The perspective of this organisation was that the members of their community, whether involved in prostitution or not, should have all the rights that any ordinary citizen enjoys. They stressed that they are professional people and their occupation is that of an artist, therefore, their contribution to the musical heritage of the country should be acknowledged. They lobbied with the government to introduce reform efforts to make their profession and their area safe, and the sex service providers secure.

Activists and academics

Somehow the women's movement in Pakistan had its hands so full with other issues related to discriminatory laws, unfair sentences for women in cases of Hadood laws, and issues of violence against women that prostitution did not really appear on their agenda. The interaction between women who were prostitutes and those who were social activists was nil. The general perception of prostitutes in society might be less condescending among the activists and they probably would be more sympathetic towards these women, but there is hardly any evidence to show that they had a real understanding of the lives of women in prostitution. Thus, although activists never took up the fight to protect the rights of women prostitutes, they also never joined hands with the government and general public in their efforts against them. In general they had a sympathetic and tolerant attitude towards them, but were never of any help either.

In recent years, a few NGOs have become involved in advocating precautions in relation to HIV/AIDS infection. This has resulted in the first interface between the residents of red-light areas and the NGO circles. Although the interventions have so far been limited, they can become a basis upon which to build stronger ties in the future.

Pakistani literature has given a realistic idea of the constraints a woman prostitute has to face. Writers like Saadat Hassan Manto and Ismat Chughtai were those who brought the sufferings – their pains as well as their human face – to people. These writings, however, were in the 1940s and 1950s.

The writers of feature films romanticised these red-light areas and presented the women as victims to the extent that it glorified their role as martyrs and perverted the reality of their condition. The film industry is responsible for creating many myths about these women and presenting an unreal picture of their lives to the public. The films presented no specific perspective for the future of this community or this occupation.

In 2001, a book entitled *Taboo!: The hidden culture of a red light area* brought in a new perspective (Saeed, 2001). Until then, the two perspectives that were commonly held were those of either total eradication or reform to make the trade safer, including decriminalisation. *Taboo*, structured as an ethnography, brought a deeper level of understanding of the phenomenon and a more human picture of the residents of the red-light areas. It shattered several myths that had become institutionalised in society. These myths strengthened the stigma that faced any person associated with the profession of prostitution. *Taboo* questioned the whole false dichotomy of good women and bad women and dared to ask society why the focus of all the debate on prostitution is on the women who provide the service and not on the men who use, nurture and sustain it. It also questioned the whole notion of the stigma and its hidden function for the patriarchal society. Thus, this book brought a unique perspective to the debate.

Laws and policies

Existing laws and policies on prostitution

To analyse the legal position of prostitution one has to look at the laws in Pakistan before and after 1979. In the pre-independence era, British law prevailed, as the areas that now make up Pakistan were a part of British India. The Penal Code, drawn up by the British in 1892, remains a core element of current Pakistani law. The 1861 Police Act of British India remained the fundamental guide for police activities until 2002.

Sexual relations between two consenting adults was never a crime in Pakistani law before 1979. A couple did not have to be married to each other to have sexual relations, whereas rape was defined very clearly on the foundation of lack of consent of one party, even if they were married. Thus the point of emphasis was consent, not marriage. The only thing that was prohibited by the law was involving minors in prostitution.

In the Pakistan Penal Code (PPC) there were two sections dealing with prostitution:

> *Section 372*
> Selling minors for purposes of prostitution etc. Whoever sells, lets to hire or otherwise disposes of any person under the age of 18 years with intent that such person shall at any age be employed or used for the purpose of prostitution or illicit intercourse with any person or for any unlawful and immoral purpose, or knowing it to be likely that such person will at any age be employed or used for any such purpose, shall be punished with imprisonment of either description for a term which may extend to ten years, and shall also be liable to fine.
>
> *Explanation 1*
> When a female under the age of 18 years is sold, let for hire, or otherwise disposed of to a prostitute or to any

person who keeps or manages a brothel, the person so disposing of such female shall until the contrary is proved be presumed to have disposed of her with the intent that she shall be used for the purpose of prostitution.

Explanation 2
For the purpose of this section 'illicit intercourse' means sexual intercourse between persons not tied by marriage or by any union or tie which though not amounting to a marriage is recognised by the personal law or custom of the community to which they belong or where they belong to different communities, or both such communities as constituting between them quasi-marital relations.

Section 373
Buying minors for purposes of prostitution, etc.
Whoever buys, hires or otherwise obtains possession of any person under the age of eighteen years with intent that such person shall at any age be employed or used for the purpose of prostitution of illicit intercourse with any person or for any unlawful and immoral purpose, or knowing it to be likely that such person will at any age be employed or used for any such purpose shall be punished with imprisonment of either description for a term which may extend to ten years and shall also be liable to a fine.

Explanation 1
Any prostitute or any person keeping or managing a brothel, who buys, hires or otherwise obtains possession of a female under the age of 18 years, shall, until the contrary is proved, be presumed to have obtained possession of such female with the intent that she shall be used for the purpose of prostitution.

Explanation 2
'Illicit intercourse' has the same meaning as in Section 372.

Zia-ul-Haq, a conservative military dictator, fiddled around with the laws and policies of the country to bring about his version of Islamisation. Women were one of the prime victims. This period is referred to in Pakistani history by the women's movement as 'the 11 dark years' (Mumtaz and Shaheed, 1984). As mentioned earlier, Hadood Ordinances were issued during this period. Zia gave them protection under the 8th amendment of the Constitution, making it difficult for subsequent governments to alter them (Weiss, 1986).

The Zina Ordinance, one of the set of ordinances under Hadood, dealt with sexual interaction of people outside the contract of marriage. It covered both sexual intercourse without consent and with consent, thus it covered rape and adultery under one ordinance. Other than its structural faults, the concept of legislation against adultery is still being protested by the Pakistani activists. It leaves women vulnerable and open to abuse. In the last 20 years, several charges of rape have been changed to adultery, and the woman has gone to prison. In the context of prostitution, this is the law that is being used to take police action against prostitutes or their clients. This, however, is used indiscriminately on all women and men for adultery and does not separate prostitutes from any other 'culprit'. In other words there is still no specific law against prostitution.

The Zina Ordinance is very similar to the older provisions of the PPC; only the definition of who is an adult and the severity of the punishment was changed in this law. Previously, the age of majority was 18 but under the Zina Ordinance, while it remained 18 for men, for women, it was reduced to 16 or puberty, which at times could be at 10 or 12. The punishment for Zina ranged from stoning to death to lashes and imprisonment.

Regarding minors, the clauses of this Zina Ordinance were almost the same as section 372 of the PPC. The only difference was the definition of the age of a minor, which in the PPC was below 18 and in Zina Ordinance, as explained earlier, was before puberty for girls.

The Zina Ordinance became the most misused law. In general, society's progressive circles and the activists questioned the morality of putting rape and adultery together. It had several loopholes, and had a damaging psychological impact on society. Sex outside marriage was a social and moral issue for society, which had now also become a criminal offence.

For prostitutes and other residents of the red-light areas this law became a nightmare. It became a licence to put any prostitute in jail. It also gave way to bribes on a regular basis from the prostitutes, just to keep themselves out of lock-ups. Although the ordinance requires very strict evidence, the police used it to throw people in jail without evidence and later release them after extorting money. The biggest complaint of the leaders of the red-light areas was that the police, if angry at the community or a particular family for not paying their monthly bribe, would pick a dancing girl up from her house and pick up any male *Kanjar* from the street and simply book them under Zina. In fact, the law made prostitution illegal and according to the perspective of the government it was acceptable for the police to use it as a beating stick. They wanted to intimidate the community to the extent that the *Kanjars* would leave both the area and the profession.

The abuse of this law was not only perpetrated on the prostitutes, but it has been used against all women. Poor women, who are inherently more vulnerable, frequently fell victim. A strange confusion between rape and adultery in the earlier years allowed the courts to change an unproven case of rape into an adultery case against the woman, taking the pregnancy of the rape victim as evidence of adultery. As the adult age according to this law could be as young as 10-12 years old, a rape case of such a girl, in light of lack of witnesses or evidence, was also seen as sex with consent and therefore she was liable to be charged with adultery.

In some of the most extreme cases, Pakistani feminists took to the streets and the punishments were stopped before execution. The liberals and women's activists of the country have fought against this law vigorously for the last 20 years to the extent that this has become an icon for the resistance against discriminatory laws. They have undertaken campaigns, organised rallies, used media for awareness raising and promoted debates on this issue. The Permanent Commission on the Status of Women (a government body) issued a brave report condemning this law and recommending that the government repeal it entirely.

In the 1950s a High Court order legitimised the dancing girls as artists and gave them permission to perform for three hours in the evening. That is the only legal cover they have obtained so far. The rest of their activities, as far as the red-light areas and tens of thousands of brothels in the country are concerned, remain illegal businesses that operate as an open secret. The usual clients know where and how to find the brothels and to some extent the police are also familiar with most of their activities. It is only bribery that enables them to continue their operation. The police obviously have an upper hand and can abuse their authority at any time.

Key issues faced

The obvious issues related to this phenomenon are the prejudice and discrimination that the community engaged in this profession experiences from the society at large. This culminates in the form of police brutality and extortion, lack of attention to the development of their residential areas by the government departments, social isolation, and extreme negative reaction if the 'stigmatised' people try to blend into the 'good' people.

Another set of issues relates to the health of this community. They have been targeted as one of the high-risk groups for HIV infection, and various organisations have started work there, not only for HIV, but for other sexually transmitted diseases (STDs) also. Other than the few HIV-oriented NGOs that have come up, hardly any group is able to organise itself to deal with the difficulties the community faces. The community is in a period of steep decline. Many are leaving their traditional workplaces and quietly moving their business to other residential areas of the cities. They are focused on immediate survival, not on fighting battles for their rights. This sense of immediacy stems from the deep social stigma that is associated with the profession. There is no concept of a 'reformed prostitute' in Pakistan. Any woman who is labelled as having been a prostitute (or even related to one) stands a minuscule chance of obtaining any other form of livelihood. The only exceptions to this rule are a few young women who with their beauty and talent have moved to the film and mainstream music industries.

The stigma itself is an indicator of the major contradictions society has had on this issue. The debate at this stage is about raising important questions: why is it that society on the one hand does not want this 'evil' and on the other hand supports this profession by not allowing women to leave it and mix with the 'good' women of society? Why does society not reprimand the male clients for making the choice of indulging in these services? Why can a male be a client and quit whenever he wants to without any stigma lurking with him throughout his life, while female prostitutes do not have the space for the same choice of leaving prostitution when they please? Why are women and people from these service-providing communities always in the spotlight for criticism, and the other party – the clients – never talked about, called names or stigmatised? They both are parties in this phenomenon of prostitution: does society protect the clients and keep the focus on the service provider just to give protection to influential clients (Saeed, 2001)?

A new wave of discussion has brought to light the whole larger backdrop of the patriarchal society and the responsibility of mainstream society in perpetuating the occupation, the abusive aspects of the profession and the stigma that weigh heavily on the women in this profession. The real debate, currently, is not around the immediate issues of how to deal with the police or how the prostitutes could make the clients use condoms. It is beginning to revolve around the whole concept of 'good women' and 'bad women'. The weight that a 'bad woman' carries – her stigma, which is bequeathed to her future generations – and the weight a 'good woman' carries – her respect and honour – is now a matter of open discussion. Thus, if we look at the phenomenon from this perspective, the main issue for those in prostitution is not why women join this profession, but why they cannot choose to leave it.

Poverty is commonly held out as the major factor inducing women to join this profession. The recent discussion on prostitution in Pakistan considers this to be a myth. This is a myth created to hide the real reasons that are more difficult to face. The analysis of the patriarchal roots of this profession is generally avoided, maintaining the focus on poverty or the morality. This trend is being changed gradually. The section below presents a brief discussion on why women join this profession, followed by why they cannot leave it at their will.

Reasons for entry into prostitution

Most of the traditional prostitutes enter the trade because they are born into the families who are involved in this occupation and they are socialised from childhood to follow this career path. Those that are in the brothels are mostly coerced into a relationship or marriage and then sold or brought to this business through kidnapping and trafficking. No research has been done to obtain any specific numbers of women inducted into the trade in this manner.

The trafficked women in Pakistani brothels can be from Bangladesh, Burma and Afghanistan. The reasons for the women coming from Bangladesh and Burma are straightforward: poverty has forced them to look for jobs outside the country, and agents then trick them into prostitution. Many Afghan women came as refugees and have been coerced into prostitution as soon as they crossed the border and were most vulnerable. This again is carried out through a series of agents who promise them jobs, but end up selling them into the business. These women are found more in the brothels of the frontier provinces and Islamabad. Pakistani women have rarely been trafficked out of the country.

In addition, there are a limited number of young women who join this occupation for pocket money. There is some unsubstantiated information that indicates that those who are in this field through traditional means, but now work out of their new homes in smart suburbs manage to convince college girls to take up the profession as a part-time job to cover the expenses of being a 'modern woman'. However, in view of the social stigma attached to this profession in this country and the emphasis given to one's past social networks it can be inferred that the tendency of women to take up prostitution out of free choice is still extremely limited.

Thus, women are mostly in prostitution because that is what they inherited as a profession from their families, or they were coerced into it. Poverty does not appear to be a major cause of pushing women into prostitution. Even when poor women are inducted there is an element of coercion or force.

Exit from the profession

In Pakistan, the questions raised by recent discussions on prostitution are focused less on the reasons for entry, but more on the reasons why women cannot leave the profession when they want to. This issue has become important whether entry was induced by a woman's socialisation process or was forced upon her. Theoretically, if poverty or free choice was the reason for getting into the profession, we need to ask why women cannot leave the profession if they feel like it. In answering this question one runs into all the abusive networks and control politics that surround them. Obviously, the pimps and management that make money directly from their activities are involved, and would go to any extreme to prevent them from quitting. However, they are aided in their control measures by a society in general that will not accept the women as normal members if they choose to leave the profession. Although the mainstream norms proclaim that prostitution is a social ill, the question arises then, why should society not welcome anyone who is willing to abandon this disreputable profession? Unfortunately, this is not the case and the stigma associated with a prostitute's past would continue to be held up against the advancement of her succeeding generations.

Conclusions

The phenomenon of prostitution in Pakistan, as in the rest of South Asia, has to be understood in the local cultural setting. There is an occupational group that identifies prostitution as a hereditary profession. Through this group, prostitution has been coupled with music, dancing and other types of entertainment. It exists also in the form of brothels, where its link to music and dancing is not retained and women are usually coerced or kidnapped into the profession.

The social conditions of South Asia, of which Pakistan is an integral part, are still dominated by an overtly patriarchal system. Regardless of the brave struggle of the women's movement in Pakistan, the overall system continues to give men the social responsibility for judging women's morality. Thus, men determine a woman's fate by categorising her as being a moral and chaste person or as having a bad character. Prostitutes are the icons for a 'bad woman' in mainstream society.

The common perspectives about prostitution that exist in Pakistani society focus either on eradication or reform of the profession. Government and mainstream society, in general, think of eradication of this profession as a solution. Activists acknowledge the abuse that women in this trade experience and are inclined more towards reforming the profession to ensure their safety and healthcare. Some progressive thinkers in the country want the government to leave prostitutes alone and not interfere at all. They think prostitution is like any other profession and that these women have the right to earn a living in any way they want. This view is held by only a minority.

Very limited research is available on the topic; however, a recent ethnography has moulded the way of thinking about this community. This research study (Saeed, 2001) questioned the double standards of Pakistani society in blaming the immorality of women who are in prostitution, and fully protecting the men who use the service and support the system. That book has questioned the stigma associated with the women in the profession (as opposed to the men who are clients), which becomes the biggest hurdle to living a normal life for these women. This stigma also plays an important role in confining them to this profession and not allowing them to move out, even if they are ready to. Another book, *The dancing girls of Lahore* (Brown, 2005) has just come out and has added to the insights into the lives of prostitutes.

In terms of action research or work on the social issues of prostitutes, the only area that has become an entry point is health, and that is specific to STDs or HIV. It is at initial stage and could be seen as foundation for future work.

Finally I will address future trends and directions, both within the trade of prostitution and related to the efforts undertaken to address this phenomenon. These trends are based on observation and not on evidence from research data.

First, the future trends in the profession of prostitution:

- The traditional form of prostitution is changing from the *kotha* system, where prostitutes operated from a red-light area in their shops, to going out on musical 'variety shows' in rural fairs, family celebrations and sometimes private sector entertainment programmes. This they consider a modern form of entertainment and use these events to access potential clients.
- Women from this group of traditional prostitutes will continue to move willingly to Dubai and other Middle Eastern countries.
- Women from Central Asia and Afghanistan are trafficked into the brothels of the country. The government has enforced a law on trafficking, but this trend will continue. Other countries might join this trend if they experience a war or political crisis situation.
- The number and forms of brothels in big and small cities will continue to increase. Women prostitutes' vulnerability will increase as the brothels increase in number compared with the family-owned *kothas*.

Second, future trends and directions in terms of government policy and the thinking of wider society:

- The government's efforts to curb prostitution have focused more on the traditional prostitutes, since that system is more visible and open. This focus will continue. The government will not bother about the brothels that are hidden and not so open as the traditional red-light areas are.
- The government has been successful in harassing the residents of the traditional red-light areas, and many of them have moved out already to other parts of the cities. Most of the bazaars where they used to have music and dancing are being replaced by shoemaking factories. This trend will continue in future.
- The social stigma placed by the traditional society continues, but there are some chances of a shift in the thinking.

- A change in thinking could be a trend in the future, where the whole concept of good and bad women is questioned, rather than keeping all the focus on prostitutes as bad women.
- In future, it is possible that the government as well as society may shift its focus from seeing prostitution as a national issue to an international issue, so that there is more learning and less tendency to deny and hide the issue with embarrassment.

It is hoped that the trend of doing research on this topic is considered crucial to developing a firm strategy and a more comprehensive perspective on the phenomenon. It is also hoped that civil society might take up the issue at a conceptual level and not only think of the communities at high risk from HIV/AIDS.

Notes

[1] Equity is also affected by the level of political participation by the poor; participation must be meaningful. 'For example, India has a long democratic tradition but since local participation depends on social caste, the poor often have little influence' (Litvack et al, 1998, p 17).

[2] Hadood Ordinances were a set of laws related to adultery, murder, alcohol drinking, theft etc. These were supposedly a part of Zia-ul-Haq's attempt to bring back 'Islamic punishments' in order to create an 'Islamic society'. The punishments prescribed were claimed to be what was in Quran or Fiqah (the Islamic law derived later on Islamic principles tailored to political pressures of the time). In general these ordinances are seen as tools for political control and influence.

Recommended further reading

If we review the literature on prostitution in South Asia we would find many books starting from 1920, even earlier. However, if we look at books published on prostitution in Pakistan, the number is amazingly low. Some of them are based on information about politicians and their affairs with prostitutes, giving it a scandalous flavour. *Taboo* was the first academic research-based book on the subject in the country. It was written in English and is available in Urdu and Hindi under the name of *Kalunk*. It is mandatory reading if researching prostitution in Pakistan. Recently *The dancing girls from lahore* has been a sound addition to the body of knowledge.

Other materials published are short stories or novels. Literature has dealt with this issue in terms of bringing out the suffering of those women living in prostitution. It has highlighted the lives of prostitute as a neglected segment of the society.

Books

Brown, L. (2005) *The dancing girls of Lahore: Selling love and saving dreams in Pakistan's ancient pleasure district*, New York: Harper Collins.

Saeed, F. (2001) *Taboo!: The hidden culture of a red light area*, Karachi: Oxford University Press, (www.pak_philes.com/taboo).

In Urdu

Hussain, M. (2001) *Pakistan men jisaam faroshi*, Lahore: Nigaarshat Publishers.

Zaheer, A.B. (2002/2004) *Parliament Se Bazaar-e-Husn Tak (pakistani siyasat daano'n ke sharamnaak scandals ki hoshruba tafseelaat),* Lahore: Shaam ke Ba'd Publications.

Literature

Kaashmiri, S. (nd) *Us bazaar men (In that bazaar)* – this book is not available any more, even for reference. However, it is well known and might be available in any private collection.

Newspaper articles

Anybody pursuing this topic in Pakistan would have to do a search on newspaper articles (news items as well as features); some organisations have electronic materials, others categorise physical clippings by theme. Some examples of articles are given below:

Aslam, S. (1990) 'Dancing girls granted bail', *Frontier Post*, 30 June.

Bhatti, M. (1989) 'Multan's candid courtesan', *Friday Times*, 20-26 July.

Bhatti, M. (1989) 'To be or not to be', *Friday Times*, 15-21 July.

References

Arif, K.M. (2001) *Khaki shadows: Pakistan 1947-1997*, Oxford: Oxford University Press.

Asian Development Bank (ADB) (2000) *Women in Pakistan,* Country briefing paper, Islamabad: Asian Development Bank.

Brody, A. (ed) (1997) *Moving the whore stigma*, Bangkok: Global Alliance Against Trafficking of Women.

Brown, L. (2005) *The dancing girls of Lahore: Selling love and saving dreams in Pakistan's ancient pleasure district*, London: Fourth Estate.

Cohen, S.P. (2005) *The idea of Pakistan*, Lahore: Vanguard Books.

Golden, A. (1998) *Memoirs of a geisha*, London: Vintage.

Hayward, F.R. (2000) *Breaking the earthenware jar: Lessons from South Asia to end violence against women and girls*, Kathmandhu: UNICEF, United Nations.

Human Rights Commission of Pakistan (2004) *State of Human Rights in 2003*, Lahore: Human Rights Commission of Pakistan

Joardar, B. (1984) *Prostitution in historical and modern perspectives*, Delhi: Inter-India Publications.

Joardar, B. (1985) *Prostitution in nineteenth and early twentieth century Calcutta*, Delhi: Inter-India Publications.

Litvack, J.J. and Bird, J.A. (1998) *Rethinking decentralization in developing countries*, Sector Studies Series, Washington, DC: International Bank for Reconstruction and Development/ World Bank.

Madhur, A.S. and Gupta, B.L. (1965) *Prostitution and prostitution*, Agra: Ram Prasad and Sons.

Mazari, S.K. (2002) *A journey to disillusionment*, Oxford: Oxford University Press.

Ministry of Women's Development (2005) *Pakistan national report Beijing +10*, Islamabad: Ministry of Women's Development, Government of Pakistan.

Mumtaz, K. and Shaheed, F. (1984) *One step forward, two steps backward*, Lahore, Pakistan: Women Action Forum.

Nyrop, R.F. (ed) (1995) *Pakistan: A country study*, Washington DC: Federal Research Division, Library of Congress.

Punekar, S.D. and Rao, K. (1967) *A study of prostitutes in Bombay*, Bombay: Lalvani Publishing House.

Rao, M.R. and Rao, J.U.R. (1969) *The prostitutes of Hyderabad*, Andhra Pardesh: Association for Moral Hygiene in India.

Rose, H.A. (1933) *A glossary of the tribes and castes of the Punjab and North-West Frontier Province*, Lahore: Asian Educational Services.

Saeed, F. (2001) *Taboo!: The hidden culture of a red light area*, Karachi: Oxford University Press.

Scott, G.R. (1976) *A history of prostitution: from antiquity to the present day*, New York: AMS Press.

Shaheed, F. and Zaidi, Y. (2005) *Pakistan: Ten Years into the Beijing Platform for Action*, Pakistan, Islamabad: NGO Organising Committee.

United Nations (2003) *Promoting the millennium development goals in Asia and the Pacific: Meeting the challenges of poverty reduction*, New York: United Nations.

Weiss, A. (1986) *Islamic reassertion in Pakistan: The application of Islamic laws in a modern state*, Syracuse, NY: University of Syracuse Press.

World Bank (2002) *Poverty and vulnerability in South Asia*, Washington, DC: World Bank.

EIGHT

Selling bodies/selling pleasure: the social organisation of sex work in Taiwan

Mei-Hua Chen

Introduction

In daily practice, prostitution is simply the explicit selling and buying of sex. However, if we reduce the complex social practices of prostitution to sex we will fail to examine the economic, political and ideological underpinnings of prostitution, that is, the social problems that underlie it. As O'Connell Davidson has argued, 'the ills associated with prostitution can be addressed only through far broader political struggles to rid the world of poverty, racism, homophobia and sexism' (1998, p 189). This chapter will discuss the historical development of prostitution in Taiwan, the legal and feminist responses to prostitution, and some projections on the future of prostitution in Taiwan.

The national context

Organising against prostitution

The social and legal status of women in Taiwan has greatly improved in the past two decades. This success can be partly attributed to the campaigns of the women's movement in Taiwan, focusing on promoting women's equal rights via an effort to amend unequal laws. Women's organisations have existed since the 1920s; however, women's organisations propagating feminist ideals and devoting themselves to radical social change did not emerge until the Awakening Foundation was founded in 1982 (Hsieh and Chueh, 2005). The first campaign against the trafficking of children was organised by the Awakening Foundation, the Taiwan Association for Human Rights and the Presbyterian Church in Taiwan in January 1987. It is generally considered the beginning of the women's movement in Taiwan. The campaign identified punters, traffickers, brothel owners, pimps and corrupt police at the centre of the abuse of child prostitutes. Moreover, inappropriate policies against the indigenous tribes that let them fall into poverty were considered as the major reason that young women and girls from these tribes were sold to brothels. Subsequently, the relatively large number of indigenous women and girls in prostitution became a public concern. Growing out of this initial campaign, the Taipei Women's Rescue Foundation was founded with the goal of eliminating trafficking of women and child prostitution. The early campaign against prostitution helped to legitimise the creation of other women's organisations, as well, which eventually led to the development of a fully fledged women's movement in Taiwan.

Legal efforts against prostitution

In the legal efforts against prostitution, since the late 1980s Taiwanese women's organisations have demanded reform of the patriarchal 1930 Family Law, which until the mid-1990s entirely denied women equal rights in marriage. Feminist scholarship has extensively documented the particular ways in which marriage in Taiwan has served as a patriarchal institution that treats women as 'household servants' (*jia nu*) and shapes women's domesticity (see, for example, Liu, 1995). Until the last decade, the Family Law gave husbands greater rights to property and to child custody than wives. In addition, regular payments of alimony to divorced women were not enforced by the legal system. Even today, women's inferior status in marriage is such that many women soon fall into poverty after divorce. Chang and Wu (2005) cite that the ratio of single mothers who become heads of households and fall into poverty is three times that of single fathers, which partly explains the femininisation of poverty. Some women have reported how they managed to get a divorce, then, finding themselves in poverty, had to turn to prostitution for survival (Hong and Tsai, 1998).

Women in the labour force

The right to work has been one of the oldest issues taken up by the women's movement in Taiwan. Women's labour-force participation has stayed at a level between 45% and 46% in the past two decades in Taiwan. Women's low rate of participation in the labour market stems in a large part from the lack of a good childcare system. According to government statistics, 4,651,000 women did not enter the labour market in 2001 because they had to do housework and childcare (DGBAS, 2002). Yet the majority of those women had at one time been in the job market. The top two reasons they gave for leaving the workplace were childcare responsibilities and marriage (Chen, 2000).

It is well documented that Taiwanese women have suffered from gendered exclusions within the labour market for many decades. Chin-fen Chang (1995), for example, argues that women are excluded from many jobs by the 'men-only' recruitment policy. In addition they are forced to tolerate sexual harassment, unequal pay for equal work, and unequal opportunities in obtaining job training and promotion. According to government statistics, in the year 2000, women's average salary only reached 74% of men's, and women occupied only 15% of managerial positions (DGBAS, 2003).

Women's legal and social status, however, has greatly changed since the late 1990s. The tragic rape and murder in 1996 of feminist activist and politician Peng Wan-ru, who devoted herself to promoting women's participation in politics, dramatically accelerated the course of the women's movement. Her death raised public awareness of all kinds of violence against women. Politicians perceived the impending political risks of failing to take serious measures to protect women from violence. Thus, soon after her death, a body of gendered legislation was removed and gender-equal legislation was passed. Several amendments to the Family Law, for instance, were passed to guarantee women equal rights in marriage. The Anti-Domestic Violence Law was enacted in 1998, and the articles in criminal law, where rape was considered as violating 'virtuous custom' rather than women's sexual autonomy, were replaced by feminist-backed sexual offence articles in 1999. Moreover, the Gender Equality Labour Law was enacted in 2002 to protect women's equal rights in employment. In a more direct move to confront gender inequality, in 1997 the central government set up the Commission on Women's Rights Promotion, composed of local women's organisations and all related governmental branches dealing with women's policies. However, it is a consulting commission on women's policies, rather than a decision-making body with real power.

A sketch of commercial sex in Taiwan

Much historical research traces the current Taiwanese sex industry back to the Japanese colonial era (for example, Lin, 1995; Huang, 1999). During the colonial period (1896-1945), Taiwan had a licensed, dual prostitution system divided by race, with one sector serving the Japanese colonists, the other the Taiwanese. Both sectors were further divided into hierarchies by types of service and the social class of clients. The purpose of licensed prostitution was to make 'safe sex' – in terms of disease transmission and social control – available to both Japanese colonisers and local Taiwanese men.

After the Second World War, policing prostitution became an issue for the Chinese Nationalist government of Taiwan, which officially took control of the island under Chiang Kai-Shek in 1945. In that year, the nationalist government prohibited prostitution in order to correct the 'improper social atmosphere' that had been brought about by Japanese colonists (Lin, 1997, p 11). Nonetheless, many cafés and bars were set up to cater underground to the undiminished demand for commercial sex. The prevailing attitude was that the sexual urges of the young Nationalist soldiers from mainland China should be satisfied; they were not allowed to get married, in order to show the government's determination to counterattack mainland China. Set up by the Nationalist government in 1945, the Taiwan provincial government, which ruled until 1997, passed laws to legalise *special bars*, which in reality were licensed brothels. The government failed to regulate these special bars, resulting in a serious sexually transmitted disease (STD) problem (Huang, 1999). In 1956, the government reacted by passing the Act of Management of Prostitution in Taiwan Province to control unruly commercial sex and STDs. According to the Act, local governments were able to issue licences to brothels and prostitutes, and prostitutes were subject to regular medical check-ups. However, it did not diminish the activities of new sex-oriented entertainment establishments. Hence, in 1962, the Regulation of Management of Special Businesses was passed to legalise the existence of four different kinds of businesses – dance halls, bars, special tearooms, and special coffee shops – and to allow the hiring of women for chatting, drinking, singing and dancing with clients. These women by law were not allowed to be involved in commercial sex or to participate in 'obscene behaviour'. Nonetheless, such behaviour permeated these sexual establishments. The decriminalisation of these special businesses turned Taiwan into a sexual haven for Japanese and Western tourists as well as American soldiers during the 1960s and 1970s. The saying was: 'Go shopping in Hong Kong, gambling in Macau, and whoring in Taiwan'. Moreover, the official tour guides of the Taiwan Tourism Bureau went so far as to suggest that tourists take a sex tour to Bei-tour, Taipei (Jiang, 1987, quoted in Du, 1998, p 45; my translation). Prostitution therefore came to be justified not only in terms of male sexual urges but also as a means of serving the state's interests in winning foreign exchange through sex tourism.

Sex tourism was tolerated until it was named and shamed in the 1960s. *Time* magazine in December 1967 reported on the sex tourism in Bei-tour and published a picture showing an American soldier bathing with two nude Taiwanese prostitutes (cited in Peng, 2004, p 51), after which, in a show of determination, the government abolished those special businesses in Bei-tour. It also stopped issuing licences to set up 'special businesses' in the 1970s. Many sexual establishments once again went underground. In seeming contradiction to the freeze on licences for existing special businesses, the government attempted to manage sexual establishments more adequately by amending the Regulation of Management of Special Businesses and legalising four more types of special businesses (massage parlours, karaoke singing halls, barber salons, and saunas). The special businesses now numbered eight and were known as the *ba da harng yeh* (literally, eight special businesses) (Liu, 1997, p 18).

The licensed prostitution that was legalised in 1956 and the 'special businesses' have constituted the two major sex sectors of the Taiwanese sex industry in the past four decades. The former is commonly known as 'body-selling' (*mai shen*) and the latter as 'pleasure-selling' (*mai xiao*). Commercial sex in the 'body-selling' sector involves providing explicit sex to clients, and relations between clients and workers are more commercialised than in the 'pleasure-selling' sector, where there is a whole range of more personalised services and relations catering to clients' diverse demands. As Hwang's (1996) research has shown, Taiwanese sex workers in the 'pleasure-selling' sector have to play a series of female roles ranging from waitress and entertainer to prostitute. The two sectors also differ from each other in terms of legal status. Women in the 'body-selling' sector, which includes streetwalking and illegal brothel work, usually suffer from police harassment since their work is directly targeted by the prostitution laws, while the 'pleasure-selling' sector is much more tolerated in the name of urban hedonism.

Debates on prostitution

Although women's organisations work enthusiastically against prostitution especially in the area of eradicating child prostitution, the majority of Taiwanese turn a blind eye to the sex industry as long as it is not too visible and does not involve trafficking in women. Hence, policing prostitution hardly constituted an important social issue until late 1997, when licensed prostitution in Taipei was abolished. The issue divided feminists and women's organisations into two camps: one demanding abolition and the other campaigning for the decriminalisation of commercial sex. Although policing prostitution has been the focus of the debate, there are several layers of conflicts between these two camps. They have, for instance, disagreed over whether prostitution is an issue of gender oppression or sexual oppression, whether doing commercial sex is nothing but sex or a kind of work, whether prostitutes come into this job by 'force' or 'free choice', and whether the third parties involved are sexual exploiters or neutral business organisers.

In the abolition camp, the major figures are Liu Yu-xiu, Lin Fung-mei and Hwang Shu-ling. Women's organisations such as ECPAT-Taiwan, the Garden of Hope Foundation, and Taipei Women's Rescue Foundation also strongly back this position. According to Lin (1998), the abolition camp thinks that sexuality should be located within the gender system as a whole. Prostitution thus is not an issue of whether women should have the right to do sex work, but 'how the sex industry produces and reproduces sexuality and allocates men and women to different positions in the sex industry' (Lin, 1998, p 63, my translation). The abolition camp defines prostitution as a gender issue in which men exploit women's bodies and sexuality, and thus what prostitution provides is considered by abolitionists as sex that men desire. Moreover, following Hwang's (1996) research and the legacy of eliminating child prostitutes in the 1980s, this camp also has emphasised the link between trafficking and commercial sex. It is claimed that prostitutes are usually controlled (either by drugs or force) by gangsters or organised criminals. Huang (1998) has taken the view that all kinds of commercial sex constitutes violence against women and violates human rights.

In contrast, 128 formerly licensed Taipei prostitutes established the Taipei Licensed Prostitutes' Self-help Association to demand their 'right to work'. Two women worker organisations, the Taipei Solidarity Front of Women Workers and Pink Collar, later joined the anti-abolition camp, claiming that former licensed brothels were just like ordinary factories and licensed prostitutes like any other workers (Wang and Ku, 1998). Apart from the grass-roots women's organisations, a few feminist scholars who advocate sexual liberation have also joined the anti-abolition camp. For example, Josephine Ho (1998) has treated the pro- and anti-abolition debates as an antagonism between the politics of 'good women' and 'bad women'. The abolition of licensed prostitution is considered a form of suppression of women who dare to transgress sexual and social taboos. Conceptualising prostitution in terms of labour, Josephine Ho (1998, p 222) offers a justification for sex work in the light of the historical transformation of labour in a capitalist market. She explains how productive and reproductive labour that was once carried out in private is now integrated into the capitalist market through the commodification of labour. Sexual labour was once provided by housewives but has been transferred into the market. Moreover, this historical change, she claims, not only serves the interests of the capitalists, but also functions to liberate women's labour and diversify women's lives.

Both camps universalise diverse forms of commercial sex, including the varied relations between sex workers and third parties. The camps are polarised into the anti-abolition view that commercial sex is organised to the satisfaction of all sides and the pro-abolition view that it benefits one party at the expense of others. In short, sex workers are either just like ordinary workers or are seriously exploited by the third parties. However, sex workers' working conditions vary in how the work is organised and in employee status (Lim, 1998; O'Connell Davidson, 1998). The anti-abolition camp is certainly correct in arguing that it is the gendered prostitution laws that constantly (re)produce the 'miserable prostitutes', and the pro-abolition camp is right in wanting to stop sexual exploitation in the sex industry. However, what is missing from this debate, and what should be of great concern for feminists, is a critical questioning of the nature of the labour, the ways in which labour is organised in the market, and how different organisation of sex work shapes diverse working conditions and work experiences among sex workers.

Laws and policies

Existing laws and policies on prostitution

Currently the major regulations regarding prostitution include criminal law, the Social Order Maintenance Act (SOM), and the Act for Prevention of Child and Juvenile Involvement in Commercial Sex (PCJICS). The criminal law does not criminalise prostitutes, but makes pimping, trafficking of women and children, and running and managing brothels felonies (Article 231). However, the SOM criminalises adult prostitutes and people who solicit for prostitution. According to Article 80 of the SOM, 'those who intend to profit by having sex with people, or those who solicit, in public or areas accessible to the public, in order to prostitute or pimp for prostitution should be punished' (my translation). Accordingly, adult prostitutes and people who solicit can be fined up to NT$30,000 or detained for three days. After having been arrested three times in a year, prostitutes can be detained and sent to government-funded shelters for six months to one year. With the legacy of rescuing child prostitutes in the late 1980s, local feminist scholars and women's organisations are very concerned about young girls' involvement in commercial sex and sex-related urban entertainments. The PCJICS was enacted in 1995 to protect children from prostitution. Buying sex from children under 18 is criminalised (Article 22). The Act not only criminalises people who pimp, lure, use, or force children under 18 to become involved in prostitution (Article 23), but also criminalises people who use any kind of media to 'circulate, broadcast, or publish any information which might lure or influence people to perform commercial sex with others' (Article 29, my translation). Moreover, children found to be involved in prostitution are to be sent to government-funded halfway centres within 24 hours of being reported, and kept in those centres for between two months and two years (Article 15).

Operation and analysis of laws and policies

Article 80 of the SOM is infamous for its gendered ideology regarding prostitution; namely, that buying sex is acceptable, while offering sex in exchange for money is forbidden. Therefore, the behaviour of men who constitute the majority of sexual consumers is acceptable, while the sex workers – for the most part women – are criminalised. The gendered legislation reflects the century-old idea that men have 'sexual urges' while women are responsible for their 'sexual attractions' (McIntosh, 1978). Indeed, using a prostitute is taken for granted as normal behaviour and widely practised as a rite of passage among young men, constituting part of the hegemonic masculinity of Taiwan (Chen, 2003a).

Criminalising prostitutes while tolerating punters not only serves to consolidate gender hierarchy, it also constantly (re)produces the 'miserable prostitutes' of Taiwan. As the literature shows (for example, COSWAS, 1998; SFWW, 1998), this situation makes sex workers suffer from repeated exploitation and oppression by, for example, allowing abusive punters to refuse payment, dubious police tactics of all kinds to arrest prostitutes, and police corruption. The risk of being arrested by undercover police puts many sex workers in a terrifying situation. Nonetheless, the degree to which sex workers take the risk of being harassed or arrested by police varies according to the work setting. In my own research (Chen, 2003b), I have found that bar girls who work in licensed special bars are happy to report that 'police raids' are indeed very perfunctory. Conversely, streetwalkers, and sex workers who run their businesses independently or work in illegal brothels or small-scale call-girl services, turn out to be soft targets for police raids. In order to work safely, many independent sex workers have to seek out third parties for protection or move to work in organised sex establishments. Criminalising prostitution therefore puts sex workers in a risky situation in which women have to choose either to work independently without safety, or to work safely without autonomy.

Criminalising prostitution makes the situation even harder for migrant sex workers. Recently, Chinese migrant sex workers either smuggled into Taiwan or brought in through phoney arranged marriages with local men, have become the most vulnerable group to suffer at the hands of traffickers, pimps and corrupt police. The biggest scandal of this kind broke out when many police officers were revealed to have been acting as gangsters kidnapping Chinese migrant sex workers and then demanding huge ransoms from their affiliated sex establishments (Chang and Hwang, 2001). Such events strongly suggest that instead of cutting down on trafficking of women, criminalising prostitution makes sex workers more vulnerable to the police and third-party exploitation, and paves the way for police corruption.

The infamous 'anti-porn ads' clause, Article 29 of PCJICS, is intended to prevent children from access to any pornographic materials that *might* lead them to become involved in commercial sex. Nonetheless, it is so strict that posting a message such as 'looking for one-night-stand' on the internet (Tsay, 2002) could be considered a form of soliciting prostitution. Thus, Ho (2002) argues that many police actions cracking down on 'porn ads', far from preventing children's involvement in the sex industry, constitute a concrete barrier for adults to engage in multiple sexual encounters.

Hughes (1999) argues that cyberspace has been one of the hottest sites for the sex industry to organise commercial sex globally. Pressured by NGOs such as ECPAT-Taiwan, the Garden of Hope Foundation, Mennonite Good Shepherd Centre and Taipei Women's Rescue Foundation, local police stations use Article 29 to hunt people who circulate seductive ads on the internet. Police usually focus on soft targets such as independent workers, underage workers and inexperienced or first-time casual workers. Compared with other performance on assignments, the police are extremely efficient and show a good record in dealing with 'anti-porn ads'. According to the Statistics of Justice (SJ, 2003), 178 people were prosecuted under Article 29 in 1998. The number of people prosecuted in 1999 rose to 345. The newest statistics show that 1,344 persons were prosecuted in 2002. However, many cases were dropped due to police abuse in executing the Article or violating the due process of law when enforcing Article 29.[1]

As abusive execution of these laws is so prevalent, human rights groups and prostitutes' rights groups strongly argue that the common practice of 'fishing' for potential targets by the police indeed violates the due process of law. Above all, the police sometimes instigate the crimes they are assigned to prevent. The accusation is indeed confirmed by my research on young girls in halfway centres. These young girls had been involved in commercial sex in diverse ways; however, they were all recorded as committing internet *yuan juh jiau jih*[2] (mutual sex aid). For example, many of the young girls had worked as hostesses in a karaoke bar, but it did not involve commercial sex. Some of the girls were victims of sexual assault, but were recorded as 'performing *yuan juh jiau jih*' because their abusers had left some money for them. The logic of the police officers was rather straightforward: since both money and sex were involved, it was considered to be commercial sex rather than sexual assault. Nonetheless, it is important to note that Taiwanese criminal law does not recognise children under 16 as sexual subjects who are able to 'consent' to being involved in any sexual relationship. Children under 16, paradoxically, are not qualified to consent to sex but can be arrested for engaging in commercial sex!

Debates on legalisation and decriminalisation, and their relevance

Current prostitution laws are extremely gendered as well as flawed. The anti-abolition camp supports decriminalising prostitution: they propose that sellers, buyers and the third parties should be decriminalised. Commercial sex is thus treated as any other business that should be subjected only to ordinary business regulations in order to de-stigmatise prostitution. On the contrary, the abolition camp welcomes policies and legislation that might function to diminish the sex industry. Adopting the Swedish legislation that makes purchasing or attempting to purchase sexual services a criminal offence punishable by fines or up to six months' imprisonment is seriously under consideration. For the abolition camp, punishing sex buyers not only serves to diminish the sex industry, but also is likely to undermine the gendered sexuality in which men have relatively unlimited access to women's bodies and sexuality in the market.

The common ground of both camps is that they also agree that the clause 'punishing prostitutes' in the SOM Act is problematic and should be subject to change immediately. Nonetheless, the abolition camp demands to change the clause into 'punishing punters while tolerating prostitutes' and tends to criminalise the third parties involved; whereas the decriminalisation camp prefers decriminalising all the parties involved in prostitution (Fan, 2004). The abolition camp wants to reduce the sex industry by punishing punters; it seems unlikely that they will achieve this end. Making punters punishable means that clients have to take a risk to purchase sexual services. Therefore, it is more likely that they will purchase 'safer' sexual services in those well-organised sexual establishments that are licensed by the government and have a good connection with the police. In other words, punishing clients simply functions to dash the existence of independent sex workers and small-scale sexual establishments, rather than diminish the sex industry. On the contrary, it is likely that the sex market would come to be monopolised by several big sexual establishments, and sex workers would feel forced to work for them.

It is important to note that these debates regarding the prostitution laws are only among feminists and women's organisations. The government in fact does not take it seriously yet. After subsidising two research projects (total grant is NT$1,500,000) conducted by Shiah et al (2002) and Lan et al (2002), the government seems to have laid aside the issue of reforming prostitution policy. The Commission on Women's Rights Promotion regularly issues White Papers on women's policies, but its most recently issued Taiwan Women's Rights Report (FWRPD, 2003) deals only with the sexual exploitation of children. It points out that current child prostitution is highly related to runaway children rather than ones trafficked into the sex market. In order to prevent runaway children from turning to prostitution, the report suggests that schools should provide adequate guidance to young students, and the government should offer proper job opportunities for young girls. However, the report does not mention anything about adult prostitutes, nor does it propose any substantial projects to prevent adult women from prostitution or to provide social services to sex workers. Currently, the Collective of Sex Workers and Supporters (composed of former licensed Taipei prostitutes and supporters of sex work) is the only organisation directly engaged in helping adult streetwalkers and former licensed Taipei prostitutes who are unemployed. Prostitution is not only about selling and buying sex. Prostitution should not be reduced to an issue of concern for only a small portion of women. It is indeed linked to some key issues in larger society. Making buyers and sellers punishable is not likely to end the 'world's oldest profession'. Poverty, gender hierarchy and the ways in which masculinity is constructed in society are the major issues we all must confront.

Key issues faced

Reasons for entry into prostitution: making sense of prostitution

Although feminists do not intend to problematise or pathologise (female) prostitutes, the question of 'why women and girls prostitute' is always at the centre of prostitution debates. The Western sex work advocates argue that gender inequality in the labour market makes prostitution a reasonable and available choice under very limited material conditions (for example, Lopez-Jones, 1988; Lim, 1998). This perspective is also adopted by the International Labour Organisation-backed report, *The sex sector* (Lim, 1998), which focuses on prostitution in four South-East Asian countries: Indonesia, Malaysia, the Philippines and Thailand. The report sees the sex industry as part of the labour market and as constituting a huge economic sector in contemporary states. Moreover, women's inferior economic situation is linked to the gendered nature of the labour market. Jones et al (1998, p 35) suggest that the low wages of the Indonesian labour market provide the incentive for female workers to become sex actors and earn instant money. Taiwanese feminist scholars in both camps report that Taiwanese prostitutes mostly come from working-class and low educational backgrounds (for example, Hwang, 1996, p 124; Ji, 1998). Many of the grief stories of former Taipei licensed prostitutes also show that 'sacrificing a girl or woman to rescue a family' is sometimes the only way for a working-class family to survive (Wang and Wang, 2000, p 80; Huang and Huang, 2000, p 93). Contesting the stigma that prostitutes are greedy, lazy and prefer to earn 'easy money' (underage girls in particular), my research (Chen, 2003b) points out that the ways in which women and girls get into prostitution are far from straightforward but instead are full of twists and turns. Almost every interviewee had worked as a low-paid, low-status factory woman or drifted among the lowest service occupations, such as cleaner, hairdresser, or waitress, for many years until they could not survive on their inadequate pay cheques. Thus, to some extent, it is the labour market that constantly produces the reserve sex labour-force for the Taiwanese sex industry.

Moreover, the underdeveloped social welfare system in Taiwan plays an important role. Writing on child prostitution, Adams et al (1997) and Pitts (1997) stressed that a lack of social benefits, independent housing and income and the criminalisation of prostitutes made British child prostitutes more vulnerable to the abuse of police and pimps. Although the British social welfare system is under attack, it is identified as an important mechanism in dealing with child prostitution. However, the language of social welfare is very much a Western concept. Apart from taking in underage girls in halfway centres and schools, Taiwan's social welfare system does not offer proper services to these girls. Unmarried teenage mothers in fact reported that they failed to get adequate support from the social welfare system, and thus some of them had to turn to prostitution for survival (Chen, 2003b).

In the name of filial piety

Prostitution is caused in Taiwan not only because of economic hardships, but also because of the cultural beliefs in which women are expected to be both good daughters and good mothers. Gates (1987) used the term 'double hierarchy' to refer to the dual disadvantages of girls and women in Chinese society that stem from these two values of goodness. Children should absolutely obey the paternal authority. Moreover, girls suffer from the prevalent gender hierarchy within Chinese society at large. Indeed, the cultural practices of *nan neu yeou bie* (men and women are different) and *nan tzuen neu bei* (men are superior and women inferior) sum up the gender division and gender hierarchy in Taiwanese society.

It is very important to differentiate between daughters who are dutiful by choice from those who are coerced into being filial by duty. In the name of 'the principle of filial piety', a former licensed prostitute named Sue-lian said that her mother contracted her out in order to support the family. Sue-lian had become the major breadwinner of her family of origin. However, it brought her more and more economic burdens rather than honour, respect or authority. She reported:

> My mum is extremely *jonq nan ching neu* [i.e. privileges boys and condemns girls] ... She sold me to the brothel. She gave money to my elder brother to run small businesses. But his businesses always failed and ended up with huge debts. I paid for his and my sister's wedding. I paid for my father's funeral, and the betterment of our house. I almost paid for everything, but I didn't complain about it. (Sue-lian, 41, trafficked for 10 years, and 18 years as a licensed prostitute, in Chen, 2003b, p 181))

Sue-lian's narrative is not extraordinary. In Hwang's (1996, p 125) research, among 41 women (involved in commercial sex during their teens), 12 were sold to illegal brothels by their families when they were teenage girls. The cultural practice of *jonq nan ching neu* not only makes women's 'sacrifices' possible, it also creates an asymmetrical political and economic worth among daughters and sons. Many studies (for example, Boonchalaksi and Guest, 1998; Watenabe, 1998) have pointed out that South-East Asian prostitutes send back money from urban to rural areas, thereby creating a flow of money, but they seldom inform us of the ways in which this money is distributed in these rural households. Sue-lian's narratives showed that the way money is distributed follows the given gendered cultural practices of *jonq nan ching neu*, and in this way serves to consolidate the gender hierarchy in the household. It thus produces a vicious circle; men keep taking and women keep making sacrifices and are subjected to endless exploitation. Working women therefore find it difficult to leave prostitution. Guillaumin (1995, p 181) lists four different ways in which women's labour is appropriated by men in the household: the appropriation of time, of the products of the body, of sexual obligation and of the physical charge of disabled members as well as the healthy members of the group of the male sex. The ways Sue-lian's sexual labour was appropriated by her family (especially her brothers) identically matches the list. Even though Sue-lian reported that 'I didn't complain about it', we can sense that the relationship between Sue-lian and her family was very complex and should not, nor could be reduced to 'self-sacrifice'.

Conclusions

In this chapter I briefly described the diverse shapes that the Taiwanese sex industry has taken from the late 19th century up to the present time. Concerning sex workers' human rights, I surveyed the ways in which gendered legislation and abusive execution of the law works against women and girls in the sex industry. I argued that the 'miserable prostitutes' are indeed produced by the gendered legislation rather than by any essential quality of prostitution. I also highlighted the ways in which underage girls are severely exploited by third parties and abused by the police because of the strict legislation on anti-child pornography.

Contesting the views that claim that prostitutes mainly come from 'dysfunctional families' or are victims of (sexual) violence, I argued that the path to prostitution, rather than being straightforward, is full of twists and turns. Although the feminist literature shows that working-class women form the majority of the labour force in the sex industry, in itself poverty is not a sufficient reason for most women and girls to engage in commercial sex. Many sex workers drift between varied low-paid and low-status (service) occupations for a few years before entering the sex industry. Moreover, the ways women and girls become involved in commercial sex are also related to Taiwanese daily cultural practices that privilege men and boys while degrading women and girls.

In terms of reframing prostitution policy in the future, I would suggest that the government should locate prostitution in a more extensive social context, in which class, gender and sexuality are seen to intertwine in the shaping of prostitution. Since gender and class still underpin the modern sex industry, the government should make an effort to improve the employment of women and girls; specifically the government should offer an adequate employment, educational and social security programme to improve the social status of disadvantaged women and girls (for example, migrants, indigenous people, single mothers). Moreover, the government should pay attention to the flaws of the strict anti-child pornography Act (the PCJICS), and immediately take the actions necessary to decriminalise commercial sex.

Notes

[1] There were only 60 and 165 persons judged have to committed the crime in 1998 and 1999 respectively. However, there were 1,116 persons who committed the crime in 2002. It seems the courts have tended to tighten up the 'anti-porn ads' clause. See www.moj.gov.tw/f7_frame.htm

[2] The term '*yuan juh jiau jih*' originally came from Japan. Literally it means mutual sex aid between two individuals. In Taiwan, it is mainly considered as commercial sex of another kind. 'Internet *yuan juh jiau jih*' refers to commercial sex that is organised through the internet.

Recommended further reading

Chen, M.-H. (2003b) 'Selling body/selling pleasure: women negotiating poverty, work, and sexuality', unpublished PhD dissertation, York: Centre for Women's Studies, University of York, UK.

Lim, L.L. (ed) (1998) *The sex sector: The economic and social bases of prostitution in Southeast Asia*, Geneva: International Labour Office.

Lin, W.-H. and Hsieh, H.-C. (eds) (2005) *Gender, culture and society: Women's studies in Taiwan*, Women's studies in Asia series, Seoul: Ewha Woman's University Press.

References

Adams, N., Carter, C., Cater, S., Lopez-Jones, N. and Mitchell, C. on behalf of the English Collective of Prostitutes (1997) 'Demystifying child prostitution: a street view', in D. Barrett (ed) *Child prostitution in Britain: Dilemmas and practical responses*, London: Children's Society Press, pp 122–38.

Boonchalaksi, W. and Guest, P. (1998) 'Prostitution in Thailand', in L.L. Lim (ed) *The sex sector: The economic and social bases of prostitution in Southeast Asia*, Geneva: International Labour Office Press, pp 130–69.

Chang, C.-F. (1995) 'Does the resentment have an end – an analysis of the predicament of women workers', in Y.-X. Liu (ed) *The white book of Taiwanese women's situation 1995*, Taipei: China Times.

Chang, C.-F. and Wu, Y.-C. (2005) 'A critical review of women's labour market experiences in Taiwan', in W.-H. Lin and H.-C. Hsieh (eds) *Gender, culture and society: Women's studies in Taiwan*, Women's studies in Asia series, Seoul: Ewha Woman's University Press, pp 301-37.

Chang, R.-Z. and Hwang, Z.-R. (2001) 'Three police officers involved in kidnapping prostitutes to extort money', *United Daily*, 9 September, p 3.

Chen, M.-H. (2000) 'Rights to Work', in M.-H. Chen (ed) *Taiwanese women's rights report 1999* (1999), Taipei: Awakening Foundation.

Chen, M.-H. (2003a) 'Les désirs sexuels masculins et leurs contradictions: masculinité, style de vie et sexualité. Le cas des clients de prostituées à Taiwan', *Travail, Genre et Sociétés,* no 10, pp 107-28.

Chen, M.-H. (2003b) 'Selling body/ selling pleasure: women negotiating poverty, work, and sexuality', unpublished PhD dissertation, York: Centre for Women's Studies, University of York, UK.

Collective of Sex Workers and Supporters (1998) 'The result of abolition – sex industry goes underground', Proceedings of the 1998 World Action Forum for Sex Worker Rights, in L.-C. Shiah (ed) *Licensed prostitutes and sex workers' rights*, Taipei: COSWAS, pp 161–89.

Directorate-General of Budget, Accounting and Statistics (DGBAS) (2002) *The general situation of women's labour power* (available at www.dgbas.gov.tw/public/Attachment/411116155771.doc).

Directorate-General of Budget, Accounting and Statistics (DGBAS) (2003) *The general situation of women's economic ability in major countries* (available at www.dgbas.gov.tw/ct.asp?xItem=835&ctNode=3259).

Du, X.-Y. (1998) 'The creation and annihilation of prostitution in a patriarchal state', *Stir*, no 5, pp 44-54.

Fan, C. (2004) 'Punishing prostitutes or punishing punters? A debate regarding policing the sex industry', *Journal of Women and Gender Studies*, vol 71, pp 109-17.

Foundation of Women's Rights Promotion and Development (FWRPD) (2003) *Taiwan women's rights report*, Taipei: Foundation of Women's Rights Promotion and Development Press.

Gates, H. (1987) *Chinese working-class lives: Getting by in Taiwan*, Ithaca, NY: Cornell University Press.

Guillaumin, C. (1995) *Racism, sexism, power and ideology*, London and New York: Routledge.

Ho, J. (1998) 'Feminists' position on pornography and sex work', in J. Ho (ed) *Sex work: Prostitutes' rights in perspective*, Chungli: Centre for the Study of Sexualities, pp 813–54.

Ho, J. (2002) 'Protecting under-age children or punishing adults', *United Daily*.

Hong, M.-J. and Tsai, X.-L. (1998) 'If you really want to help, please listen to us', in L.-C. Shiah, S.-S. Chen and T.-C. Cheng (eds) *The homework of Taipei citizen: Is it right for A-bian to abolish Taipei licensed prostitutes,* Taipei: Taipei Licensed Prostitutes' Self-help Association, Solidarity Front of Women's Workers, and Pink Collar Press.

Hsieh, H.-C. and Cheuh, C. (2005) 'The development of the women's movement and women's/gender studies in Taiwan', in W.-H. Lin and H.-C. Hsieh (eds) *Gender, culture and society: Women's studies in Taiwan*, Women's studies in Asia series, Seoul: Ewha Woman's University Press, pp 301-37.

Huang, S.-Y. (1998) 'Go-whoring violates human rights', *Liberty Times*, 9 March, p 11.

Huang, X.-T. and Huang, X.-T. (2000) 'Chen-chen's story', in Collective of Sex Workers and Supporters (ed), *Ri-Ri-Chun: The stories of the Nine Taipei licensed prostitutes*, Taipei: Collective of Sex Workers and Supporters.

Huang, Y.-L. (1999) 'Women, state, and sex work', paper presented in seminar series held by Feminist Scholars' Association, Taipei, Taiwan.

Hughes, D. (1999) 'The internet and the global prostitution industry', in S. Hawthorne and R. Klein (eds) *CyberFeminism: Connectivity, critique, and creativity*, North Melbourne: Spinifex Press.

Hwang, S.-L. (1996) 'Women in sex industries: victims, agents or deviants?', *Taiwan: A Radical Quarterly in Social Studies*, vol 22, April, pp 103-52.

Ji, H.-W. (1998) *The stories of 12 prostitutes – A study of prostitutes' moral lives*, Taipei: Tonsan Books.

Jones, G.W., Sulistyaningsih, E. and Hull, T.H. (1998) 'Prostitution in Indonesia', in L.L. Lim (ed) *The sex sector: The economic and social bases of prostitution in Southeast Asia*, Geneva: International Labour Office.

Lan, K.-J., Jou, W.-C. and Huang R.-M. (2002) *Beyond the binary opposition: On Taiwanese commercial sex policies and its regulation regime*, term paper issued by Commission on Women's Rights Promotion (CRWP), Executive Yuan, Taipei: CWRP Press.

Lim, L.L. (ed) (1998) *The sex sector: The economic and social bases of prostitution in Southeast Asia*, Geneva: International Labour Office.

Lin, F.-M. (1998) 'The identity politics of the women's movement in contemporary Taiwan: the example of the debates of the abolition of Taipei licensed prostitution', *Chung Wai Literary Monthly*, vol 27, no 1, pp 56-87.

Lin, H.-X. (1995) 'The social bases of the sub-culture of prostitution in Taiwan', unpublished MA thesis in Sociology Department, Taipei: Soochow University.

Lin, H.-X. (1997) 'The abolition of Taipei licensed prostitution and the history of prostitution in Taiwan', *Historical Monthly*, no 122, pp 106-15.

Liu, C.-D. (1997) *A comparative study of special entertaining businesses*, Taipei: Executive Yuan.

Liu, Y.-X. (1995) 'Men's law and men's country: an ideological analysis of the Family Law', in Y.-X. Liu (ed) *The white book of Taiwanese women's situation 1995*, Taipei: China Times Press.

Lopez-Jones, N. (1988) 'Workers: introducing the English Collective of Prostitutes', in F. Delacoste and P. Alexander (eds) *Sex work: Writings by women in the sex industry*, London: Virago Press.

McIntosh, M. (1978) 'Who needs prostitution? The social construction of male sexual needs', in C. Smart and B. Smart (eds) *Women, sexuality and social control*, London: Routledge & Kegan Paul.

O'Connell Davidson, J. (1995) 'British sex tourists in Thailand', in M. Maynard and J. Purvis (eds) *HeteroSexual politics*, London: Taylor & Francis.

O'Connell Davidson, J. (1998) *Prostitution, power, and freedom*, Cambridge: Polity Press.

Peng, Y.-W. (2004) 'Deliberating prostitution policy: frame critical analysis for intractable policy controversies', unpublished PhD dissertation, Urban Planning and Policy Development, New Brunswick, NJ: Rutgers, State University of New Jersey.

Pitts, J. (1997) 'Causes of youth prostitution, new forms of practice and political responses', in D. Barrett (ed) *Child prostitution in Britain: Dilemmas and practical responses*, London: Children's Society Press.

Shiah, J.-J., Yan, J.-A., Wang, T.-Y. and Wang, J.-S. (2002) *Progress report on the Taiwanese sex industry and policy of commercial sex*, Taipei: Executive Yuan.

Solidarity Front of Women Workers (1998) 'Sex work and sexual violence', in J. Ho (ed) *Sex work: Prostitutes' rights in perspective*, Chungli: Centre for the Study of Sexualities, pp 164-7.

Statistics of Justice (JS) (2003), *The statistics of local courts hearing cases of the Act for Prevention of Child and Juvenile Involvement in Commercial Sex* (available at www.moj.gov.tw/f7_frame.htm).

Tsay, K.-L. (2002) 'Internet male prostitute encounters female police', *China Times*, 24 March 2002.

Wang, F.-P. and Ku, Y.-L. (1998) 'My work is my dignity: sex work is work', in J. Ho (ed) *Sex work: Prostitutes' rights in perspective*, Chungli: Centre for the Study of Sexualities.

Wang, F.-P. and Wang, C.-P. (edited and interviewed) (2000) 'I want to find success some day: Ms. Guan's story', in Collective of Sex Workers and Supporters (ed) *Ri-Ri-Chun: The stories of nine Taipei licensed prostitutes*, Taipei: Collective of Sex Workers and Supporters.

Watenabe, S. (1998) 'From Thailand to Japan: migrant sex workers as autonomous subjects', in K. Kempadoo and J. Doezema (eds) *Global sex workers: Rights, resistance, and redefinition*, New York and London: Routledge.

NINE

Prostitution in Thailand: perceptions and realities

Alyson Brody

Introduction

An article published in the *Financial Times* in 1987, describing Bangkok, remarked that 'there are marvellous restaurants wonderful shopping … and, of course, there is the sex …' (*Financial Times*, 1987). In the intervening years, this perception of Thailand has prevailed, despite the efforts of the Thai government to play down this association.

While this chapter talks about prostitution in Thailand, it also highlights certain tensions involved in attempting to say what Thai prostitution is, and how and why people become involved in prostitution. The chapter stresses that, while it is possible to make broad statements about prostitution in Thailand and to sketch out certain commonalities, it is important to remember that 'facts' about this phenomenon have been motivated in particular ways and often present prostitution as a singular reality, as if 'it', once located and defined, can be assessed and contained.

In particular, many of the narratives that frame the issue in Thailand fail to convey the reality of prostitution as a negotiated process that is the sum of various intersecting relationships. In addition, existing research and writing on the issue are gendered in certain ways, almost always produced by women and focusing on adult female prostitutes serving men. Male prostitution is a growing industry in Thailand, and research shows that clients are both men and women (see *The Nation*, 2003, and *Bangkok Post*, 2003, for example); yet a disproportionate amount of literature has been produced on the subject, and tends to be couched within analyses of Thai homosexuality (see, for example, Jackson, 1995; Jackson et al, 1995). Is this because it is harder to gather information on male sex workers; is it because men working in prostitution are regarded as less vulnerable; or is it because there is a fundamental unwillingness to accept this aspect of the industry where explanations are blurred and do not always fit the neat rationales framing Thai prostitution? Missing too are detailed studies of children and teenagers working in prostitution, although the reason for this may be – as I note later in this chapter – that a heavy-handed approach to this issue has driven these activities underground, requiring more investigative approaches to research that many are unwilling or unable to undertake. Studies of child prostitution instead centre on the mechanisms that sustain trafficking of children into the sex industry. Finally, the voices and experiences of those engaged in the sex industry are a notable absence in much of the literature; their views are paraphrased or edited, but the humanity of those involved – their personalities and aspirations – is often obscured by a generic image of 'the Thai prostitute', whose role in the literature is often to exemplify qualitative differences from 'other' types of sex workers elsewhere.

My approach in this chapter is to reflect on the material that is available and, thus, it reproduces many of the silences mentioned earlier. I would urge the reader to be aware of what is not being said or included and to interrogate these gaps as thoroughly as the material presented. The chapter starts by discussing aspects of the Thai sex trade, as explained through various discourses with varying perspectives and motivations. I argue that the choices made in circumscribing the issue may reveal as much about the authors as it does about the set of practices to which they refer.

Next, I consider prostitution as the object of particular laws and policies, showing how the legal response to prostitution is largely a function of where particular lines are drawn: between innocent victim and willing prostitute, between passivity and agency. I explore the centrality of these definitions to debates about sex trafficking and the decriminalisation of prostitution. These debates highlight the fact that individual stories of entry into the sex trade inevitably affect the way each sex worker views her- or himself, and the types of interventions they may require or desire. I also touch on the more hazy reality of policing an industry that is theoretically illegal, despite its high visibility. This issue of policing is closely connected to the rights of sex workers, and particularly to their right to be respected for the choices they have made, in many cases, and the work they do.

Finally, I examine reasons for entry into the industry, although the routes into prostitution and the accompanying motivations are difficult to summarise in one chapter. I have focused on women, but – as indicated earlier – it is important to remember that there are also men, boys and girls involved in the sale of sex. Although the circumstances and conditions are often similar, these cases need to be understood within their own particular contexts, but should definitely form the basis of further work[1].

The national context

Like many of its neighbours in the area known as the 'Mekong region' of South-East Asia, Thailand has been a predominantly rural economy until very recently. Cultivation took off in earnest during the 18th century with the state endorsement of a pioneering mentality, whereby people were awarded ownership over land they had claimed if they could tame it and put it to productive use. Mainly a subsistence economy with surpluses going to feed the much smaller urban population, rural agriculture did not move into larger-scale commercial production until the 1950s. As part of a wider national development strategy, revenue from exported produce helped to finance the growth of an industrial base and of a burgeoning infrastructure. Farmers received subsidies to buoy up production. In tandem, development policies advocated new technologies and high-yield seed varieties, while farmers were rewarded for concentrating on a single crop rather than practising the multiple cropping methods that were the foundations of a self-sufficient lifestyle. Money was introduced into the rural economy, and farmers were lauded as the 'backbone of Thailand' (see, for example, Phongpaichit and Baker, 1995).

Yet, as Thailand's five-year development plans were implemented, backed by the World Bank, Asian Development Bank and the International Monetary Fund (IMF), among others, and focused on the development of an industrialised urban-based economy, the gap between the rural and urban population grew exponentially. As prices of produce were kept low to encourage overseas sales and to sustain the growing urban population, the distribution of income became increasingly skewed. Coupled with this, in the last few decades, large-scale agro-industries have dominated the agricultural market and government subsidies have been withdrawn from smaller enterprises. One visible effect of the small farmers' economic marginalisation has been the exodus of rural Thais both to urban and to other rural areas, as a means of entering the wage economy. Bangkok – as the main core of Thailand's accelerated modernisation and as the nation's administrative heart – has typically attracted the largest number of migrants, drawn to opportunities in manufacturing, construction and service industries. According to Phongpaichit and Baker, 'over two million people came to the city from rural areas in the 1980s and possibly a further million entered the urban workforce on a temporary basis' (1995, p 153). Notably at least half of migrants in recent years have been women; a percentage of these women migrants in Bangkok and in other areas, such as popular tourist destinations, work in the sex trade.

It is difficult to generalise about women's status in Thailand, since levels of gender equality and the ways in which they are manifested vary according to religion[2], place, class and level of education. However, a central characteristic that separates Thai gender norms from many other countries in the region is the relative mobility of Thai women and their visibility in public spaces. Although migration of women to major cities is a fairly recent phenomenon linked to rapid development (see Fuller et al, 1983; Phongpaichit and Baker, 1995), poorer women in urban and rural centres have traditionally been engaged in trading, selling produce from their farms, or hand-crafted items. Debates revolve around the extent to which this may be regarded as gendered equality, given that – in the Buddhist context – trading is considered an earthly pursuit that suits women's lack of spirituality, and that marks their lower status[3]. Significantly, this perceived lack of spiritual understanding results in women's restriction from being ordained as monks, which is a means of bestowing karmic merit on oneself and one's family in addition to being a mark of social prestige[4].

Despite the expectation that women will provide financial support to their families, boys have traditionally been favoured for education. However, over the past few decades the number of girls attending school has risen dramatically, as has the percentage of girls going on to higher education[5]. The legal situation for Thai women has also improved in recent years; both men and women have the right to vote in elections, and Thai women now have the same rights of divorce as men[6]. Women are able to stand for parliamentary seats, although their level of political representation is still minimal compared to men. One of the arenas where inequalities are still prevalent is in the workplace. Despite the increase in female-dominated employment, such as garment production, women's wages are still below those of men, and there is a tendency to foist redundancy on women before they reach the age of 30, as a way to maintain levels of unskilled, cheap labour (see Bell, 1992; Chouwilai, 2000).

Estimating the number of commercial sex workers in Thailand has proved an evasive and inexact process. The estimates have varied greatly in magnitude with – at one extreme – a child protection agency announcing the existence of two million sex workers, of whom a significant percentage were under the age of 15, and at the other, government figures that give a far more conservative estimate of 75,000 (see Boonchalaksi and Guest, 1994). Boonchalaksi and Guest (1994) have taken a more practical approach to the question. Their figure of 175,000 represents 2.1% of the 2.8 million women aged between 15 and 29 – the age group for which prostitution is most likely. It is also 7.3% of women in this age group who are living in the urban places where most commercial sex workers (CSWs) are employed. The majority of women working in prostitution are from the northern and the north-eastern regions of Thailand, which are also the poorest. The average age of 106 sex workers interviewed for Boonchalaksi and Guest's study was 23, but they found that that there was a high concentration of women under the age of 21 in massage parlours. This is linked to the fact that the majority of massage parlour workers are from the north and it is common for northern Thai girls to enter the industry at a very young age (13-15), for reasons that will be explained later in the chapter.

The Thai sex industry

Before launching into a discussion about prostitution in Thailand, it is important to disaggregate the notion of the 'sex industry' and ask what it means in practice. Most of the literature on prostitution makes the point that the image of girls sold into sex 'slavery', forced into servicing many customers every day under intolerable circumstances is a reality, but represents a small part of a diverse and complex whole. At the 'high' end of the market are massage parlours, ranging from elaborate and extremely visible establishments, often occupying prime land, to smaller, more inexpensive, places. Phongpaichit notes that 'the massage parlour provides a society and environment which is often safer and more comfortable than other forms of organised prostitution' (1982, p vii). Services in massage parlours range from straight massage to massage with 'special (sexual) services'. These services can sometimes involve more than one girl (see Boonchalaksi and Guest, 1994). Prostitution also operates from bars. Its most visible manifestation in Bangkok is Patpong, a brightly lit street in the centre of the city where downstairs young women gyrate and 'pole dance' to music and upstairs various shows are often offered, such as women shooting objects from their vaginas – from ping-pong balls to razor blades[7] – or live sex shows. Patpong, and other streets like it in Bangkok and other popular tourist destinations, cater mainly to tourists and expatriates, predominantly male. Prostitution does not usually happen on the premises. Customers are expected to buy a drink and if they wish to take a girl out of the bar, they must pay a fee – usually about 200 Baht (£5) – to the bar. Anything that happens between the customer and the girl from that point is negotiated between them. There are bars in other less central areas of Bangkok that are frequented more typically by Thais, and where the women are more likely to be acting as hostesses than providing erotic entertainment, but where customers can also pay a fee to take a girl out of the bar.

At the lower end of the market are brothels, where customers choose from girls sitting behind a window – sometimes one-way glass – with numbers pinned to their clothes. The customer selects a girl and pays for her services for up to an hour, sometimes more. The girls usually service customers in the brothel, often in the rooms in which they sleep.

Prostitution also operates from less well-recognised locations, such as restaurants, beauty salons, coffee- and tea-shops, discotheques and through escort agencies and call girls, both of which are often advertised in Thai-based English-language newspapers. There are also 'indirect' sex workers, who are employed as singers or hairdressers.

Boonchalaksi and Guest's comprehensive study (1994) found that the women working in the establishments mentioned above were mainly from the northern and north-eastern regions of Thailand, which are also the poorest. There is a high concentration of northern women in massage parlours, catering to a local Thai clientele, for two linked reasons: women from the north are considered the most beautiful in Thailand, renowned for their fair complexions; as a result the networks through which many women are recruited into the sex industry provide a direct link from the north to these establishments. By contrast, women serving customers in bars predominantly frequented by foreigners are typically from the north-east. As is explained below, these links are due to the movement of north-eastern women from establishments that served American soldiers during the Vietnam War, to tourist areas like Patpong in Bangkok.

Development of the Thai sex industry

The evolution of this multifaceted multimillion dollar industry has been predicated on a number of interlinked factors, which are played up or down depending on the source describing them. Typically, external influence has been blamed for the introduction of commercial sex to Thai society. For example, Phongpaichit links the sex trade to the start of the export of rice and other commodities in the 18th century. She notes that immigrant traders brought with them practices of polygamy and the collection of concubines 'as part of the status symbolism of wealth' (1982, p 4) and that these legitimised the commodification of women as an expression of power. The implication is that the traders were from other parts of Asia, but rich Europeans also increased their contact with Thailand as a result of colonisation in the surrounding countries.

Thitsa (1980) locates the origins of prostitution in Thai Buddhism, which – she claims – perpetuates a gender hierarchy through which women are devalued and doomed to a life of slavery as a 'good' wife or a 'bad' prostitute. Others note that Buddhism itself is an import that corrupted what they see as a pristine system of equal and mutual respect between the sexes, and contributed to shifts in male behaviour and expectations - particularly in urban areas - which took root in Thai society (see, for example, Tantiwiramanond and Pandey, 1991; Phongsapich, 1997).

Lyttleton suggests that the issue needs to be rooted in an understanding of local culture. Focusing on the particular context of north-eastern Thailand, Lyttleton draws attention to a fining system for sexual transgression that 'bridges ideology and capital and provides a strong impetus for the commodification of female sexuality' (2000, p 215). According to north-eastern village culture, men are expected to pay fines for inappropriate sexual activity, on an escalating scale depending on the severity of the crime. In this way, argues Lyttleton, 'sexual relations outside marriage are imbued with an intrinsic element of financial exchange' (2000, p 216). Boonchalaksi and Guest focus on the influence of urban-centric Thai upper-class values that emphasised beauty as women's main asset, thus leading to their commodification (1994, p 6). Another strand identified in the growth of prostitution is the abolition of slavery in 1909, which led to former female slaves going into the sex trade (Asia Watch Women's Rights Project, 1993).

Despite these cultural and historical precedents the Thai sex trade has only developed into a full-scale industry in the past few decades, as an effect of two separate, but interconnected events: the Vietnam War and the explosion of tourism. The role of Thailand in providing a haven of 'Rest and Recreation' (henceforth, the R & R industry) for American soldiers stationed in Vietnam and on the north-eastern border with Vietnam has been well documented. A visible effect of the R & R industry was the development of the neon-lit bar scene, exemplified by Patpong in Bangkok, mentioned earlier, which was later transformed into a centre for high-profile 'a go-go bars', and which today remains the focus of foreign interest in the sex scene. Other areas in which Americans invested include Soi Cowboy, a bar strip in an area predominantly populated by foreigners and rich Thais.

The other, and possibly the most significant, factor in the promotion of the sex trade is tourism. The R & R industry played a role in attracting visitors to Thailand, but the rapid expansion of tourism can be attributed to deliberate policies linked to an overall plan for Thailand's development and supported by international donors. Tourism was identified as a key means of attracting foreign capital into the underdeveloped Thai economy, and donor money was invested in improving the infrastructure. That there was money to be made from a sex trade catering to foreign tourists had been evidenced by the R & R scene. Despite its essential illegality – a point the next section expands on – prostitution became a defining feature of the way Thailand was packaged as a tourist destination. Sex tours were run from Europe and East Asia, particularly Japan, and the delights of Thai women were promoted in holiday brochures catering mainly to male tourists. As Boonchalaksi and Guest point out: 'the bodies of Thai women have become one of the bases of growth of the Thai economy' (1994, p 1).

Truong (1990) takes a strategic approach in explaining the growth of sex tourism. She considers ways in which politics and commercialism have conspired to promote and sustain sex tourism. She emphasises the role of prostitution as a vehicle for massive investment of Thai and Western capital, noting the high level of foreign investment in bars, massage parlours and hotels. She provides an in-depth analysis of the role played by hotels in the chain of circumstances engendering the sex trade, noting that, in order to ensure full occupancy, many hotels are included in sex tour packages. This builds on an existing tendency of some hotels to permit short-term letting of rooms for the purposes of prostitution. Truong also makes the point that many escort agencies are linked to hotels, even the most luxurious first-class establishments.

Earlier, I discussed the economic and social conditions that foreground the Thai sex industry. A conspicuous absence in much of the literature and policy on prostitution, however, is a reflection of the complex 'demand side' of the industry – the male clients (see De Zalduondo, 1991, p 23).

This omission is largely predicated on the basic understanding that male desire is a deterministic response that is so overpowering that it alone drives men to visit CSWs. As I have argued: 'desire is neither a given, free-floating biological instinct, nor is it always the same', and, from this perspective: 'more care should be taken to differentiate between foreign and local clients on the level of motivation and practices' (Brody, 1994, p 19). Manderson's study of 'public sex performances' in Patpong, Bangkok, illustrates the role of the imagination in sex shows aimed at tourists, stressing that the performances are 'a commentary on the presumed nature of Western and Japanese male desire' (1992, p 457), playing on their preconditioned ideas about 'exotic', Eastern women and sexuality.

At the same time, it is important not to overstate the differences between Thai and Western men, since the available literature has also exoticised and 'otherised' them as amoral, sexually promiscuous and chauvinistic (see Lyttleton, 2000). It is undeniable that the Thai sex industry is largely sustained by a local clientele; the figures commonly quoted are that 96% of Thai men have had sex with a CSW, while 48% had their first intercourse with a sex worker.[8] Yet, as Lyttleton points out, these figures tell us little about what Thai men actually do in practice, or their motivations for visiting prostitutes. His own interviews with Thai men revealed a 'lack of enthusiasm for commercial sex' (2000, p 231), indicating a disjuncture between male scripts about visiting prostitutes and male *behaviour*. Some of the men he interviewed indicated that they wanted romance, and were keen to 'win the women over', to elicit some response other than indifference (Lyttleton, 2000, p 231). Similar themes are reflected in Cohen's work on farang (foreign) men. He argues that the sexual transactions between tourists and sex workers cannot always be considered as only a 'neutral economic exchange', referring to the 'edge of ambiguity' in relationships where foreign men are looking for companionship as well as sex, and the money involved takes on the character of a gift, with women not stating a price but leaving it up to the client (Cohen, 1996, p 255). Seabrook's (1996) narratives of foreign males who have been involved with Thai sex workers also indicate a high level of emotional dependency for some of these men. He notes, however, that it is difficult to generalise; some men simply want to use the women for sex, while others are more vulnerable and likely to become hurt when they realise the women they have fallen in love with see them as clients and nothing more.

Laws and policies

That the drive for foreign capital through capitalism was accompanied by the introduction of a legislative instrument known as the 1966 Service Establishments Act, commonly referred to as the Entertainments Act, was no accident. This legislation effectively legitimised places where CSWs could be sought, offering a subtle challenge to an existing law that had made prostitution illegal in 1960. Prior to that, prostitution had been legal, regulated by the 1909 Control and Prevention of Venereal Disease Act, which introduced licensing for brothels and required brothel owners to ensure that the CSWs were free of sexually transmitted diseases (STDs). The 1960 Suppression of Prostitution Act criminalised prostitution, penalising procurers and pimps, as well as CSWs, whether or not they had been forced into sex work. The aim of imprisoning CSWs was to engender their 'moral rehabilitation', so that CSWs could gain adult education, vocational training, counselling and follow-up services so they could take up alternative employment (Boonchalaksi and Guest, 1994, p 23).

In the last two decades, changes to the Thai Penal Code have responded to the reality of a continuing sex trade, and the weak laws that neither protect CSWs nor adequately chastise procurers or customers. These shifts have chiefly come about because of concern over AIDS and because of outrage over revelations of the increasing numbers of girls under the age of 15 who had been sold into the industry – a phenomenon I will explore in the next section. Certain authors have maintained that it was at this point that prostitution was framed as a 'problem'. According to Bishop and Robinson: 'it is fair to say that without AIDS and child prostitution the sex industry would continue to receive as little attention in the popular press as it did in earlier decades. It would not be cast as a "problem"' (1998, p 87). These concerns were compounded by the increasingly negative representations of Thailand as a place where young girls were exploited for sex, and where AIDS was rampant; an image that did not fit with the desire to project Thailand as a world-class tourist destination.

In response to these concerns, the 1982 Penal Code increased penalties for procurers of girls under 18. The 1996 Code went further, imposing strict penalties not only for procurers but also for the parents who had sold their daughters, and for the clients of child prostitutes.

Laws and policies in practice

The 1966 Entertainments Act is ostensibly 'designed to control the operations of establishments which endanger the morals of the community through empowering the police to close a place in which commercial sex is offered' (Boonchalaksi and Guest, 1994, p 20). In reality, what the Act does is to provide loopholes for owners of bars, brothels and other establishments to operate, without the expectation that the CSWs who work for them will be protected. Under the 1966 Entertainments Act, these owners are able to run such establishments, providing they are legally registered, and to employ women to 'attend male customers' in private if necessary. The Act does not overtly permit prostitution, but many establishments evade prosecution by expecting customers to pay a fee for taking a girl or boy off the premises. As noted earlier, any further negotiation for sex or other services is between the CSW and the client. What this Act has done is to encourage a double standard whereby police are often notoriously willing to turn a blind eye to the activities of many establishments, in return for a 'protection' fee. CSWs, who have no legal status through this Act, are particularly vulnerable to these forms of collusion.

It is equally difficult to ensure the implementation of the revisions to the Penal Code, particularly when the police, military and even governmental officials are involved in this lucrative trade (see Asia Watch Women's Rights Project, 1993, for example). Furthermore, the rights of CSWs are still not covered under these laws and the prostitution of boys – a growing phenomenon – is not acknowledged. As noted earlier, prostitution takes many benign forms in Thailand and remains hidden within the legal definitions of 'places of prostitution'. An ironic and unintended effect of such severe penalties on those working in child prostitution may have been to drive the problem deeper underground. The focus on an internal problem also draws attention away from the issue of trafficking in women, an issue that will be explored in the coming sections.

Analysis of policies and interventions

While the revised legislation is designed to punish those who control or abuse aspects of the sex trade, there are notable silences around the issue of protection or rights for sex workers themselves. One complaint is that, although the Penal Code is in place, the legislation has not been implemented and therefore young victims of forced prostitution have no real recourse, while their procurers continue to go free (Asia Watch Women's Rights Project, 1993). Others have been calling for the existing legislation to be reviewed altogether, arguing that the only law to offer sex workers themselves any protection – the 1949 UN Convention for the Suppression of Traffic in Persons and of the Exploitation of the Prostitution of Others – is inadequate, for several reasons. The main issue is that the law does not recognise the complexities involved in a trafficking situation. It does not take into account other forms of trafficking besides prostitution, such as of mail-order brides, domestic workers or factory labour; it does not set out any regulations that protect trafficked victims from immediate deportation. Most notably, the Convention does not protect women who voluntarily enter into an agreement with a trafficker, knowing the type of work they would be doing, to find themselves then working under coercive conditions. It does not accept that women may choose to become sex workers (see GAATW, 1997).

Debates around legalisation and decriminalisation

The Global Alliance Against Traffic in Women (GAATW), with its headquarters in Bangkok, argued that the 1949 Convention was both too narrow to be useful, and too moralistic in its conflation of trafficking with prostitution, because it required that sex workers prove that they were deceived into entering prostitution, rather than choose to do so. They campaigned for new legislation that would recognise the rights of sex workers as workers and decriminalise prostitution, since they were the most likely to be arrested under current law. These changes would enable sex workers to seek protection under the labour laws, rather than having to appeal through the channels of a Convention that portrayed them at best as victims and at worst as bad, 'fallen' women in need of rehabilitation. Their report states that: 'a consensus is being formed on the recognition that women may consent to prostitution but not to slavery-like conditions in prostitution' (GAATW, 1997, p 32). In tandem with this call to decrimimalise prostitution, the report called for international trafficking law to reflect diverse situations of trafficking, including forced prostitution. As a result of campaigning and increased international awareness of trafficking, in 2000 a new United Nations Convention against Transnational Organized crime was launched. Over 80 countries signed one of its supplementary protocols – the Protocol to prevent, suppress and punish trafficking in persons, especially women and children. The new protocol, which has yet to be ratified by all countries, broadens the definition of trafficking and protects women and children who consented to enter into prostitution or other work. The protocol also states that people do not necessarily have to cross international borders to be trafficked.

Yet the debates over the issue of consent continue. Taking a strongly opposed stance to GAATW, the Coalition Against Trafficking in Women (CATW) maintains that prostitution is inherently exploitative and therefore always a form of trafficking. It views consent as a form of false consciousness, arguing that 'trafficking for the exploitation of prostitution and other forms of sexual exploitation can occur not only under conditions of force or coercion but through the abuse of a victim's vulnerability' (Raymond, 2003, p 7). It maintains that prostitution should not be decriminalised and/or recognised as a form of work, with the implication that the trafficking protocol would be the only means for sex workers to seek protection. This challenges GAATW's position that women *can* make a choice to enter prostitution and should be treated as agents in the process.

Key issues faced

Reasons for entry into prostitution

As Lyttleton notes, prostitution is 'not a single phenomenon understood by singular explanations'. Likewise, motivations for entry cannot be boiled down to a single cause. Poverty or gender roles 'cannot adequately explain the range of engagements, premises and strategies that make prostitution such a powerful aspect of Thai society' (Lyttleton, 2000, p 17). It is difficult to discuss the economic and social reasons for women's and men's entry into prostitution apart from the ways in which these have been discursively framed, since the narratives have also been motivated in certain ways. That prostitution is linked to the status of women and to their socio-economic situations is axiomatic. At the same time, as I pointed out in my introduction, to try and pin prostitution down to a few simple causal factors would be to undermine a complex web of practices and relationships. Prostitution has, to an extent, become a locus for many diverse strands and pathologies emerging from the changing Thai society and economy and from tensions between old, embedded expectations and more recent opportunities and developments. As Jeffrey points out, it is also important to recognise that the notion of 'the Prostitute' is a construct that has been 'made visible discursively through discussions about sex workers as "silent, or victims, or greedy consumers"' (2002, p xi), which rarely include sex workers' voices. Jeffrey notes that debates around prostitution as a 'problem' for policy have little to do with the realities of sex workers' lives or self-perceptions, yet they derive their persuasiveness from the creation of this essentialised 'prostitution'. She sees prostitution as a focus for anxieties over the penetration of Western values into Thai society, where the bodies of Thai women are equated with national boundaries.

Discourse of sex workers as victims of culture and capitalism

Thitsa's widely cited paper on 'providence and prostitution' in Thailand portrays Thai women as victims of imported Western corruption in the form of capitalism, and of indigenous traditional attitudes 'inculcated through the family and the process of socialisation' (1980, p 4). In her perception, Thai women are already devalued through the low position ascribed to them by Buddhism, the main religion of Thailand that forms the fundamental basis of a social and cultural, as well as a spiritual life. Her essentialised reading of Thai Buddhist beliefs posits that male authority rests in the expectation that they will take on lofty spiritual and governmental roles, while women are consigned to the baseness of 'secular ... trading and marketing' (1980, p 5). These conclusions are based on the fact that all male Buddhist Thais are expected to join the Buddhist monk-hood – a highly esteemed role – even if only for a short time, whereas the same privilege is not granted to women, because of their insufficient karma. Thai women are expected to support their families financially and are more likely to be in business than men. In the face of escalating rural poverty, Thitsa views these economic imperatives as a prime factor in women's inevitable migration to an ever corrupt Bangkok and in their choice of prostitution as the most obvious and lucrative choice of career.

According to Thitsa's argument, that women fall naturally into the role of sex worker is justified by entrenched Buddhist beliefs that women's sexuality is dangerous and latent and that women walk a thin line between being a 'good' and devoted wife and a 'bad', sexually manipulative prostitute. Women are forced into prostitution because of the expectation that they are sexually weak and likely to become temptresses – 'with the low value attached to the female body and the female spirit by Buddhism, she has been sufficiently degraded already to enter prostitution' (Thitsa, 1980, p 23). At the same time, using prostitution as a means to support her family can earn a woman merit, enabling her to climb the karmic ladder and possibly be reborn as a man. Thitsa's explanations, though influential, are problematic in many ways. First, she denies Thai women any agency in their lives or in the choices they make. Her argument fails to account for the thousands of rural women who migrate to Bangkok and other places yet do not become involved in prostitution, while still managing to support their families by other means. Furthermore, Thitsa's claim that Thai women are denied social status has been overturned by several critics who note that men and women can earn equal respect if they fulfil the social roles available to them (see Kirsch, 1985 and Van Esterick, 1996, for example). Finally, Thitsa's work is imbued with moral outrage, and the patronising assumption that entry into sex work could not possibly be a choice, that women who do it are by definition powerless.

Discourse of sex workers as agents and entrepreneurs

Phongpaichit responds to this moralistic stance that renders women helpless. She critiques also an anthropological trend that defined Thailand as a 'loosely structured society' (see Embree, 1950, for this argument). She states that 'there is nothing especially "loose" about Thailand's rural women', criticising any attempt to seek 'an explanation for this in any eternal characteristics of Thai culture' (Phongpaichit, 1982, p 75). Phongpaichit's work remains largely unrivalled in its grounding in sex workers' stories and words. Like Thitsa, she stresses that they seek work in Bangkok out of a sense of duty and responsibility to their families, and because of 'the economic responsibility imposed on them by their social role' (Phongpaichit, 1982, p 2), with one important difference: she views prostitution as a pragmatic choice for rural Thai women in the face of other limited and low-paid employment such as factory work, where women are expected to endure long hours and uncomfortable conditions for minimal wages. She is keen to critique the notion that these women are merely self-interested, noting that 'perhaps the most remarkable thing about the sample girls was their conception of themselves as family breadwinners. They were not, like so many young people, making for the bright lights of the city, extracting themselves from their family background' (Phongpaichit, 1982, p 25)[9]. From this perspective, Thai women derive agency from fulfilling their duty and responsibility to their families, in response to the 'obligations' they feel they owe them[10]. By viewing the meeting of obligations as a source of pride, Phongpaichit's perspective is that doing sex work is an entrepreneurial move. Above all, she is keen to stress that these girls are not prostitutes in the 'usual sense', but that there is something 'specific and unusual' about the Thai girls (1982, p 71). Hence, she in many ways mirrors Thitsa's moral judgment about sex work.

Focus on socio-cultural roots of prostitution

As noted earlier, the majority of sex workers are from the rural north and north-east of Thailand, the poorest areas. Yet, of these two broad regional groups, northern Thai women account for the largest percentage of very young, unmarried women, and are most likely to be aged between 13 and 15 on entry into sex work (Boonchalaksi and Guest, 1994). This phenomenon has been explained with reference to the practice of meeting obligations to parents described earlier. The studies indicate that this practice is particularly strong in the north, and is a major contributing factor to the entry of young girls into the industry. By contrast, research indicates that women from the north-east of Thailand tend to enter the industry at a later age. They are likely to be from failed marriages, supporting children through their work. Certain authors have pointed to more relaxed morals in the north than in the north-east as a major factor explaining these demographic variations. Lyttleton (2000) stresses that reactions to sex work and to women working as CSWs vary according to region, and are informed by the ways in which sexuality and relationships are understood and experienced. He notes the significance of precedence in the north, where there is a high preponderance of agents seeking the renowned 'northern beauties' who are considered so valuable in the sex industry, as mentioned earlier. Women who have worked in Bangkok usually return to the villages, and their sophisticated clothes and the beautiful houses they build act as magnets for younger girls. Sometimes these returnees are actively involved in recruiting. An important difference from the north-east seems to be that these returning women are not stigmatised and there are no boundaries to their marrying men from their home village. The merit the women acquire overrides the means by which they acquired it.

In the north-east, Lyttleton observed a stricter sense of morality. Former CSWs found it difficult to return to their villages if it was known what work they had been engaging in. Phongpaichit also notes that 'fundamental views about sex and marital relations are more relaxed in the North than the Northeast' (1982, p 47). Lyttleton adds the caveat, however, that materialistic gains are beginning to temper this moral stricture. Recruiting mechanisms also differ for north-eastern women. Considered less classically beautiful, north-eastern women are less likely to be sought by agents and tend instead to move into the sex industry from other work, such as factory employment. North-eastern women tend to work in foreign-oriented bars, since many of their predecessors were engaged in a local sex industry catering to US troops and later moved to Bangkok after the war, when areas such as Patpong began to develop.

Discourses on trafficking and prostitution

Earlier, I dealt chiefly with the group of women who have some agency over their entry into prostitution. An issue that has probably attracted the most media attention is trafficking of children into the sex trade, and particularly of young girls who have been 'sold' to procurers by their parents. As mentioned earlier, forced prostitution represents a small percentage of the industry, although its illicit nature means that much of it remains to be uncovered, particularly in the light of strict laws. A typical pattern sees recruiters targeting very poor families, often in the rural north of Thailand, and offering relatively large sums of money that daughters or sons are expected to pay back with interest through their sexual labour. While many parents have been deceived by recruiters into believing their children would be working under legitimate circumstances, others have knowingly sold them into prostitution. The conditions they work under are usually appalling. Often forced to service several customers a day, they are virtually prisoners, not permitted to leave the brothel in case they run away.

Publicity has also focused on women trafficked across borders, particularly from Burma and Cambodia. These women and young girls are also part of a slave trade, often working 10–18 hours a day, 25 days a month and servicing up to 15 clients per day (see Asia Watch Women's Rights Project, 1993). According to one high-profile report, trafficked Burmese women received little or no healthcare or birth control and were forced to abort illegally, or continue to work if they became pregnant. The report found that 50%-70% of the women interviewed were HIV-positive and had been tested without their consent but denied the results. In Thailand illegally, they would face deportation if they tried to escape; the involvement of the police and military in trafficking (Asia Watch Women's Rights Project, 1993) compounds this risk. Once back in Burma, the likelihood was that they would be arrested and – reputedly – even executed if found to be HIV-positive.

Conclusions

In this chapter I have shown that the phenomenon of prostitution is a product of several overlapping strands, of which economic factors are perhaps the most powerful. These economic forces include the relative poverty that makes prostitution a viable and even attractive option for a percentage of poor, rural Thai women, as well as a smaller number of men and parents of young girls. They encompass also rapid growth at the opposite end of a massively skewed economic order. I also demonstrated that prostitution takes myriad forms in Thailand, each with its own specific set of conditions.

I have argued that the reasons for entry into prostitution are as difficult to pin down as the reasons for the sex trade itself. There are as many reasons as there are people taking up sex work, whether voluntarily or not. I highlighted some of the key perceptions as to what motivates entry into prostitution, drawing on available material. I stressed that an author's own assumptions or intentions are bound to shape the approach they take and the choices they make in emphasis.

I mapped out various responses to the issue of prostitution, exposing particularly the complexities of a debate that revolves around whether prostitution is inherently exploitative or can be viewed as a conscious choice and right in some cases. I also argued that the demand side of prostitution – the predominantly male customers using the services – is a notable absence in most of the work explored. Much of the material is predicated on essentialised *ideas* about male behaviour, without really telling us what maintains prostitution as a lucrative industry. Sex is a powerful marketing tool, of course, but the little evidence available indicates that the negotiated relationships between sex workers and their clients often belie simple explanations.

In conclusion, it is fair to say that a great deal of time, space and paper have been devoted to the topic of prostitution in Thailand, to which I am adding here. Given this situation, I feel we should be asking ourselves why the topic is so compelling. While I was working in a child protection agency in Bangkok, the insistent interest of journalists and filmmakers in child prostitution and those who had been prostituted often felt more like voyeurism and morbid fascination with the illusive topic of sex than pure interest in the plight of the children. It is to be hoped that academics can claim to be less self-serving in our own coverage of the sex trade, but I would argue that there are many topics equally deserving of our attention and rooted in the same inequalities and mechanisms, but which are rather less sensational or topical. I suggest that we need to examine our own motives in wishing to understand the Thai sex industry and those who work in it. Is there a latent morality in our fascination, or are there deeper feelings of discomfort about dangerous sexuality that offers a threat to our social fabric and to our physical integrity in the shape of AIDS? By defining 'it' and making 'it' visible are we satisfying an urge to control and contain 'it'?

If there is a need to talk about prostitution, whose voices should be the loudest? In all of the available literature on Thailand, there is a notable lack of opinions from sex workers themselves. Even when they are permitted to speak, their words are framed by an author's own position. In my view, if we are to approach a truly informative, useful and inclusive study of the Thai sex trade and Thai CSWs, we need to support a participatory study, the terms of which are developed and agreed by the women themselves, and whose conclusions are their conclusions.

Notes

[1] In this chapter I have used various terms, for particular reasons. I use the term 'prostitution' to refer to a set of practices and ideas that relate to the commercial sale of sex. The 'sex industry' relates more specifically to the mechanisms and transactions that underpin the sale of sex. I also use 'sex trade' to emphasise the fact that prostitution is a business, dependent on particular enabling factors and involving

financial exchange on various levels. I use the phrase 'commercial sex worker' (CSW) rather than 'prostitute', since the second term has become an overburdened metaphor, with associations ranging from bad, promiscuous woman to victim.

[2] The dominant religion of Thailand is Buddhism, but there is a significant Muslim population in the south of Thailand and there are also Christian minorities as well as Animist beliefs among some hill tribes.

[3] See Thitsa (1980), Keyes (1984) and Kirsch (1985) for a debate over the degree to which Thai women are able to enjoy equal prestige with men.

[4] Thai men are expected to ordain as a monk for at least ten days, at around the age of 20. This is seen as a transition from being 'raw' to being 'ripe' – gaining the necessary maturity and wisdom to move into adulthood (see Keyes (1987) for further explanation).

[5] See, for example, Yoddumnern Attig (1992) for an assessment of women's 'changing roles and statuses' in Thailand.

[6] Until relatively recently, women were not able to file for divorce on the grounds of adultery unless they could prove that their husband had been keeping another woman as his minor wife.

[7] The razor blades are withdrawn on a clear nylon thread from a film canister contained in the vagina, rather than being shot in the same way as ping-pong balls.

[8] The high numbers of Thai males visiting sex workers has been used as an argument to counteract accusations that the sex trade is a Western import. For example, Wilson states: 'US Marines on R and R, together with sex tourists, cannot be held solely responsible for corrupting Thailand's morals and spreading prostitution - only for making things uglier, more obvious and worse' (D. Wilson and D. Henley, in *Bangkok Post*, 25 December 1994).

[9] Phongpaichit interviewed 50 masseuses from nine establishments in Bangkok.

[10] Thais are expected to repay the debt of love and care bestowed on them by their parents, by remitting money to them to support them in their old age and/or by looking after them later in life. In practice, men are not expected to take these obligations as seriously as women.

Recommended further reading

Asia Watch Women's Rights Project (1993) *A modern form of slavery: Trafficking of Burmese women and girls in brothels in Thailand*, New York: Human Rights Watch.

Bangkok Post (2003) 'More family men paying for gay sex', 29 May.

Boonchalaksi, W. and Guest, P. (1994) *Prostitution in Thailand*, Bangkok: Institute for Population and Social Research, Mahidol University.

Brody, A. (1994) 'Problematising Thai masculinity with specific reference to prostitution in Thailand', unpublished MA thesis, London: School of Oriental and African Studies.

References

Asia Watch Women's Rights Project (1993) *A modern form of slavery: Trafficking of Burmese women and girls in brothels in Thailand*, New York: Human Rights Watch.

Bell, P. (1992) 'Gender and economic development in Thailand', in P. and P. Van Esterick (eds) *Gender and Development in Southeast Asia*, Montreal: Canadian Asian Studies Association, pp 61–82.

Bishop, R. and Robinson, L. (1998) *Night market: Sexual cultures and the Thai economic miracle*, London: Routledge.

Boonchalaksi, W. and Guest, P. (1994) *Prostitution in Thailand*, Bangkok: Institute for Population and Social Research, Mahidol University.

Brody, A. (1994) 'Problematising Thai masculinity with specific reference to prostitution in Thailand', unpublished MA thesis, London: School of Oriental and African Studies.

Chouwilai, J. (2000) 'Life after redundancy: the effects of the termination of employment of Thai workers', in A. Brody (ed) *Uniting voices: Asian women workers' search for recognition in the global marketplace*, Bangkok: Committee for Asian Women, pp 85–98.

Cohen, E. (1996) *Thai tourism, hill tribes, islands and open-ended prostitution*, Bangkok: White Lotus Press.

De Zalduondo, B. (1991) 'Prostitution viewed cross-culturally: towards recontextualising sex work in AIDS intervention research', *Journal of Sex Research*, vol 28, no 2, pp 223–48.

Embree, J. (1950) 'Thailand: a loosely structured social system', *American Anthropologist*, vol 52, pp 181–93.

Financial Times (1987), July 10.

Fuller, T., Peerasit, K., Lightfoot, P. and Rathanamongkolmas, S. (1983) *Migration and development in modern Thailand*, Bangkok: Chulalongkorn University.

Global Alliance Against Traffic in Women (GAATW) (1997) *Report from regional meeting on trafficking in women, forced labour and slavery-like practices in Asia and Pacific*, Bangkok: GAATW.

Jackson, P. (1995) *Dear Uncle Go: Male homosexuality in Thailand*, Bangkok: Bua Luang Books.

Jeffrey, L. (2002) *Sex and borders: Gender, national indentity and prostitution policy in Thailand*, Vancouver: UBC Press.

Keyes, C. (1984) 'Mother or mistress but never a monk: Buddhist notions of female gender in rural Thailand', *American Ethnologist*, vol 2, no 2, pp 223–41.

Keyes, C. (1987) *Thailand: Buddhist Kingdom as modern nation-state*, Boulder, CO: Westview Press.

Kirsch, T. (1985) 'Text and context: Buddhist sex roles/culture of gender revisited', *American Ethnologist*, vol 12, no 12, pp 302–30.

Lyttleton, C. (2000) *Endangered relations: Negotiating sex and AIDS*, Bangkok: White Lotus Press.

Manderson, L. (1992) 'Public sex performances in Patpong and explorations of the edges of the imagination', *Journal of Sex Research*, vol 2, no 4, pp 451–75.

The Nation (2003) 'Male prostitution: clientele growing, varied', 29 May.

Phongpaichit, P. (1982) *From peasant girls to Bangkok masseuses*, Geneva: ILO.

Phongpaichit, P. and Baker, C. (1995) *Thailand: Economy and politics*, New York: Oxford University Press.

Phongsapich, A. (1997) 'Feminism theories and praxis: women's social movement in Thailand', in V. and S. Theobold (eds) *Women and gender relations and development in Thai society, Vol 1*, Chiang Mai: Chiang Mai University Women's Centre, pp 34–42.

Raymond, J. (2003) *Guide to new UN trafficking protocol*, Canada: Coalition Against Trafficking in Women (available at action.web.ca/home/catw/attach/un-protocol.pdf).

Seabrook, J. (1996) *Travels in the skin trade: Tourism and the sex industry*, London: Pluto Press.

Tantiwiramanond, D. and Pandey, S. (1991) *By women, for women: A study of women's organisations in Thailand*, Singapore: Institute of Southeast Asian Studies.

Thitsa, K. (1980) *Providence and prostitution: Image and reality for women in Buddhist Thailand*, London: CHANGE International Reports.

Truong, T.-d. (1990) *Sex, money and morality: Prostitution in Southeast Asia*, London: Zed Books.

Van Esterick, P. (1996) *Women of Southeast Asia*, Dekalb, IL: Northern Illinois University Center for Southeast Asian Studies.

Yoddumnern-Attig, B. (1992) *Changing roles and statuses of women in Thailand: A documentary assessment*, Bangkok: Mahidol University.

Relevant Acts

1909 Control and Prevention of Venereal Disease Act.

1960 Suppression of Prostitution Act.

1966 Service Establishments Act.

UN Conventions

1949 Convention for the Suppression of the Traffic in Persons and of the Exploitation of the Prostitution of Others.

2000 Protocol to Prevent, Suppress and Punish Trafficking in Persons, especially Women and Children.

Index

Locators shown in *italics* refer to boxes and tables.

R

S